DICTIONARY OF STOCK MARKET TERMS

DICTIONARY OF STOCK MARKET TERMS

by Peter Wyckoff

PRENTICE-HALL, INC.
Englewood Cliffs, N.J.

LIBRARY OF CONGRESS
CATALOG CARD NUMBER: 64–16432

Second printing ....April, 1968

PRINTED IN THE UNITED STATES OF AMERICA

21081—B&P

To
ALLETHY *and* JACK

By the Same Author

The Psychology of Stock Market Timing

PREFACE

Every business and profession has its own special language, but the vernacular of the stock market is especially full and rich. In addition to many technical terms and expressions, it has an argot of slang often very descriptive of the meaning to be conveyed, yet sometimes confusing to the uninitiated.

Some terms describe the people who operate in stocks: speculators, investors, traders, the public, bulls, bears, scalpers, plungers, professionals, specialists and brokers. Others refer to the character and price action of stocks themselves: firm, steady, soft, sick, erratic, inactive, weak, dull, sensitive, churning, or slipping; during a recovery, boom, recession, or panic; in a thin, top-heavy, liquidating, oversold, or buoyant market.

Stocks may be bought long or sold short. They may be crossed, dumped, or accumulated by insiders and outsiders, who are realizing, scalping or discounting the news, bucking the trend, selling against the box, or evening up. They rally or react, appreciate or slump, slip or stiffen, spurt or fall out of bed in terms of points or fractions of points.

The shorts may be squeezed and forced to buy back. The lambs have been sheared. A speculator has hedged his position with a put, call, spread, straddle, strip or strap. And a head and shoulders pattern on a point and figure chart may indicate to a technician that a selling drive is imminent.

This is the language of the marketplace, the talk of the ticker as it is heard and spoken everyday by a large segment of the 19 million persons reported to own American securities.

Between the covers of this book are more than 1,200 terms. They are defined with many cross references and numerous examples intended to inform the novice or assist the professional wishing to supplement his knowledge. Although they have long been buried under the law, terms such as pool, corner, manipulation and bucketshop are included. They are historically important. No effort has been spared to retain the color and humor which might further convey the meaning of a term or typify the lingo used continually on Wall Street.

Indeed, the sole requirement for admission of a term has been whether it has a place in the vocabulary of floor brokers, clerks, customers' brokers, Board Room habitués and that vast and growing army of investors and speculators—The Public.

While it cannot be guaranteed that an intimate knowledge of these expressions will facilitate "a killing" in the stock market, it is to be hoped that a more complete understanding of them will prevent some costly headaches.

ACKNOWLEDGMENTS

The author expresses appreciation and thanks to M. C. Horsey & Co. for permission to reproduce various chart formations appearing in the text, to the *Financial Analyst's Journal* for allowing certain excerpts from the magazine to be reprinted and to Dorothy Fossen for many long hours spent typing the manuscript.

DICTIONARY OF STOCK MARKET TERMS

A

A. 1. The TICKER abbreviation for The Anaconda Company.
2. When printed on the upper line of the TICKER TAPE and accompanied by other letters, it means Class "A," or Series "A."

ABOVE PAR. 1. A price above the FACE VALUE (PAR VALUE) of a security.
2. A price above $100 per share. Thus, if a stock is selling at 100, it is selling *at par;* if the price is 100⅛, it is said to be selling *above par* or *at par and one-eighth.*

ABSORB. To assimilate (absorb) the volume of sell orders with offsetting buy orders. "Yesterday's late selling pressure was well absorbed and the market closed virtually unchanged."

ABSORPTION POINT. A level at which the market is unable to absorb more selling without moving downward.

ACCELERATED DEPRECIATION. An unusually rapid decrease in the value of an asset caused by carelessness, unskilled labor, or poor maintenance of equipment. See DEPRECIATION. In order to take advantage of rapid write-off privileges, the property must meet certain qualifications: (A) It must be tangible, having buildings and equipment; (B) It must have a useful life to the taxpayer of 3 years or more; (C) It must be new property acquired after 1953. Rapid methods may not be applied to used or second-hand property (although the so-called "150% declining balance method" may be so applied). Also, the taxpayer must be the original user and the use must begin after 1953; (D) The property must have been constructed or reconstructed after 1953. Accelerated rates may be used only for that portion of the cost of construction attributable to periods after 1953. Of course, where construction was started after 1953, the entire cost can be written off under the accelerated methods. But, the *first use* of the property must have begun with *you.* If you make any additions to property that was not new when you bought it, or if you convert a residence or a personal auto which was purchased by you since 1954 to business use, you can use accelerated depreciation methods on the additions or converted portions. The outstanding factor about accelerated methods is that the taxpayer has additional money in hand in the early years which may provide required funds for outside investment, business investment, an accelerated replacement program, or for placing a business in position to profit from short-term financing. (For more detailed information consult Prentice-Hall's Special Report "The Revolutionary New Tax Rules for Depreciable Property"—November 10, 1962 Section 3).

ACCOUNT. 1. A broker's record of the cash and/or securities deposited with him by a client on which future orders to buy or sell for the client's account are based. See ACTIVE ACCOUNT; BROKERAGE ACCOUNT; CASH ACCOUNT; CLOSED ACCOUNT; DISCRETIONARY ACCOUNT; DORMANT ACCOUNT; ERROR ACCOUNT; FROZEN ACCOUNT; HOUSE ACCOUNT; JOINT ACCOUNT; LONG ACCOUNT; MARGIN ACCOUNT; SHORT ACCOUNT.

2. See PROFIT AND LOSS STATEMENT.

3. In England, the term applies to the period when securities contracts must be settled. Account Day (also Settling Day or Pay Day) is the last day of the period. It usually occurs twice monthly, and such days are determined a year in advance.

ACCOUNT AND RISK. The understanding between a broker and his client upon which all securities transactions are based. It means that the broker, acting as agent in the transaction, will execute orders for the *account and risk* of his client, who acts as principal.

ACCOUNTS PAYABLE. The amounts credited to others as shown by the records of a business; liabilities for goods or services purchased and other unclosed accounts—except for such things as notes, drafts, acceptances, and bonds. The aggregate sum due to creditors that must be settled to close an account. Accounts payable are included under CURRENT LIABILITIES in a corporate BALANCE SHEET.

ACCOUNTS RECEIVABLE. The amounts due from customers as shown by the records of a business but excluding notes, drafts, acceptances, and bonds. Accounts receivable are included under CURRENT ASSETS in a BALANCE SHEET.

ACCRUED DIVIDENDS. Dividends which have accumulated on a CUMULATIVE PREFERRED stock since the last payment was made. The buyer pays the price of the stock, plus any accrued dividends.

ACCRUED INTEREST. Interest which has been earned and has accrued on a bond since the last regular payment date, but which is not yet payable. If a bond paying interest on January 1 and July 1 is bought on February 3, the buyer will receive on July 1 an interest coupon for one-half year. However, since he did not own the bond for the full six months, he must pay back the interest which accrued for 34 days from January 1 to February 3 to the seller. *With Interest, And Interest* or *Interest Added* may be used in the same sense as accrued interest.

ACCRUED LIABILITIES. The aggregate sum of wages, taxes, and insurance incurred but not payable until a future date. This is mostly a bookkeeping item, useful for improving the perspective of the periods such liabilities will affect. They are included under CURRENT LIABILITIES in a BALANCE SHEET.

ACCUMULATED DIVIDENDS. Dividends which have remained unpaid as of the date they fell due and have accumulated over a period of time.

ACCUMULATED INTEREST. Periodic interest payments which are past due and unpaid.

ACCUMULATED SURPLUS. An excess accumulated by a corporation from its profits. See SURPLUS.

ACCUMULATION. The purchase of securities quietly and gradually in anticipation of rising prices. Accumulation usually takes place after a long decline, such as in a BEAR MARKET, when public confidence and corporate profits are at a low ebb and the market's action is characterized by dullness and stagnation. The opposite of DISTRIBUTION. See TAKE ON A LINE.

ACROSS-THE-BOARD. Term referring to the unified price action of the general market list: "Today's market was strong (weak) *across-the-board.*"

ACTION. 1. A general term alluding to the movements of volume and prices.

2. The French word for a share of stock.

ACTIVE ACCOUNT. A brokerage account with securities which are bought and sold frequently. An active MARGIN ACCOUNT is usually given preferential interest rate treatment.

ACTIVE ASSETS. Assets used continuously for productive purposes such as operating a business. The opposite of DEAD ASSETS.

ACTIVE CAPITAL. Capital that is steadily employed in profit-making ventures.

ACTIVE MARKET. A market where securities are heavily traded and the volume of sales is above normal. On the New York Stock Exchange when volume for a day tops 5 million shares, the market is considered to be active. See VOLUME.

ACTIVE PARTNER. An officer, or partner, of a brokerage firm who is active in formal association with others in the management of the firm for the mutual benefit of all. See GENERAL PARTNER, LIMITED PARTNERSHIP, SILENT PARTNER, SPECIAL PARTNER.

ACTIVE SECURITIES. Frequently traded securities experiencing daily sales for which QUOTATIONS are readily available.

ACTUAL PRICE. The price at which a deal for the transfer of ownership is formally closed. In the stock market, it means the actual price at which a transaction between a buyer and a seller is made.

ACTUARIAL BUYING. See DOLLAR COST AVERAGING.

ADJUSTMENT BOND. A bond on which interest is payable only when earned. Failure to pay such interest is no cause for foreclosure. Adjustment bonds are generally considered synonymous with INCOME BONDS. They are a claim on earnings against stock issues only and are seldom issued for public subscription, because they usually result from a reorganization of a company's finances.

ADMITTED TO DEALINGS. Term meaning that a security has been officially *admitted to the list;* that is, it has been granted the privilege of being traded on an exchange with the approval of that exchange and the SECURITIES AND EXCHANGE COMMISSION. See LISTING REQUIREMENTS.

ADR's. See AMERICAN DEPOSITARY RECEIPTS.

ADVANCE. 1. A rise in security prices.

2. A loan, or deposit, paid before the legal due date of a contract.

ADVANCE-DECLINE LINE. An index which indicates how closely the action of the general market conforms with that of the DOW-JONES Industrial Average. It is computed by taking a discretionary number and *subtracting* from it if declines predominate, or *adding* to it if advances predominate, the net difference between the total number of stocks which close higher and those which close lower each day on the New York Stock Exchange. For example, if the number is 10,000 and on the first day there are 700 advances and 300 declines the Line rises to 10,400. When this Line plotted on a chart coincides with the action of the D-J Industrials over a period of time, it is said to be "conforming." But if the Line "peaks out" and turns downward while the Industrials are still advancing, it will indicate a deteriorating market situation. The reverse holds true if the Line moves upward, contrary to a declining trend shown by the Dow Industrials.

AFFILIATED COMPANY. According to the SECURITIES AND EXCHANGE COMMISSION, a company which "directly, or indirectly, through one, or more, intermediaries controls, or is controlled by, or is under common control with another." The SEC further defines control as "the power to direct, or cause the direction of, the management and policies . . . (of a corporation) whether through the ownership of voting securities, by contract, or otherwise." The principal difference between an affiliated company and a SUBSIDIARY company is that the latter is more completely controlled.

AGENT. Term synonymous with BROKER.

AGENT DE CHANGE. The French term for stockbroker.

AGGRESSIVE PORTFOLIO. A securities portfolio containing issues held primarily on the assumption that they will appreciate in value, as opposed to securities which provide greater yield, or have good defensive qualities. The opposite of DEFENSIVE PORTFOLIO. See INVESTMENT PORTFOLIO.

AIRDALE. Slang expression for a fast-talking, sharply dressed salesman such as might be associated with a BUCKET SHOP.

ALLIED MEMBERS. Partners, or voting stockholders, in a stock exchange member organization who are not entitled to transact business on the trading floor of an exchange but are subject to the same rules and regulations as exchange members.

ALL, OR ANY PART. A phrase which may accompany an order to buy or sell. It is a discretionary privilege given by a client to his broker allowing the broker to execute all of the original order, a small part of it or any amount he sees fit, but only at the client's specified price limit.

ALL, OR NONE. A stipulation which sometimes accompanies an order to buy or sell at a specified price. It is understood that the client will accept an execution only for the number of shares stated in the original order and no less than that amount. *All or none* may also mean that any sales made by the UNDERWRITERS, or other brokers, of a new issue of securities to the public will become final, only if the entire issue is sold within a specified time period.

ALLOTMENT. The amount of a new issue of securities which is assigned (allotted) to a subscriber to that issue by a SYNDICATE, or

Investment company. If the issue is unusually popular and there are many subscribers, the amount allotted may be less than the amount applied for. See Hot issue.

AMALGAMATION. A union or combination of two or more businesses.

AMERICAN DEPOSITARY RECEIPTS (ADR's). American certificates of deposit issued by an approved New York bank or trust company against the deposit of the original (foreign) shares with a European branch of the New York institution. These receipts facilitate the financing of foreign companies in this country. As foreign shares are deposited abroad, the equivalent ADR's are issued to buyers in New York. When transactions are made, the ADR's change hands, not the certificates. This eliminates the actual shipment of stock certificates between the U.S. and foreign countries and expedites Arbitrage transactions in securities traded on foreign exchanges.

AMERICANS. The London Stock Exchange term for American securities. Also called "Yankees."

AMERICAN STOCK EXCHANGE. A leading securities exchange located in New York City and the largest market for foreign securities in the United States. Formerly known as the Outdoor, or New York Curb, Market because its operations were originally conducted outside at Wall and Hanover Streets and later on Broad Street below Exchange Place. In June, 1921, the market moved indoors to its present location at 86 Trinity Place. In 1929, it adopted the title, New York Curb Exchange. This was changed officially to American Stock Exchange on January 5,

1953. The Exchange has a regular membership of 547 of which 156 are SPECIALISTS.

AMORTIZATION. 1. Reducing, extinguishing, wiping out; gradually liquidating a future debt or obligation (especially long-term debts) by creating a SINKING FUND to meet current interest payments and to pay off the principal on a bond at maturity.

2. To gradually charge off and extinguish the premium paid for a bond. (The premium is that part of an investment paid at the time of purchase that will not be returned at maturity.) A certain part of the cash interest paid at each interest date is set aside; the amounts being so determined in advance that when the bond matures, they will equal the premium paid at the time of purchase.

ANALYST. A trained person who investigates all the facts concerning a security or industry under study and reaches a dependable conclusion about its merits that may help an actual or potential investor to decide what action he should take. Many brokerage firms, banks, institutions and large corporations maintain investment research departments where certain analysts specialize in one or several industries: the steel analyst, the utility analyst, the railroad analyst, for example.

AND INTEREST. Term denoting that ACCUMULATED (ACCRUED INTEREST) must be added to the fixed or quoted price of a bond. The fixed price plus interest equals the full price.

ANNUAL REPORT. A detailed printed statement issued annually by the management of a corporation to its stockholders, which describes progress made during the year under review and indicates prospects and company plans for the future. The report includes a statement by the independent accounting firm that audited the company's books and also, a PROFIT AND LOSS STATEMENT and a BALANCE SHEET describing its financial condition.

ANNUAL YIELD. The money income or percentage of return in dividends or interest received annually from an investment.

ANNUITY. A fixed sum of money paid to, or received by, a beneficiary (annuitant) at regularly spaced time periods during his lifetime or for a specified number of years. Annuity also refers to the contract under which the payments are made. It represents a form of retirement planning offered by life insurance companies. The first U.S. life insurance company policy written in 1759 was an annuity.

ANNUNCIATORS. Two large boards bearing plates with a number assigned to each FLOOR BROKER, which face each other from the North and South walls of the New York Stock Exchange trading floor. When a broker's presence with his firm's booth on the rim of the trading floor is requested, the telephone clerk presses a button which drops a disk revealing the broker's number—"puts his number up." If the request is urgent, the number will be "flashed" (moved up and down rapidly several times). The broker is expected to report to the booth himself or send a page whenever his number appears. Annunciator boards were first introduced on January 29, 1881.

ANTHRACITE ROAD. Any railroad whose major freight tonnage consists of hard (anthracite) coal.

ANTI-TRUST. Any policy or action opposed to monopolistic power, restraint of trade or unfair practice in interstate commerce. Federal statutes designed to prevent such things include: *The Sherman Act* (Anti-trust Act of 1890), *The Clayton Act* and the *Federal Trade Commission Act* (both passed in 1914), *The Robinson-Patman Act* (amending *The Clayton Act* in 1936), *The Miller-Tydings Act* (amending the *Sherman Act* in 1937) and *The Wheeler-Lea Act* (amending the *Federal Trade Commission Act* in 1938).

APPLICATION FOR LISTING. See LISTING REQUIREMENTS.

APPRECIATION. Term synonymous with price improvement, one of the fundamental investment objectives. A stock advancing from 70 to 80 is said to have appreciated ten points.

ARBITRAGE. The purchase of a security or commodity in one market and the almost simultaneous sale (or a SHORT SALE and then a purchase) of the same security or commodity in another market at a different price. The object is to profit from any price difference between the two markets. For example, if International Paper stock could be bought in London at a price which showed a profit when sold in New York, business could be negotiated to bring this about. If the stock could be bought in New York and sold in London at a profit, business could again be negotiated. The London and New York Stock Exchanges define arbitrage as "The business of buying or selling securities in one market with the intent of reversing such transactions in a market in a country different from that in which the original transaction has taken place, in order to profit from price differences between such markets." Both exchanges require that members or firms which propose to operate in international arbitrage must first obtain permission from their respective exchanges.

ARBITRAGE HOUSE. A firm specializing in ARBITRAGE business.

ARBITRAGIST. An individual who conducts an ARBITRAGE business.

ARREARS. An unpaid debt which is overdue (as when the issuing company of a CUMULATIVE PREFERRED stock is unable to pay dividends at the proper time). A corporation must pay in full any arrears existing on its cumulative preferred stock before it may declare dividends on the common stock.

ASKED (ASKING) OR OFFERING PRICE. The lowest quoted ROUND-LOT price which any potential seller will accept for a security at any given time. It is synonymous with LOWEST OFFER and the opposite of BEST BID price. See FIRM OFFER; OFFER.

ASSENTED STOCKS OR BONDS. Securities deposited under an agreement with a banking house or trust company with the owners' assent to exchange their securities for a new issue. Changes in the status of securities often occur during a reorganization of the issuing company, where an assessment is made of the securities according to a definite plan.

ASSESSABLE STOCK. Stock which is liable to an ASSESSMENT in the case of insolvency or reorganization of the issuing company.

ASSESSMENT. 1. An amount which the security owners of a corporation must pay in order to raise capital during a period of financial stress such as insolvency or reorganization.

2. An official valuation for tax purposes; any fixed tax.

ASSETS. The total property which belongs, or is due, a person, a corporation, or an estate. Assets are plus factors. They signify property and claims against others as opposed to LIABILITIES, or minus factors, which represent debts or other obligations due others. See CAPITAL ASSETS; CASH ASSETS; CURRENT ASSETS; DEAD ASSETS; DOUBTFUL ASSETS; FIXED ASSETS; FLOATING ASSETS; FROZEN ASSETS; HIDDEN ASSETS; INTANGIBLE ASSETS; LIQUID ASSETS; QUICK ASSETS; TANGIBLE ASSETS.

ASSIGNED IN BLANK. A formal transfer, or assignment, of title to a stock, or bond, or other property, in which the space for inserting the new owner's name is left blank. STREET CERTIFICATES are assigned in blank, yet it is generally unwise to accept, or purchase, most securities so assigned, especially from an unknown party, without proper identification and signature guarantees.

ASSIGNMENT SEPARATE FROM CERTIFICATE. See STOCK (BOND) POWER.

ASSUMED BOND. A bond of a corporation that has been secured by another corporation. This may result from a merger or from one corporation's assumption of another's debts.

AT A DISCOUNT. Below PAR VALUE. A security is said to be selling at a discount, when the market value is below the par value of the security. A bond selling at 85 (worth $850) with a par value of $1,000 is selling at a 15%, or $150, discount from par value. A $25 par value stock selling at 23 is selling at an 8% or $2.00 discount.

AT A PREMIUM. 1. Above FACE VALUE (PAR VALUE). A security is said to be selling at a premium when its market price is above its par value. A $50 par value stock selling at 55 is selling at a 10% or $5 premium. See PREMIUM.

2. Term referring to a condition that exists when an extra amount is charged to borrow stock in order to make delivery on a SHORT SALE. This *premium rate* is in addition to the regular rate, and is charged when a stock is particularly scarce and therefore difficult to borrow.

3. The REDEMPTION VALUE of a security, if such price is higher than the market price or FACE VALUE of the security.

AT, OR BETTER. Term which sometimes accompanies an order to buy or sell. When attached to the buy order, it requires purchase at the price limit specified or below that limit. When attached to the sell order, it requires sale at the price limit specified or above. Since brokers, as agents, are obligated to execute their client's order at the best price obtainable, the stipulation *at, or better* is actually superfluous.

AT PAR. 1. The price which equals the FACE VALUE (PAR VALUE) of a security.

2. A market price of 100. A stock selling at 100 is said to be selling *at par.*

AT THE CLOSE. An order calling for an execution at the best price obtainable *at the close* of the market on the day it is entered, except on the American Stock Exchange where Rule 130 would be violated.

AT THE MARKET. An order which the broker will execute at the best price obtainable after it is received by him on the trading floor. Synonymous with MARKET ORDER. See LIMIT ORDER.

AT THE OPENING. Term designating an order to be executed at the best price obtainable as soon as the market opens; no actual price limit is set. ODD-LOT orders to be executed *at the opening* are contingent upon the opening price of the related ROUND-LOT.

AUCTION MARKET. A market where goods are freely sold to the highest bidder. The New York Stock Exchange is the world's largest auction market for securities. When a broker receives an order to buy a stock, he goes to the location on the trading floor where that stock is traded and bids for the amount he wishes to buy. There he will meet other brokers with orders to buy or sell in the same issue. When the bid and offer coincide in price a transaction is effected. The SPECIALIST in a stock acts as an auctioneer, receiving running bids from would-be buyers and offerings from would-be sellers of that stock.

AUDIT. An official examination of the books and records of a business enterprise made periodically by an outside agency to determine its financial status, uncover clerical errors, discrepancies, and misstatements respecting funds or resources.

AUTHORIZED CAPITAL STOCK. The total number of shares of CAPITAL STOCK a company may issue in accordance with its charter.

AUTHORIZED ISSUE. An issue of securities which has been authorized by the charter of a corporation, the amount of which can be changed only by amending the terms of the charter. See OUTSTANDING SECURITIES.

AVERAGE OUT. To conclude a trade or commitment in the market without loss, or at a profit, by the process of AVERAGING.

AVERAGE PRICE. The mean, or average, price obtained in the purchase, or sale, of a security by the process of AVERAGING.

AVERAGES. See MARKET AVERAGES.

AVERAGING. The purchase, or sale, of additional shares of a given stock at successively lower (averaging down) or higher (averaging up) prices in order to establish an average price on the total transaction. See SCALE ORDER.

The holder of 100 shares of a stock at 20, who buys 100 additional shares of the same stock at 10, would thus own 200 shares at an average price of 15. Hence if the stock recovers to 16 he would show a profit. Conversely, anyone selling 100 shares at 20 and an additional 100 shares at 30 would obtain an average price of 25 on the 200 shares. See BUY ON SCALE; SELL ON SCALE.

B

B. 1. The TICKER abbreviation for Baldwin-Lima-Hamilton Corporation.

2. When printed on the upper line of the TICKER TAPE and accompanied by other letters, it means Class "B," or Series "B." When printed on the lower line, preceding prices, it means "Bid" or "Buyer."

BABY BOND. A bond issued in denominations smaller than the standard $1,000 bond. A bond whose FACE VALUE is $500, $100, $50 or, in the case of U.S. Savings Bonds, $25. Baby bonds usually sell AT A DISCOUNT because of their limited MARKETABILITY when compared with the standard bond.

BACKDOOR LISTING. The ability of a company that failed to meet the original LISTING REQUIREMENTS of a stock exchange to become listed, nevertheless, by acquiring a smaller, listed company and merging itself into the acquisition.

BACKLOG. The total or accumulation of unfilled merchandise orders existing on a corporation's books.

BAD DELIVERY. A delivery of securities which is not properly in accord with specific regulations respecting days, hours, assignment and power of attorney. Also, a delivery made impossible by titling, transfer or physical inadequacies.

BALANCED FUNDS. INVESTMENT COMPANIES, which diversify their portfolio holdings over a wide list of common stocks, bonds and/or preferred issues. Holdings of defensive securities (good-grade bonds, preferreds) are proportionately increased when the market is considered high, and decreased in favor of more aggressive issues (common stocks) when the market appears to be low.

BALANCE OF PAYMENTS. The relationship between total payments to foreigners and total receipts from foreigners. On balance, every nation is either a debtor or a creditor.

Balance of payments and balance of trade should not be confused. The latter merely represents the difference between import values and export values. The former consists of (A) Current transactions: those involving international payments (excluding capital), such as tourist spending, merchandise import and export payments, interest payments, freight charges; (B) Gold movements resulting from foreign exchange shortages; (C) Capital transactions, meaning the investments made by one country in another country.

Balance of payments is a key factor in international finance. It is a good indicator of a nation's credit standing. The flow of gold and goods and services has a profound influence on prices all over the world.

BALANCE SHEET. An itemized statement published in tabular form, showing the financial condition of a corporation as of a specific date. Assets (credits) are shown on the left side; liabilities (debits) appear on the right. The term is derived from the fact that the two sides equal, or balance, each other. It is also known as FINANCIAL STATEMENT, STATEMENT OF CONDITION, or simply, THE STATEMENT.

BALLOONING. Term denoting manipulation of the price of a single stock, a group of stocks, or the entire market, to over-inflated levels far above their intrinsic worth. This practice is strictly outlawed.

BANKER'S POOL. Prominent financial and banking interests, who combined their resources during the 1929 market break and entered supporting bids on certain key stock issues in a futile attempt to stabilize the market.

BAR CHART. See LINE CHART.

BARGAIN COUNTER. An imaginary place where great values are available at very cheap prices. In the stock market, it means that securities are selling at unreasonably low levels relative to their intrinsic worth.

BARGAIN HUNTER. A person who delays purchases until he believes prices have reached an extreme low.

BARRON'S CONFIDENCE INDEX. A ratio of Barron's highest-grade corporate bond yield average to the Dow-Jones composite bond yield average. The latter, which is the denominator of the ratio, includes lower-grade bonds. Thus, when high-grade bond yields rise faster, or fall more slowly, than lower-grade bond yields, the ratio rises. And when high-grade bond yields rise slower or fall faster than lower-grade bond yields, the ratio declines. Since yields move in an opposite direction from prices, the relationship can be readily expressed in terms of price. The Confidence Index rises when lower-grade bond prices outperform high-grade bond prices, and falls when high-grade bond prices outperform lower-grade bond prices.

Users of the C.I. reason that its movement reflects changes in the attitudes of "smart money." It is claimed that when professional investors are relatively gloomy about business and financial prospects, they emphasize high-grade bonds in their operations. This causes high-grade bond prices to outperform the prices of lower-grade bonds and the C.I. falls. When emphasis shifts toward lower-grade bonds, investors become more optimistic. This causes lower-grade prices to outperform high-grade prices and the C.I. rises. The Index is compiled by *Barron's Magazine* and quoted each week in their publication.

BASIC CROPS. A commodity market term including certain agricultural commodities (corn, wheat, rice, tobacco, peanuts, cotton), which are subject to price supports under the *Agricultural Act of 1954* and the *Soil Bank Act of 1956.*

BASIS VALUE. The rate of the interest on a bond or obligation that serves as the basis on which bond values are compared. Bonds are generally bought according to basis, as "a 5% basis", or "to yield ——%".

BEAR. A market pessimist; a believer in lower prices. The opposite of BULL.

In basing his operations on that assumption, the bear sells stock SHORT (sells that which he does not own at the time of sale) hoping eventually to cover or BUY BACK the same stock at a lower price. The difference between the higher selling price and the lower purchasing price represents his profit on the transaction. See COVERING; SHORT SALE.

The term originated on the London Stock Exchange. Since the bear seeks depressed prices, his name may be derived from the verb *to bear,* meaning to press heavily upon. It may also be derived from the adjective *bare,* because the bear—having sold short—is bare of stock. The term for bear on the Paris Bourse is "baissier."

BEAR ACCOUNT. The aggregate of shares "sold short" by those who are pessimistic on the future price trend of securities or commodities. The term is synonymous with SHORT ACCOUNT. See SHORT POSITION; SHORT SALE.

BEAR CAMPAIGN. Same as BEAR RAIDING.

BEAR CLIQUE. An informal group of individuals or interests which strives to depress security or commodity prices by selling short. See SHORT SALE.

BEARER BOND. A bond made payable to its holder. The opposite of REGISTERED BOND.

BEARER FORM. A note or bond payable to the bearer of the instrument. COUPON BONDS fall into this classification.

BEARING THE MARKET. Forcing down by artificially depressing market prices. A form of manipulation currently made impossible by the ONE-EIGHTH RULE. Synonymous with BEAR RAIDING.

BEARISH. The prevailing psychology or market position of one who is pessimistic on the future trend of prices, or the future outlook for a corporation or industry. Also, any adverse news, or development; a protracted decline in market prices resulting therefrom.

BEAR MARKET. A market where prices decline sharply against a background of widespread pessimism, growing unemployment and business recession. The opposite of BULL MARKET.

The highest level achieved by each intermediate rally (see INTERMEDIATE TREND) in a bear market is below the high reached on the previous rally, and the lowest level attained on each decline is below the preceding low. Bear markets usually end sooner than bull markets; stocks tend to go down much faster than they go up.

BEAR POOL. A formally organized fund contributed by BEARISH market operators or interests for the purpose of forcing prices downward. The operation of the pool is entrusted to a manager and the members agree to share profits or losses. It is prearranged also that, while the agreement is in force, no pool member may operate individually in the same security that the pool is exploiting. A form of manipulation currently prohibited. See POOL.

BEAR POSITION. Same as SHORT POSITION.

BEAR RAIDING. Aggressive SHORT SELLING directed against one or more stocks, or the entire market, by a group of BEAR operators; their intention being to scare the BULLS and force liquidation from over-extended MARGIN ACCOUNTS that will enable them to close out their short selling contracts at a profit. Rules against bear raiding were enacted in the early 1930's and the practice is prohibited, in fact impossible, today. See ONE-EIGHTH RULE.

BEAR SQUEEZE, OR PANIC. A condition existing when the BEARS, who have been working for lower prices, suddenly find the market advancing rapidly to levels where they may be forced to close out their SHORT SELLING contracts at a loss. See SHORT SALE.

BELOW PAR. A price below the FACE VALUE (PAR VALUE) of a security.

BENEFICIARY. An individual in whose interest an instrument conferring value is drawn.

BEST (ALFRED M.) CO. INC. A publisher since 1906 of comprehensive statistical reports upon the financial position, history and operating results of legal reserve life insurance companies, fraternal benefit societies and assessment associations operating in the United States and Canada. Home Office: Best Building, 75 Fulton Street, New York 38, New York. See FITCH INVESTOR'S SERVICE; MOODY'S INVESTOR'S SERVICE; STANDARD & POOR'S CORPORATION.

BEST BID. The bid which tops all others at a specific moment; a written, or verbal, statement of the highest price any prospective buyer will pay for something being offered for sale. The best bid is what really establishes the market in a stock. The opposite of "best offer" or LOWEST OFFER.

BID AHEAD. Term which indicates to the prospective buyer of a security that a bid, or bids, to buy the same stock at the same price, or a higher price, were received on the trading floor before his order; these naturally take precedence over his bid.

BID AND ASKED (OFFER). The highest quoted price that any potential buyer will pay for a security, coupled simultaneously with the lowest quoted price that any seller of the same security will accept as a basis of negotiation.

Bid and asked prices are known collectively as *quotes* or QUOTATIONS. They are furnished by broker-members of the Stock Exchange called SPECIALISTS and are liable to frequent change during the business day, especially in very active securities.

BIDDING UP. Raising the price bid for a security or commodity to successively higher levels; a method followed usually by anxious buyers, who are afraid they might MISS THE MARKET (fail to act) before an advance gets underway.

BID PRICE. The highest quoted price that any prospective buyer will pay for a security at a specific moment of time. The *bid price* is the real established market for a stock, regardless of the price of the last sale. See FIRM BID.

BID WANTED. Request made by a seller of a security who is anxious to find a buyer for it. See OFFER WANTED.

BIG BOARD. The New York Stock Exchange; it is so called, because it is the largest securities market. The term is also partially derived from its earlier title, The New York Stock and Exchange Board. The American Stock Exchange is sometimes called the "Little Board."

BIG STEEL. Nickname formerly applied to the preferred stock of the United States Steel Corporation but now referring more to Steel common or to the company itself.

U.S. Steel was formed by J. Pierpont Morgan from a super-trust, which owned or controlled some 785 plants. It was incorporated February 25, 1901, and was ready for business on April 1 of the same year with an authorized CAPITALIZATION of $1,400,000,000.

BIG THREE. The three largest companies in any leading industry. The Big Three of the automobile industry are General Motors, Ford and Chrysler.

BIRD DOG. Slang expression meaning a tout, who receives a commission for furnishing fraudulent, high pressure, securities salesmen with new prospects. When used as a verb, it means to ferret out, or explore; to search for facts, which may help in analyzing the status of a company, or its future earnings or dividend trend.

BLACK FRIDAY. Any one of several famous Fridays when a financial disaster occurred. In the United States it generally denotes Friday, September 24, 1869, when an attempt by Jay Gould and James Fisk, Jr., to CORNER (gain control of) gold ended in failure.

Gould, Fisk and their allies bought gold in quantity in the Gold Room of the Stock Exchange and rocketed the price straight up. While they were still buying, the U.S. Treasury suddenly entered the market and purchased with gold $4 million worth of its own bonds. This surprise action broke the intended corner and caused a collapse in gold; leaving suicide, failure and wreckage strewn everywhere.

BLIND POOL. A formally organized fund contributed by market operators or interests the control of which is vested in a single person, usually a member of the POOL, for a specified period of time.

By prearrangement, no instructions may be submitted by other pool members nor may information be handed down by the controlling member while the pool is in force, unless its object has been completed beforehand. Only the manager knows what is being done, hence the term, *blind pool.*

BLOCK. A large amount of stock, usually representing at least 1,000 shares. Where a stock is relatively low in price, a block is 5,000 shares or more.

BLOTTER. A detailed book of original entry; a temporary record in which security or commodity transactions are first listed, pending eventual transfer to a more permanent ledger. It is also known as *journal* or *register.*

BLOW OFF. A temporary buying or selling climax; accompanied usually by heavy volume and taking place after an extended advance or decline.

BLUE CHIP. The stock of a leading company which is known for excellent management and a conservative financial structure. It deals in some necessity of life that is a household word. The company's prospects for future growth should be favorable and its dividend considered secure, regardless of normal changes in the BUSINESS CYCLE. It normally takes many years for a stock to build up a reputation strong enough to acquire *blue chip* status.

BLUE LIST. A list of MUNICIPAL BOND offerings published daily by Blue List Publishing Co., a subsidiary of STANDARD & POOR'S. A bond trader's equivalent of PINK SHEETS, except that only OFFERING prices are quoted.

BLUE-SKY LAWS. Laws designed to shelter the investing public from unscrupulous securities salesmen and promoters who actually offer a piece of *blue sky* and nothing more.

They are enacted in various forms by nearly all states. The first state to enact such a law was Kansas in 1911. By 1922, 37 states had blue-sky laws; but not until passage of the *Securities Act of 1933* were most of the loopholes plugged.

BOARD. The trading room of an exchange; also applies to the BOARD OF DIRECTORS of a corporation. Thus, *on the Board* means on the Exchange, or on a Board of Directors—a member of the DIRECTORATE.

BOARD LOT. The accepted UNIT OF TRADING on an exchange; usually 100 shares of stock and $1,000 PAR VALUE of bonds.

BOARD OF DIRECTORS. A body of individuals responsible for managing the affairs of a corporation. It is also referred to as the DIRECTORATE, or the BOARD.

BOARD OF GOVERNORS. Government of the New York Stock Exchange is vested in a Board of Governors, each member of which must be a United States citizen. The Board consists of: (A) Chairman of the Board, who must be a member of the Exchange; (B) President of the Exchange, "who shall not engage in any other business during his incumbency and who, if a member of the Exchange at the time of his election, shall promptly thereafter dispose of his membership; (C) Thirteen members residing and having their principal place of business within the metropolitan area of the City of New York, of whom not less than seven shall be general partners of member firms engaged in a business involving direct contact with the public, and of whom not less than ten shall spend a substantial part of their time on the floor of the Exchange; (D) Six members, or allied members, residing and having their principal place of business within the metropolitan area of the City of New York who shall be general partners in member firms engaged in a business involving direct contact with the public, of whom five shall be allied members and one a member of the Exchange; (E) Nine members or allied members of the Exchange residing and having their principal places of business outside of such metropolitan area who shall be general partners in member firms engaged in a business involving direct contact with the public, of whom not less than two shall be members of the Exchange; (F) Three representatives of the public." The first Governing Committee was elected in 1868.

BOARD ROOM. 1. The trading room of an exchange. See FLOOR.
2. A room in a broker's office in which are located many facilities for keeping abreast of changes in the securities or commodity markets.

Before automatic electric stock quotation boards were introduced, price changes were recorded in chalk on a blackboard by a "Board Boy"; hence the term BOARD ROOM. Also known as "Customer's Room."

BOBTAIL POOL. An informal group of brokers, speculators, or other financial interests whose members operate independently of each other and not through a single member. Having acted together in manipulating a security or commodity up or down any member may terminate his individual interest without permission from the other members. See POOL.

BOILER ROOM. Space in a BUCKET SHOP allocated to high-pressure securities salesmen.

BONANZA. A Spanish word meaning prosperity. The term originally referred to an unusually rich mine, which made the discoverer or owner immediately wealthy. Today, it applies more to a highly profitable investment or speculation.

BOND. A certificate of debt; an IOU issued by a government, municipality, or corporation. It represents a binding agreement between the issuing company and the bondholder, whereby the issuer promises to pay interest (usually semi-annually) to the holder in return for the loan of his money and to repay the face amount, or PRINCIPAL, on a certain date.

Unlike stockholders, who are part owners of the company,

bondholders are creditors of the company. As such, they are entitled to payment, even if assets must be sold to raise the required funds. However, the term "bond" is no synonym of safety. See ADJUSTMENT BOND; ASSENTED BOND; ASSUMED BOND; BABY BOND; BEARER BOND; CALLABLE; CLASSIFIED BOND; COLLATERAL TRUST BOND; CONVERTIBLE BOND; CORPORATE BOND; COUPON BOND; DEBENTURE; DEFERRED OR EXTENDED BOND; DEFINITIVE BOND; GENERAL MORTGAGE BOND; GUARANTEED BOND; HIGH GRADE BOND; INCOME BOND; INSTALLMENT BOND; INTERCHANGEABLE BOND; INTERIM BOND; MORTGAGE BOND; MUNICIPAL BOND; OPTIONAL BOND; PARTICIPATING BOND; PERPETUAL BOND; REDEEMABLE BOND; REGISTERED BOND; REVENUE BOND; SECURED BOND; SERIAL BONDS; TAX EXEMPT BOND; TAX FREE BOND; UNSECURED BOND.

BONDED DEBT. The debt owed by a state, a city, or a corporation, as represented by bonds and as distinguished from FLOATING DEBT.

BOND HOUSE. An institution whose principal business is selling bonds.

BOND INDENTURE. The contract or deed under which bonds are issued. It describes such terms of the agreement as rate of interest and date of maturity. See INDENTURE.

BOND QUALITY RATINGS. A system of gradation for measuring the relative investment qualities of bonds by the use of rating symbols, which range from the highest investment quality (least investment risk) to the lowest investment quality (greatest investment risk). These ratings according to STANDARD & POOR'S CORP.

are: Al+, highest grade; Al, high grade; A, upper medium grade; Bl+, medium grade; Bl, lower medium grade; B, speculative; Cl+ and Cl outright speculations; C, income bonds paying no interest and the best defaulted bonds; and Dl and D, in default, with the D symbol assigned to issues, which appear to have little recoverable value.

The ratings according to MOODY'S INVESTOR'S SERVICE are:

Aaa

"Bonds which are rated Aaa are judged to be of the best quality. They carry the smallest degree of investment risk and are generally referred to as "gilt edge." Interest payments are protected by a large or by an exceptionally stable margin and principal is secure. While the various protective elements are likely to change, such changes as can be visualized are most unlikely to impair the fundamentally strong position of such issues.

Aa

"Bonds which are rated Aa are judged to be of high quality by all standards. Together with the Aaa group they comprise what are generally known as high grade bonds. They are rated lower than the best bonds because margins of protection may not be as large as in Aaa securities or fluctuation of protective elements may be of greater amplitude or there may be other elements present which make the long term risks appear somewhat larger than in Aaa securities.

A

"Bonds which are rated A possess many favorable investment attributes and are to be considered as higher medium grade obligations. Factors giving security to principal and interest are considered adequate but elements may be present which suggest a susceptibility to impairment sometime in the future.

Baa

"Bonds which are rated Baa are considered as lower medium grade obligations, *i.e.*, they are neither highly protected nor poorly secured. Interest payments and principal security appear adequate for the present but certain protective elements may be lacking or may be characteristically unreliable over any great length of time. Such bonds lack outstanding investment characteristics and in fact have speculative characteristics as well.

Ba

"Bonds which are rated Ba are judged to have speculative elements; their future cannot be considered as well assured. Often the protection of interest and principal payments may be very moderate and thereby not well safeguarded during both good and bad times over the future. Uncertainty of position characterizes bonds in this class.

B

"Bonds which are rated B generally lack characteristics of the desirable investment. Assurance of interest and principal payments or of maintenance of other terms of the contract over any long period of time may be small.

Caa

"Bonds which are rated Caa are of poor standing. Such issues may be in default or there may be present elements of danger with respect to principal or interest.

Ca

"Bonds which are rated Ca represent obligations which are speculative in a high degree. Such issues are often in default or have other marked shortcomings.

C

"Bonds which are rated C are the lowest rated class of bonds and issues so rated can be regarded as having extremely poor prospects of ever attaining any real investment standing."

BONUS STOCK. Stock given as a bonus to persons aiding a corporation. It also is sometimes given as a bonus to purchasers of a corporation's bonds or preferred stock. See TREASURY STOCK.

BOOKS. Journals, ledgers, registers, or records, containing the accounts of an individual, a firm, or a corporation. See SPECIALIST'S BOOK.

BOOKS (CLOSE). Term denoting the day when a corporation's transfer books close; so that the TRANSFER AGENT can check the list of stockholders who are entitled to vote or to receive declared but unpaid dividends.

BOOKS (OPEN). Term indicating the day when the transfer books of a corporation are open after having been closed to check the dividend or voting list. The normal business of transferring stocks may be resumed on this day.

BOOK VALUE. The net worth of a corporation as shown by its records.

To determine the book value per share of common stock: 1. Add up the assets (generally excluding INTANGIBLE ASSETS); 2. Subtract all liabilities and the liquidating value of any preferred stock; 3. Divide the result by the number of common shares OUT-

STANDING. Book value is really a nominal value; it has virtually no connection with MARKET VALUE.

BOOM. A period of time notable for active business conditions, rising prices, widespread optimism and increased speculative activity. Booms may be localized or confined to certain things: stocks, commodities, real estate, for example; but a general boom means prosperity all around.

BOOTH. A communications room, or private area, maintained by a MEMBER FIRM on the rim of a stock exchange trading floor, which serves as the focal point for orders to buy and sell securities received from the ORDER ROOM of that firm.

BORROWED STOCK. The stock a broker borrows to fulfill the obligations of a SHORT SELLING contract assumed by his customer. See LOANED STOCK.

BOTTOM. The price level reached by the market at the end of a long decline.

BOTTOM DROPPED OUT OF. When the price of a stock declines so suddenly and abruptly as to convey the idea that it will carry to zero, it is said that "the *bottom has dropped out* of the market" for that stock.

BOTTOM OUT. The gradual leveling of market prices after a long and steep decline. Not all securities reach their lowest prices simultaneously; hence, a *bottoming out* process in the general market may extend over several weeks or months before a position has been established stable enough for any strong and sustained recovery. The opposite of this is TOP OUT.

BOTTOM PRICE. The lowest price. To *get in at the bottom* means to buy at the lowest level possible.

BOURSE. An exchange located in Continental Europe where securities or commodities are bought and sold. See PARIS BOURSE.

BOX. A metal container in which securities are deposited for safekeeping.

BOX COUNT. A periodic accounting made of the securities held by a broker in the names of his customers or in a STREET NAME (the name of his own firm or another firm). Securities are stored in vaults in large metal containers during non-business hours. Hence, the term "box count" is used when a check of their contents is made.

BRANCH OFFICES. Other offices of the same firm located in another city or foreign country or in some other location in the same city as the main office. Branch offices are subject to Stock Exchange approval. They must bear the same name as the parent firm and be administered by qualified persons acceptable to the Exchange.

BREAK. A sudden and abrupt decline in price.

BREAK EVEN. To terminate a transaction with neither a profit nor a loss.

BREAKOUT. The action of the general market, or a particular stock, in advancing above a level where strong selling resistance is indicated, or declining below a level of strong indicated buying support.

BREAK-UP VALUE. The amount, or value, of the available assets of an investment trust, or HOLDING COMPANY, after taking into account the value of its marketable securities.

BRING OUT. To introduce or offer a new issue of securities to the public.

BROAD MARKET. A market in which an unusually large number of stocks is traded, generally on heavier volume and with increasing participation by the public.

BROAD TAPE. A machine operated by Dow-Jones & Co., which prints all the important news, especially relating to finance, on an enlarged form of TICKER TAPE. Broad tapes are located in most brokers' offices and many banks and occasionally, in business offices, restaurants, and private clubs. They are not permitted on the trading floor of the New York Stock Exchange. Such easy access to the news would give on-the-spot traders too much advantage in buying or selling securities.

BROKE. 1. To lack money; to be bare of funds.

2. The action of a declining market: "The market *broke* badly today."

BROKEN LOT. Any unit of trading smaller than the standard unit. In stocks—an ODD-LOT, or *fractional lot;* in bonds—an amount less than $1,000 PAR VALUE.

BROKER. One who acts as agent or intermediary between the buyers and sellers of securities or other property and charges a commission for his services. See FLOOR BROKER; MONEY BROKER; ODD-LOT BROKER; OUTSIDE BROKER; PUT AND CALL BROKER; REGISTERED REPRESENTATIVE; SPECIALIST; TWO-DOLLAR BROKER.

BROKERAGE. 1. The business of a broker, i.e., the brokerage business.

2. The fee or commission a broker charges for executing his client's order.

BROKERAGE ACCOUNT. An account maintained with a broker which enables him to buy and sell securities or commodities, for cash or on MARGIN on his client's behalf and subject to his order.

BROKER'S FREE CREDIT BALANCE. The amount of money standing idle in brokerage accounts, reported monthly by the New York Stock Exchange.

BROKER'S LOANS. The money a broker borrows to help finance "underwritings," investments, inventories of stocks and/or the purchase of securities made on a MARGIN basis by his customers. See UNDERWRITE.

BUBBLE. A fraudulent or illusory scheme; an unsound business venture. The most famous bubbles in financial history are the

Mississippi Bubble (France) and the South Sea Bubble (England); both of which collapsed in the 1720's.

BUCKETING. Term referring to sales made by a broker for his own account against customer's purchases or purchases by the broker against customer's sales. The practice of speculating against his customer's trades by a broker is strictly prohibited.

BUCKET SHOP. An illegal establishment run by irresponsible brokers, who are not members of an exchange. *Bucketeers* virtually bet against a customer, without his consent, that a given stock will go up, or down. If the customer buys, the broker sells an equal amount of the same stock ("short") against him; if he sells, the bucketeer purchases an equivalent amount of the same stock. See SHORT SALE. Orders are executed theoretically and not legitimately, i.e., they are *bucketed.* Should its customers win too often, the bucket shop closes overnight and moves elsewhere.

The term originated in London around 1825 and stemmed from the beer swillers' practice of going from street to street with a bucket and draining every keg they found. Gathering later around a table in their den, they passed the bucket for each to take his "draw." The den eventually became known as a bucket shop, and the term later was applied to establishments where counterfeit dealings were conducted in securities and commodities.

In the United States, where the term first became popular around the time of the panic of 1873, a bucket shop keeper was actually a dealer in broken lots (ODD-LOTS). In those days most brokers refused to accept orders for less than 100 shares. This caused a new class of broker to spring up. This class was not a member of the Exchange, but would accept odd-lot orders and combine them, until they totaled 100 shares, or a multiple thereof.

This practice of combining or bunching orders together as the staves of a bucket are combined to make a bucket caused the brokers to be nicknamed *bucket shop keepers.*

BUCK THE TREND. To SELL SHORT in a market where the trend is upward, or buy LONG in a downtrending market.

BULGE. A small, sudden and usually temporary rise in security prices.

BULL. An optimist on business and the stock market, who buys and holds a position in securities or commodities in anticipation of advancing prices. The opposite of BEAR. Stock market bulls out number the bears by an estimated ten-to-one. The term originated on the London Stock Exchange. The tendency of a bull to lift and throw an object up with his horns may be the reason why his name is linked with speculators who buy for an uplift of prices. The term for bull on the Paris Bourse is *haussier.*

BULL ACCOUNT. The grand total of securities held in anticipation of higher prices. The participation in the market which believes stocks will move upward.

BULL COMPAIGN. A sustained effort made by a group of market operators or financial interests to push security prices upward without joining a formal POOL.

BULL CLIQUE. An informal group of individuals or interests that works for an advance in prices.

BULL MARKET. A market featured by security prices advancing against a background of higher earnings and dividends, a favorable employment level, easy credit conditions, increased speculative activity and a feeling of prosperity for all.

The highest level attained by each INTERMEDIATE rally in a bull market generally carries above the previous high, and the lowest level reached on each setback holds above the preceding low. Bull markets invariably last longer than BEAR MARKETS.

BULL POOL. A formerly organized fund contributed by a group of individuals or interests for the purpose of buying one or more securities or commodities and manipulating the price upward. The operation is in charge of a pool manager, and the members have a pre-arranged agreement about the division of profits or losses. No member of the pool may trade individually in the same security or commodity that the pool is exploiting while such agreement is in force. This is a form of manipulation currently prohibited. See POOL.

BULL POSITION. The prevailing market status of the BULLS, as opposed to the BEARS, at a given moment of time. The bull position is said to be strong when the majority of market activity leans toward the buying side, and leading securities are being acquired for cash by INSTITUTIONAL or individual investors.

BUNCHED. Term referring to consecutive sales of the same security appearing in a string on the TICKER TAPE at identical, or different, prices. See PAINTING THE TAPE.

Also, an order consisting of two or more orders from different customers which the broker has combined and entered as one order for execution on an exchange. Although payment of the usual ODD-LOT DIFFERENTIAL can be avoided by *bunching* separate

ODD-LOT orders to make a ROUND-LOT, the regular commission must be paid on each odd-lot contributing to the round-lot order, under the rules of the Stock Exchange.

BUOYANT. Having a tendency to rise. When stocks are *buoyant* they are advancing.

BUSINESS BAROMETERS. Various published statistics which are useful for forecasting business, credit or stock market trends. They include: electric power production, steel and automobile output, rail freight carloadings, business failures and currency in circulation.

BUSINESS CYCLE. A regularly recurring period of undetermined scope and origin embracing prosperity, recession, depression and recovery.

BUSINESSMAN'S RISK. The risk involved in any securities or business venture which a businessman seems justified in taking. It is based on the idea that a businessman's association with business and economic matters and his ability to withstand a possible monetary loss, render him better equipped to assume a risk than others who might not be as well situated emotionally or financially.

BUTTONWOOD TREE. A spacious tree beneath whose branches gathered on May 17, 1792, a group of twenty-four gentlemen (the founders of the New York Stock Exchange) who declared themselves "Brokers for the purchase and sale of public stocks." On May 17, 1956—the 164th anniversary of that occasion—a young buttonwood (sycamore) was planted outside the Broad Street entrance to the Exchange and a plaque was installed in front of 68 Wall Street, where the original buttonwood stood.

BUY AND PUT AWAY. An expression which coincides with the old Wall Street maxim that the way to win success in the stock market is to *"buy good stocks, put 'em away and forget 'em."* The latter part of this aphorism has been often disproven, most recently by a Stock Exchange study. This study shows that the buyers of General Motors, du Pont, or National Lead in 1927 would have profited handsomely today by putting them away and forgetting them, but anyone who purchased Western Union, R. H. Macy, or General Signal would now show only a loss.

BUY BACK. The purchase of an identical amount of the same security that was previously "sold short" in order to satisfy the terms of the seller's contract and complete the transaction. Better known as SHORT COVERING. See SHORT SALE.

BUY IN. The enforced purchase of a security or commodity to satisfy the terms of a contract previously undertaken, but which cannot be fulfilled owing to an inability to make a good delivery or the insolvency of one of the contracting parties.

BUYING ON A SHOESTRING. Purchasing securities on very thin, or barely adequate MARGIN, the value of a *shoestring* (shoelace).

BUYING POWER. The cash or free credit balance existing in an account which may be applied toward the purchase of securities.

BUY ON BID. See ON BID, OR OFFER.

BUY ON MARGIN. See MARGIN.

BUY ON SCALE. A method of averaging down (reducing) the total cost of purchasing several hundred shares of the same security. It is based on the principle that anyone buying a stock should automatically assume it will decline below the level he considers to be low—that no one catches the exact bottom price, unless he is lucky.

The system involves purchasing additional shares of the same stock at fixed intervals and to a prescribed point below the price of the initial purchase. For example: a trader wishing to buy 1,000 shares of XYZ stock on a ¼ point scale down from 47, will enter ten separate, 100 share buy orders starting with 47 and continuing to 44¾. The advantage is that following purchase of the final 100 shares, a 50% recovery of the decline from 47 will leave the trader owning 1,000 shares of XYZ at 45⅞ without a loss. Purchases may also be *scaled up* in a rising market. The same principle applies to SELL ON SCALE. See SCALE ORDER.

BUY ON THE OFFER. A method of buying an ODD-LOT (usually 1–99 shares) without having to wait for a ROUND-LOT sale (100 shares, or any multiple) to take place in the same stock.

The price at which an odd-lot order is executed, if entered AT THE MARKET, depends on the price of the first round-lot sale after the odd-lot dealer receives the order on the trading floor. However, if the stock is seldom traded, the order may not be filled for hours, or even days. In order to avoid delay in purchasing an odd-lot of a relatively inactive issue, an order may be entered to "Buy on the Offer." This will be executed immediately at a price 12½ cents per share above the lowest quoted asking price at the time the order is received by the broker, if such price is below $40; or the order will be executed at 25 cents per share above the asking price if such price is $40 or above. The same principle applies to "sell on the bid." See ON BID; OFFER.

BUY ORDER. An order given to a broker or a bank authorizing the purchase of a specified amount of securities or commodities. Unless otherwise stipulated as to time, all orders are treated as DAY ORDERS, good only on the day they are given. However, orders may also be placed with a time limit: G.T.W. (Good This Week); G.T.M. (Good This Month); GOOD THROUGH——(A Specified Date); and OPEN, or G.T.C. (Good 'Till Cancelled, or Countermanded).

Regarding a price limit, the order may be entered AT THE MARKET (the best price obtainable) or limited to a specific price.

BUY OUTRIGHT. To purchase securities on a 100% cash basis paying the full price. This is the opposite of buying on MARGIN and generally considered synonymous with buying for investment.

C

C. 1. The TICKER abbreviation for Chrysler Corporation.

2. When printed on the lower line of the TICKER TAPE, following prices, this letter means "cash."

CALL. 1. A STOCK OPTION CONTRACT which obligates the writer, or the seller thereof, to deliver upon demand 100 shares of a particular stock at a set price within a specified time limit. The opposite of PUT. Calls on such things as grain, cotton, coffee, are based on the same general principles.

2. See MARGIN CALL.

CALLABLE. Term applying to bonds or preferred stocks which contain a conditional clause giving the issuer the right to retire, (redeem) the security before its stated maturity. Such issues are described as being SUBJECT TO CALL; SUBJECT TO REDEMPTION. The opposite of NON-CALLABLE, or NOT SUBJECT TO CALL.

CALL LOAN. A loan bearing no fixed maturity date or interest rate which is payable on demand.

THOMAS, HAAB & BOTTS

Member Put and Call Brokers and Dealers Association, Inc.

PUT AND CALL OPTIONS

GUARANTEED BY MEMBERS N. Y. STOCK EXCHANGE

50 BROADWAY, N. Y. C. 4 BOWLING GREEN 9-8470-5

New York, N. Y.____________19____

For Value Received, the BEARER may CALL on the endorser for ONE HUNDRED (100) shares of the____________

stock of the____________

at____________Dollars ($____________) per share

ANY TIME WITHIN____________days from date.

THIS STOCK OPTION CONTRACT MUST BE PRESENTED, AS SPECIFIED BELOW, TO THE ENDORSING FIRM BEFORE THE EXPIRATION OF THE EXACT TIME LIMIT. IT CANNOT BE EXERCISED BY TELEPHONE.

DURING THE LIFE OF THIS OPTION:

1. (a) — the contract price hereof shall be reduced by the value of any cash dividend on the day the stock goes ex-dividend; (b) — where the Option is entitled to rights and/or warrants the contract price shall be reduced by the value of same as fixed by the opening sale thereof on the day the stock sells ex-rights and/or warrants.

2. (a) — in the event of stock splits, reverse splits or other similar action by the above-mentioned corporation, this Option shall become an Option for the equivalent in new securities when duly listed for trading and the total contract price shall not be reduced; (b) — stock dividends or the equivalent due-bills shall be attached to the stock covered hereby, when and if this Option is exercised, and the total contract price shall not be reduced.

Upon presentation to the endorser of this Option attached to a comparison ticket in the manner and time specified, the endorser agrees to accept notice of the Bearer's exercise by stamping the comparison, and this acknowledgment shall constitute a contract and shall be controlling with respect to delivery of the stock and settlement in accordance with New York Stock Exchange usage.

EXPIRES____________19____
3:15 P. M.

PUT AND CALL BROKERS & DEALERS ASSOCIATION, INC. CORPORATE SEAL

SOLD BY MEMBER
PUT & CALL
BROKERS & DEALERS
ASSOCIATION, Inc.

The undersigned acts as intermediary only, without obligation other than to obtain a New York Stock Exchange firm as Endorser.

S No. 591

CALL OPTION

CAPITAL. (A) From an economic standpoint, manufactured goods are *capital;* (B) From an accounting standpoint, the term is synonymous with NET WORTH and means the excess of assets over liabilities; (C) From a business standpoint, capital is money —such as funds invested in an industry, a business, or a partnership. Also, in a corporate sense, capital is represented by various stock issues, surplus and undivided profits. According to W. W. Carlile in *Economic Method and Economic Fallacies:* "Capital is wealth which is devoted or intended to be devoted to the production of fresh wealth." See ACTIVE CAPITAL; FIXED CAPITAL; FLOATING CAPITAL; RISK CAPITAL; VENTURE CAPITAL; WORKING CAPITAL.

CAPITAL ACCOUNT. Term referring to a corporation's investments in real estate, fixtures, machinery and other CAPITAL or FIXED ASSETS.

CAPITAL ASSETS. Term generally synonymous with FIXED ASSETS.

CAPITAL EXPENDITURES. Capital spending by corporations for new plant and equipment and for modernizing and replacing obsolete facilities. The level of such expenditures usually depends upon the degree of business optimism in the near-term and long-range outlook. This capital spending takes into account such factors as growth of population, increased consumer demand, and expanded sales in new products in the years ahead. In recent years American Telephone & Telegraph has dwarfed all other corporate spending programs by a wide margin.

CAPITAL GAIN. A profit derived from the sale of capital assets such as securities or real property. The gain may be classed as a long-term capital gain, or a short-term capital gain. Short-term gains (6 months, or less) are taxed according to the full income tax rate of the individual. Long-term gains (more than 6 months) are taxed at a maximum rate of 25% and less, if the taxpayer is in a lower tax bracket.

CAPITAL GAIN DISTRIBUTION. A payment made to shareholders from net long-term capital gains realized from the sale of securities or other CAPITAL GOODS.

CAPITAL GOODS. Material goods (factory buildings, equipment and other instruments of production) used to produce wealth. See CONSUMER GOODS.

CAPITALIZATION. The aggregate PAR VALUE of a corporation's stock OUTSTANDING: plus any borrowed capital, as represented by bonds or other comparable long-term debt. A business may be capitalized by placing a value on it, and then issuing securities to represent that value. Although bonds signify indebtedness, a company's capitalization (the amount for which it is capitalized) usually means the amount of its bonds and its stock added together.

CAPITAL LIABILITIES. Term virtually synonymous with CAPITALIZATION and meaning the long-term debt of a corporation, as represented by its combined bonded indebtedness and usually including CAPITAL STOCK, although the latter represents ownership and is not claimable by creditors.

CAPITAL LOSS. A loss derived from the sale of capital assets such as securities or real property. Up to $1,000 of such loss may be deducted from taxable income for the year reported. If the loss exceeds $1,000—in each of the following five years, up to $1,000 may be deducted.

CAPITAL STOCK. All shares representing ownership in a company including common and preferred stock. If there is no preferred stock, the company may classify its only issue of stock as capital stock. If so, the capital stock is the same as common stock, and the dividend can be increased or decreased depending upon how profitable the corporation's operations are.

CAPITAL STRUCTURE. Same as CAPITALIZATION.

CARE OF SECURITIES. The first thing an investor should do after buying and paying for a stock is to have it registered in his name. There are two ways of safeguarding it after that: (1) when he has the certificate actually in his possession; (2) when he leaves it for safekeeping with a bank or brokerage firm. From a safety standpoint, the difference between a bank and a broker is inconsequential.

There is no substitute for caution, and anyone electing to guard his own securities should (A) never mail a certificate, except by registered mail; (B) never sign his name on the back of a certificate, until it is necessary to do so; (C) keep a separate record of all certificate numbers, names of companies and the exact number of shares held in each. See LOST CERTIFICATES; STOCK POWER.

CARLOADINGS. An important statistic published weekly by the Association of American Railroads, which gives the total number of freight cars loaded by CLASS ONE RAILROADS during the week.

CARRY. 1. To maintain a position in securities or commodities in expectation of an advance in price.

2. To furnish the difference between the price of a security bought on margin and the amount of the customer's down payment. See CARRYING CHARGES; MARGIN.

CARRYING CHARGES. The interest charged by a broker for carrying his customer's securities on MARGIN. In order to compensate for the expense and responsibility of obtaining the money necessary to carry a MARGIN ACCOUNT, brokers usually charge their clients a slightly higher rate than the brokers are charged by the bank.

CASH ACCOUNT. An account maintained entirely on a cash basis: i.e., all securities held therein are fully paid for. The opposite of MARGIN ACCOUNT.

CASH ASSETS. Assets consisting of cash, or the equivalent as, for example, government bonds or other negotiable instruments generally accepted as money.

CASH COMMODITY. See SPOT.

CASH DIVIDEND. A dividend paid on a security in cash or by check.

CASH EARNINGS. Net income or profits of a corporation including DEPRECIATION and AMORTIZATION accruals.

CASH FLOW. The measure of a company's ability to pay dividends and its power to invest in expansion after deducting for dividends. For example, the net profits of a company may be only moderate, yet cash may flow into its treasury at a steady rate because large amounts are being written off for DEPRECIATION, or AMORTIZATION. These funds do not really represent a profit, but they are nevertheless available to the company for improvements, debt retirement, working capital, or other purposes, and are considered an excellent barometer of fiscal health. Cash flow plays an important role in facilitating financing for corporations.

CASH-INS. See REDEMPTIONS.

CASH ITEMS. Refer to certain items in a corporate statement which are considered the equivalent of cash (bank deposits, U.S. Government bonds or notes, and marketable securities).

CASH SALE, or TRADE. A transaction calling for delivery of the securities on the day of sale. See REGULAR WAY; SELLER'S OPTION.

CATS AND DOGS. A slang expression meaning highly speculative, and generally low-priced, stocks paying no dividend.

CAVEAT EMPTOR. Latin expression meaning: "Let the buyer beware," i.e., investigate *before* you invest.

CAVEAT VENDITOR. Latin expression meaning: "Let the seller beware."

CERTIFICATE. See STOCK CERTIFICATE.

CERTIFICATES OF INDEBTEDNESS. Unsecured, short-term notes issued mainly by the Government to raise funds to meet current expenses.

CHARGE OFF. See WRITE OFF.

CHARTIST. Term synonymous with TECHNICIAN and meaning a person who makes, interprets, or follows the bars and lines, numbers or x's, drawn on graph paper to indicate what a stock, a group of stocks, or the general market has done and what it may do in the future. See CHARTS; LINE CHART; POINT AND FIGURE CHART.

CHARTIST'S LIABILITY. The estimated degree of risk involved in buying a stock or selling it SHORT as calculated by studying its chart pattern.

CHARTS. Pieces of graph paper on which are recorded (usually each day as they occur) the price changes that have taken place in a particular stock, a group of stocks, or the general market, with attendant volume of buying and selling. See LINE CHART; POINT AND FIGURE CHART.

Following are typical chart formations which trained CHARTISTS, or TECHNICIANS study for clues to future market action.

CHEAP MONEY. See EASY MONEY.

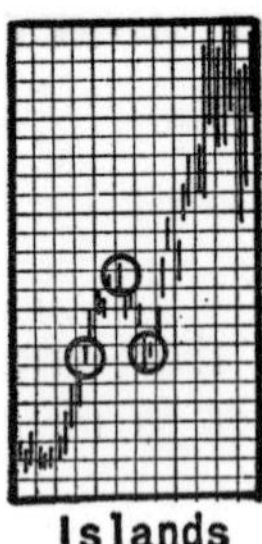
Islands

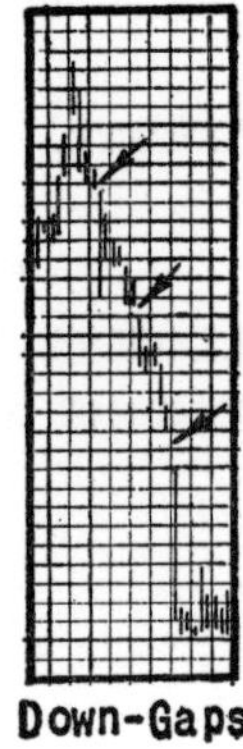
Down-Gaps

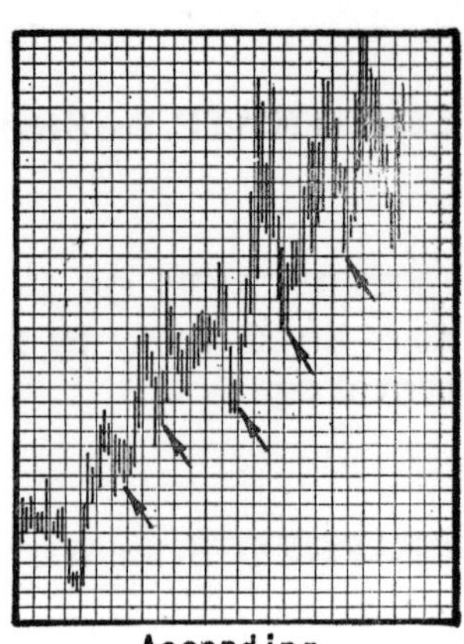
Ascending
Support Levels

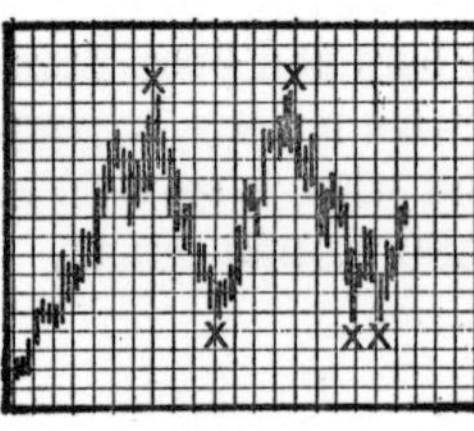

Double Top
and
Triple Bottom

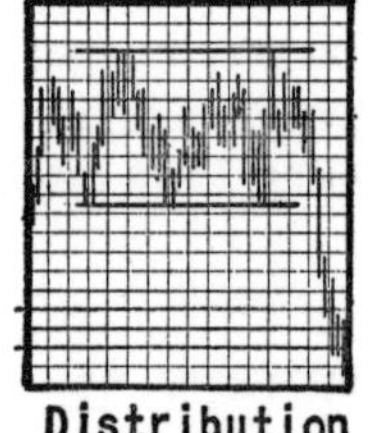
Distribution
Rectangle

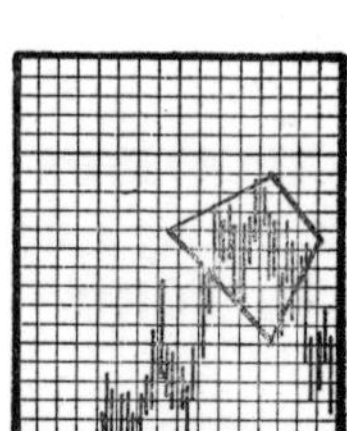
Diamond
Reversal
Formation

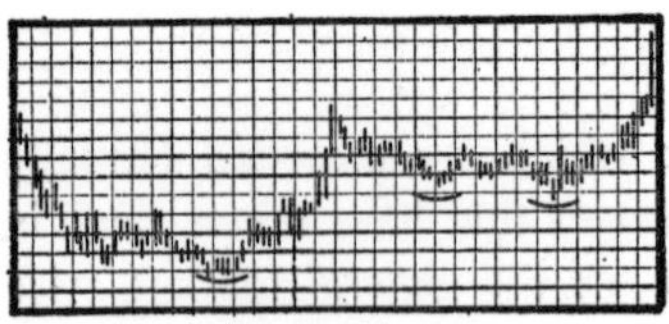
Round or
Saucer Bottoms

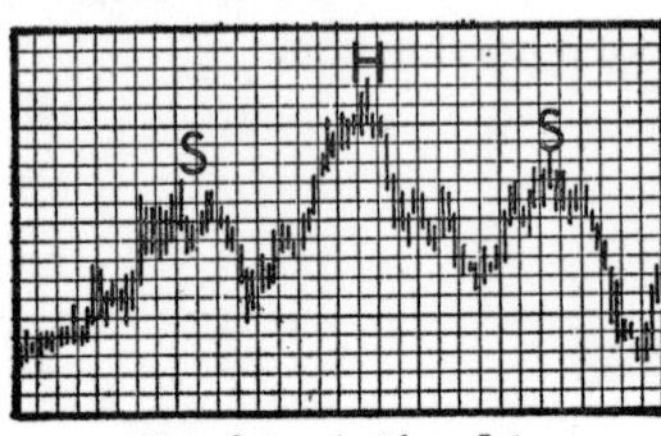

Head and Shoulders

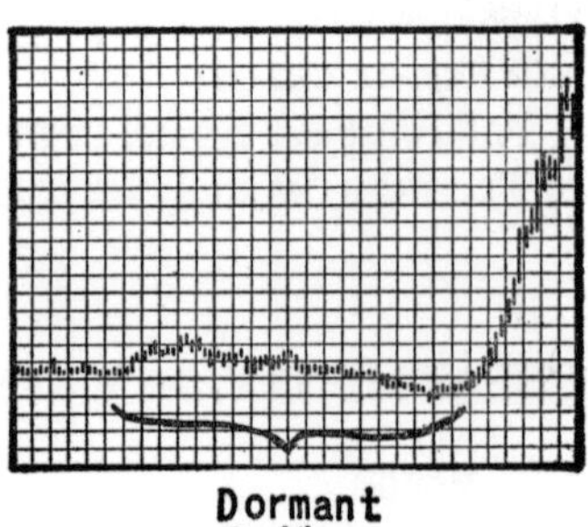
Dormant
Bottom

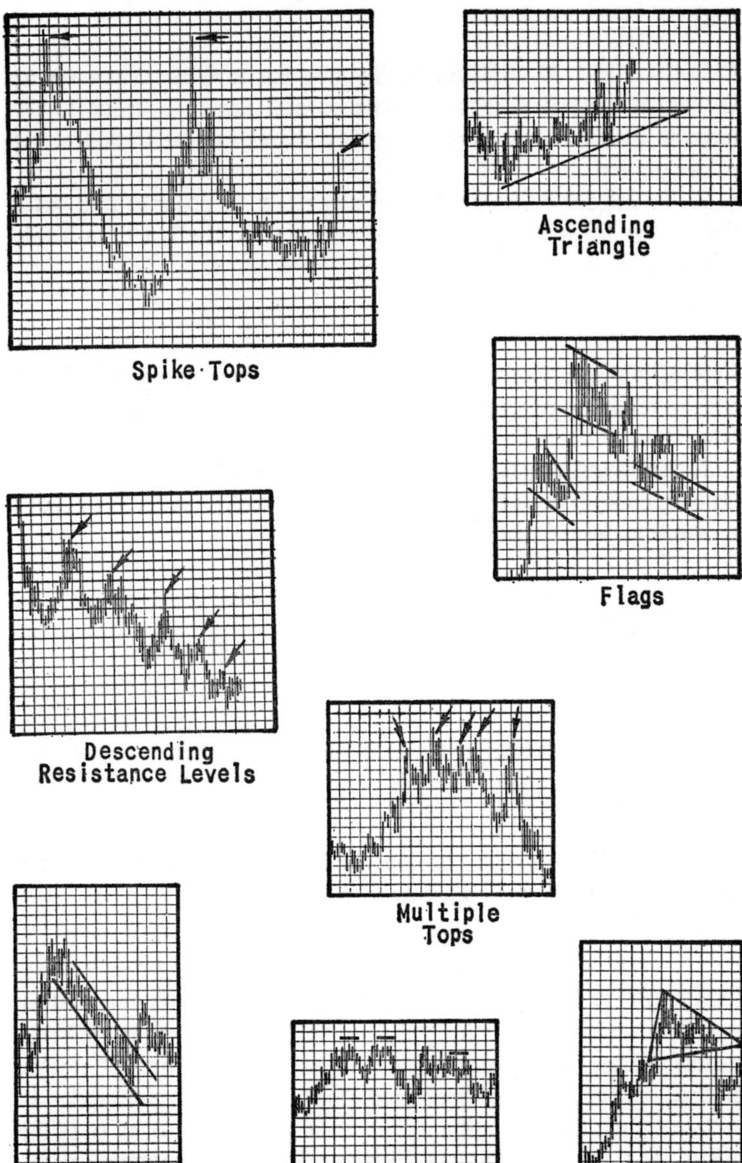
Spike·Tops
Ascending Triangle
Flags
Descending Resistance Levels
Multiple Tops
Falling Wedge
Flat Tops
Triangle Top

CHECK THE MARKET. 1. To ask for a QUOTATION on an OVER-THE-COUNTER security from several firms, in order to determine which is best and how many shares can be traded at the prices quoted.

2. To ask for a QUOTATION on any stock, in order to find out if the market for it has changed very much since the last time it sold or was quoted.

CHURNING. 1. Continuous buying and selling among speculators with virtually no progress being made by the market in either direction.

2. An illegal practice referring to a broker's attempt to build up his own commissions by buying and selling securities for his client's accounts as frequently as possible.

CIRCULATING CAPITAL. See FLOATING CAPITAL.

CLASS A—CLASS B. See CLASSIFIED BOND; STOCK.

CLASSIFIED. Securities are *classified* when any particular issue is divided into two or more classes.

CLASSIFIED BOND, STOCK. Securities of the same corporation issued in series. Class "A," "B," or "C" bonds vary as to issue, maturity date, or interest payment. Class "A," "B," or "C" stocks, or first, second, or third preferred stocks vary as to preference in certain rights; the first in the series usually having priority over the others. See FIRST PREFERRED STOCK; PRIOR PREFERRED STOCK.

CLASS ONE RAILROAD. A railroad with gross annual revenues totaling $3 million or more.

CLEAN UP. To win a large profit.

CLEARED. Securities are *cleared* (freed from encumbrance) when the person who has contracted to buy them pays for and receives delivery. Some brokerage firms make a specialty of CLEARING transactions for other brokers for a commission or fee which varies with the price of the security and the status of such brokers (members of the same exchange, out-of-town members, or non-members). Members obtain a special rate, but non-members pay full commission.

CLEARING. The physical transfer of cash and securities between buyers and sellers including the related bookkeeping.

CLEARING HOUSE. See STOCK CLEARING CORPORATION.

CLIMAX. The culmination of an extended upward or downward price movement, usually accompanied by a large volume of trading—also called BLOW OFF.

CLIQUE. An informal group of speculators formed for the purpose of manipulating a stock or group of stocks. A clique has no formal written agreement, hence it differs somewhat from a POOL. Also, its management is not entrusted to a single member.

CLOSE (CLOSED) CORPORATION. A corporation whose stock is in the hands of only a few persons and is seldom, if ever, offered for public sale.

CLOSED ACCOUNT. 1. An account which has been liquidated for lack of sufficient margin. See MARGIN REQUIREMENTS.

2. An account from which all cash and securities have been withdrawn by the owner.

CLOSED-END FUND. An INVESTMENT COMPANY whose shares are traded on a securities exchange, or the OVER-THE-COUNTER market. The number of shares OUTSTANDING is limited by the company's charter and their value is determined in the open market. See MUTUAL FUND.

CLOSED TRADE. A transaction which has been consummated by selling a security that was previously bought LONG, or "buying in" a security previously sold SHORT. See SHORT SALE; SHORT COVERING.

CLOSELY HELD. Term indicating that a certain percentage of a company's common stock is known to be held for long-term investment purposes, as by a family or another company, and is therefore unlikely to come on the market for immediate sale.

CLOSE MARKET. The opposite of WIDE MARKET and meaning that the BID and ASKED prices quoted for a stock are unusually near together.

CLOSE OUT. To finally dispose of, such as when the last shares of a large BLOCK of stock are sold.

CLOSE, THE. The period at the end of a trading session, officially designated by the Exchange. All transactions are considered made *at the close* when made during this period.

CLOSING OF THE EXCHANGE. See HOURS OF BUSINESS.

CLOSING PRICE. The price at which the final transaction in a security took place on a particular business day. Stock prices are quoted daily in the financial pages of leading newspapers, where number of shares traded and the opening, high, low and last sale (closing) prices, plus net change from the previous day, are printed from left to right in that order.

COALER. A railroad whose freight loadings consist largely of coal.

COLLATERAL. Securities or other property pledged against the payment of borrowed money.

COLLATERAL TRUST BOND. A bond secured by a pledge of other securities, either bonds or stocks, rather than by real property.

COMMERCIAL PAPER. Unsecured, short-term negotiable instruments, promissory notes, bills of exchange or acceptances sold by industrial concerns and finance companies which call for a fixed sum of money at a specific time.

COMMISSION. The charge made by a broker for executing his client's order. For commissions on the New York Stock Exchange, involving $100 or more, the minimum commission charge ranges between $6.00 and $75 per transaction provided the number of shares involved in the transaction does not exceed 100. Also, within these limits, the minimum charge shall not exceed $1.50 per share. If the money involved is less than $100, the commission is mutually agreed upon between the customer and the broker. Commissions are basically calculated as a percent of the money involved, plus a stated dollar amount per transaction. Commissions must be charged and collected on all purchases and sales of securities on the Exchange under all circumstances. Higher commission rates last went into effect on the New York Stock Exchange May 1, 1958.

COMMISSION HOUSE. A brokerage firm, or WIRE HOUSE, which furnishes investment information, accepts and executes orders, receives and delivers securities, etc. and maintains a close contact with the investing public.

COMMITTEES. In addition to the BOARD OF GOVERNORS, the following are among the more important committees of the New York Stock Exchange: Admissions—considers applications for membership on the Exchange; Business Conduct—reviews matters connected with the business relationship between members and customers, and guards against improper transactions, which might be resorted to; Stock List—considers applications for "listing" securities on the Exchange. See LISTING REQUIREMENTS.

COMMODITY. A transportable article of commerce, or trade; such as corn, wheat, cotton, sugar, coffee, oats.

COMMODITY EXCHANGE. An organized exchange where commodities are traded. They are usually located near adequate transportation facilities and generally in cities through which a substantial portion of the actual commodity passes each year. The leading domestic grain futures exchanges are in Chicago, Minneapolis and Kansas City. Canada has an important grain futures exchange: The Winnipeg Grain Exchange. The leading cotton and cottonseed oil exchanges are in New York and New Orleans. Coffee, sugar, cocoa, rubber, hides, potatoes and metals have futures markets in New York City. Egg futures markets are in Chicago.

Commodity exchanges, like stock exchanges, are member organizations. Most members are businessmen engaged in producing, marketing or processing commodities; and brokers whose principal activity is to execute orders for others. Non-members trade through brokerage firms which hold memberships through partnerships or officers. The exchanges are supported by dues and assessments on members.

Each exchange, like the Stock Exchange, has its own governing board which sees to it that business is carried out fairly and efficiently under the rules. These rules are designed for equal fairness to large and small business interests and speculators, whether members or non-members. The exchanges do not buy, or sell, or set prices. All prices are established through open trading around the trading rings, PITS provided by the exchanges.

COMMON MARKET. A group of West European countries which advocates a gradual tearing down of tariff barriers among its members and calls for a common tariff wall against goods coming onto the market from other lands. The Common Market or European Economic Community which came into existence in Rome, Italy on March 25, 1957, has a considerable influence on business decision-making. American manufacturers are increasing their investments in the member countries by establishing or enlarging local subsidiaries, or by arranging licensing and royalty agreements with local firms.

COMMON STOCK. That part of a company's CAPITALIZATION which is not preferred. Dividends may be paid only after the requirements of FLOATING DEBT, bond interest, and PREFERRED STOCK have been met.

COMPARISON. A memorandum made up in duplicate, which includes all data relative to a securities transaction. Referred to both the buyer and the seller, it is stamped if found to be correct; one party keeps the original, the other the duplicate for their records. If the trade is unknown, it is marked "D.K." (Don't Know) and returned.

COMPLETES. A term included in a FLOOR REPORT from a broker, which indicates that an order to buy, or sell, a block of securities has been filled, or completed. See TO COME—TO GO.

COMPOUND INTEREST. The interest upon principal which is being increased, or augmented, periodically by interest paid on the previous amount of principal. Interest may be compounded monthly, quarterly, semiannually, or annually. See EXACT INTEREST; ORDINARY INTEREST; SIMPLE INTEREST.

CONFIRMATION. A formal memorandum delivered to a client of a brokerage firm, which bears all data relevant to any securities contract which the client may have assumed.

CONSOLIDATED BALANCE SHEET. A statement presented in tabular form showing the combined financial condition of two, or more, corporations which are closely related, or whose businesses are conducted as a unit. See BALANCE SHEET.

CONSOLIDATION. The reorganization and strengthening of a price level recently attained. "The market is trying to *consolidate* its gains achieved during the past few days of advancing action." See MERGER.

CONSUMER CREDIT. Credit extended to consumers through charge accounts, installment plans or money loans which enables them to purchase CONSUMER GOODS and services.

CONSUMER GOODS. Economic goods which satisfy human desires. An automobile, when used for pleasure, is a consumer good; when used for business, it is a CAPITAL GOOD. Consumer goods are generally classified according to durability—for example: durable—automobile; non-durable—food.

CONTINGENT FUND. A fund set aside to cover contingent or possible liabilities, such as might result from a lawsuit, a decline in the value of foreign investment or some other chance happening. Any number of funds or reserves may be set up, depending on the nature and extent of the costs or losses anticipated.

CONTINGENT LIABILITIES. Potential, or secondary, liabilities which can become actual only upon the occurrence of some uncertain event.

CONTINGENT ORDER. An order to buy or sell a stock at a certain price which is contingent upon the prior execution of another order. "Buy 100 OPQ at ____, if you can sell 100 XYZ at ____."

CONTINUOUS MARKET. A market where there is always a seller available during regular business hours. The SPECIALIST in a stock acts as an auctioneer, receiving running bids from potential buyers and sellers of the stock in which he specializes. A continuous market was first established on the New York Stock Exchange in September, 1871.

CONTRACT. A written, oral, or implied, agreement between two or more parties.

CONTRARY MARKET. A market which moves contrary to general expectations. For example, when World War II began the Dow-Jones Industrials advanced 23%, but when the Korean War broke out it dropped 14%. From January–June, 1959 when steel-labor negotiations were underway, the market went up, but early in 1962 when steel was again a dominant factor, the market went into a steep decline.

CONTROLLING INTEREST. One person, or a number together, is said to have a *controlling interest* when he has obtained by ownership, or by "proxies," the right to cast the votes for a majority of stock of a corporation. See PROXY.

CONVERSION PRICE. The price for which a CONVERTIBLE BOND of a corporation may be exchanged for stock of the same corporation. See CONVERSION RATIO.

CONVERSION RATIO. The number of shares of common stock for which a CONVERTIBLE BOND, or CONVERTIBLE PREFERRED STOCK, of the same corporation can be exchanged. The conversion price is usually indicated at the time the bond is issued, and it may differ from the price of the stock when the right to convert is exercised. See CONVERSION PRICE.

CONVERTIBLE BOND. A bond which carries with it the privilege of conversion or exchange for common stock of the same company at a fixed price for the common, whenever the investor considers this would be to his advantage. In other words, the privilege is exercisable at the option of the bondholder. Not only does he have an interest bearing bond, but if the common shares rise, he will benefit also since his bond represents a "call" on a certain number of shares. Because the credit rating of industrial corporations is often lower than that of utility companies, convertible bonds are more commonly used by the former than the latter. See DEBENTURE.

CONVERTIBLE PREFERRED STOCK. A stock which may be exchanged at the holder's option for a specified number of common shares of the same company.

COOLING OFF PERIOD. The 30-day waiting period required by the SECURITIES AND EXCHANGE COMMISSION before the registration of a new issue of securities becomes effective. See REGISTRATION OF SECURITIES.

CORNER. A *corner* in a security or commodity is said to exist when an individual or group has bought a majority of the FLOATING SUPPLY (purchasable stock) of a company and intends to profit by advancing the price. The speculators, who have sold the stock short cannot, by reason of the corner, acquire enough stock to make delivery to the buyers or return the stock which they have borrowed, and are thus forced into a corner and "squeezed." In order to fulfill their contracts, they must pay the prices demanded by those in control of the corner. A court witness once described a corner as "a . . . combination to prevent people short of stock from buying them." This is a form of manipulation currently prohibited. However, a corner in a security may also be brought about accidentally. See BLACK FRIDAY; SHORT SALE.

CORPORATE BOND. An instrument written under seal whereby a corporation acknowledges a stated sum is owed, which it will repay at a specified date. It also obligates itself to pay a stipulated amount of interest to the bondholders for the privilege of using their money.

CORPORATE SHELL. A company with no FIXED ASSETS except cash, a name, and sometimes a stock exchange listing. See LISTED SECURITIES.

CORPORATION. An artificial being composed of one or more individuals and established by law for some specific purpose or purposes whose existence, power and scope of action are determined by its charter.

CORPORATION SECURITIES. The securities of business corporations, as compared with government or municipal securities.

CORRECTION. A price reaction in the general market, a specific group of stocks or an individual specialty stock which causes it to lose perhaps ⅓ to ⅔ of its previous gain.

CORRESPONDENT FIRM. A brokerage firm which carries on a mutually advantageous business and financial association with another firm. This usually takes the form of an out-of-town New York Stock Exchange MEMBER FIRM having its business executed and CLEARED by a member firm located in New York City.

COST OF GOODS SOLD. An item appearing in the PROFIT AND LOSS STATEMENT of a corporation, which includes all expenses connected with the manufacture of the products the company sells. Expenses such as freight, power, raw materials, rent and wages would be included.

COST OF SALES. An item characteristic of the PROFIT AND LOSS STATEMENT of a manufacturing company, which refers to expenses and other operating charges; COST OF GOODS SOLD, selling, administrative and general expenses, DEPRECIATION, maintenance and repairs, and taxes (other than Federal income taxes) would be examples. The Profit and Loss Statement of a railroad or utility company would label these items OPERATING EXPENSES.

COUNTERMAND. To cancel an order which has been entered, but not yet executed. See G.T.C.; G.T.M.; G.T.W.; OPEN ORDER.

COUPON. A certificate attached to a bond, which represents an obligation for interest on the bond. The coupons are in ticket form so they can be clipped off as they become due; and sold, or deposited, in a bank the same way as cash or a check.

COUPON BOND. A negotiable bond, the regular interest on which is payable to the person who clips the coupon and deposits it at his bank for collection. Upon maturity, the bearer is paid the FACE VALUE of the security. See REGISTERED BOND.

COVERING. Terminating a SHORT SALE contract by buying back a security or commodity; that is, to repurchase securities previously sold, but which were not actually in the seller's possession at the time of sale.

CREDIT BALANCE. The balance remaining in an account after all claims, such as interest and commissions have been settled. When securities are sold short, an account may show a credit balance. However, this is only a false credit created by the SHORT SALE.

CROP YEAR. A commodity term indicating the period from the harvest of a crop to the corresponding period of the following year, as used statistically. The U.S. wheat crop year begins July 1 and ends June 30; cotton begins August 1 and ends July 31; other commodities have varying dates.

CROSSING. Executing both sides in a brokerage transaction, with one broker performing the simultaneous functions of buyer and seller of the same stock. When a broker-member of the Stock Exchange has such an order, he must publicly offer the security for sale at a price that is enough higher than his bid price to meet the minimum "variation" permitted in the security, before consummating the transaction with himself. See VARIATIONS IN PRICE.

CROWD. The aggregate of brokers—SPECIALISTS, FLOOR TRADERS, ODD-LOT DEALERS who transact business in stocks on the floor of the Stock Exchange. Brokers dealing exclusively in bonds are referred to collectively as the BOND CROWD. They deal in over 1,180 bond issues. Brokers who lend money or securities to other brokers comprise the LOAN CROWD.

CUM-DIVIDEND. With the dividend. The London Stock Exchange equivalent of DIVIDEND ON.

CUMULATIVE DIVIDEND. A dividend, which if not paid regularly, or in full, becomes a liability and must be paid in the future by a corporation before dividends can be paid on the common stock. See ARREARS.

CUMULATIVE PREFERRED STOCK. A stock on which the dividends accumulate if not paid in full. Such dividends are said to be in ARREARS, and must be paid before any disbursement can be made on the common stock.

CURB BROKER (CURBSTONE BROKER). A member of the old New York Curb Market (now the American Stock Exchange), which moved indoors in 1921.

CURB EXCHANGE. See AMERICAN STOCK EXCHANGE.

CURRENT ASSETS. Cash, or other assets which will be eventually converted into cash, such as raw materials, accounts and notes receivable. These are also known as FLOATING ASSETS or QUICK ASSETS.

CURRENT LIABILITIES. Liabilities which become due, usually within a year, such as accounts and notes payable, accrued expenses, unearned income, taxes payable. Also revenues earned in advance for services yet to be performed or merchandise to be delivered in the future.

CURRENT PRICES. The last sale prices prevailing in the market at a specific moment of time.

CURRENT RATIO. The mathematical relationship (ratio) between CURRENT ASSETS and CURRENT LIABILITIES. It strikes the balance between what a company owns and owes and what it is owed on a short-term basis, and is one of the ways of determining a credit risk.

$$\frac{\text{Current Assets}}{\text{Current Liabilities}} = \text{Current Ratio}$$

CUSTOMER'S AGREEMENT AND CONSENT. A form requiring the signature of any client maintaining a MARGIN ACCOUNT with a MEMBER FIRM, whereby the client agrees to abide by certain rules and regulations of the New York Stock Exchange, the SECURITIES AND EXCHANGE COMMISSION, the FEDERAL RESERVE BOARD and others respecting the account.

CUSTOMER'S BROKER, OR CUSTOMER'S MAN. Same as REGISTERED REPRESENTATIVE.

CUSTOMER'S FREE CREDIT BALANCE. The cash credit balance remaining in a customer's account that may be used as he sees fit. This does not include a credit balance created by a SHORT SALE.

CUSTOMER'S ROOM. Same as BOARD ROOM.

CUTTING A LOSS. The decision to close out an unprofitable market position and take the loss involved before it becomes larger.

CYCLICAL STOCKS. Stocks which move directly with the BUSINESS CYCLE; generally they advance as business conditions improve and decline when business slackens. Steel, chemical, textile and machinery stocks are included in this category. To offset cyclical factors, many companies today are striving to diversify their operations among other fields and products.

CYCLICAL THEORY. A theory which holds that the volume of trade rises and falls in regular cycles, which can be identified fairly accurately, and this in turn is reflected in the stock market. Generally speaking, there are three kinds of cycles: (A) The Major Cycle spanning about 30 years, during which business volume and commodity prices, move either up or down, one movement following the other; (B) The Minor Cycle covering 8–11 years, during which there is a clearly defined trend within the Major Cycle; (C) The Short-Term Cycle, running from 20–24

ASEF—Form 101—Revised July, 1955

CUSTOMER'S AGREEMENT

DOE, ROE & CO.,
WALL STREET,
NEW YORK, N. Y.

Gentlemen:

In consideration of your accepting one or more accounts of the undersigned (whether designated by name, number or otherwise) and your agreeing to act as brokers for the undersigned in the purchase or sale of securities or commodities, the undersigned agrees as follows:

1. All transactions under this agreement shall be subject to the constitution, rules, regulations, customs and usages of the exchange or market, and its clearing house, if any, where the transactions are executed by you or your agents, and, where applicable, to the provisions of the Securities Exchange Act of 1934, the Commodities Exchange Act, and present and future acts amendatory thereof and supplemental thereto, and the rules and regulations of the Federal Securities and Exchange Commission, the Board of Governors of the Federal Reserve System and of the Secretary of Agriculture in so far as they may be applicable.

2. Whenever any statute shall be enacted which shall affect in any manner or be inconsistent with any of the provisions hereof, or whenever any rule or regulation shall be prescribed or promulgated by the New York Stock Exchange, the Federal Securities and Exchange Commission, the Board of Governors of the Federal Reserve System and/or the Secretary of Agriculture which shall affect in any manner or be inconsistent with any of the provisions hereof, the provisions of this agreement so affected shall be deemed modified or superseded, as the case may be, by such statute, rule or regulation, and all other provisions of the agreement and the provisions as so modified or superseded, shall in all respects continue and be in full force and effect.

3. Except as herein otherwise expressly provided, no provision of this agreement shall in any respect be waived, altered, modified or amended unless such waiver, alteration, modification or amendment be committed to writing and signed by a member of your organization.

4. All monies, securities, commodities or other property which you may at any time be carrying for the undersigned or which may at any time be in your possession for any purpose, including safekeeping, shall be subject to a general lien for the discharge of all obligations of the undersigned to you, irrespective of whether or not you have made advances in connection with such securities, commodities or other property, and irrespective of the number of accounts the undersigned may have with you.

5. All securities and commodities or any other property, now or hereafter held by you, or carried by you for the undersigned (either individually or jointly with others), or deposited to secure the same, may from time to time and without notice to me, be carried in your general loans and may be pledged, re-pledged, hypothecated or re-hypothecated, separately or in common with other securities and commodities or any other property, for the sum due to you thereon or for a greater sum and without retaining in your possession and control for delivery a like amount of similar securities or commodities.

6. Debit balances of the accounts of the undersigned shall be charged with interest, in accordance with your usual custom, and with any increases in rates caused by money market conditions, and with such other charges as you may make to cover your facilities and extra services.

7. You are hereby authorized, in your discretion, should the undersigned die or should you for any reason whatsoever deem it necessary for your protection, to sell any or all of the securities and commodities or other property which may be in your possession, or which you may be carrying for the undersigned (either individually or jointly with others), or to buy in any securities commodities or other property of which the account or accounts of the undersigned may be short, or cancel any outstanding orders in order to close out the account or accounts of the undersigned in whole or in part or in order to close out any commitment made in behalf of the undersigned. Such sale, purchase or cancellation may be made according to your judgment and may be made, at your discretion, on the exchange or other market where such business is then usually transacted, or at public auction or at private sale, without advertising the same and without notice to the undersigned or to the personal representatives of the undersigned, and without prior tender, demand or call of any kind upon the undersigned or upon the personal representatives of the undersigned, and you may purchase the whole or any part thereof free from any right of redemption, and the undersigned shall remain liable for any deficiency; it being understood that a prior tender, demand or call of any kind from you, or prior notice from you, of the time and place of such sale or purchase shall not be considered a waiver of your right to sell or buy any securities and/or commodities and/or other property held by you, or owed you by the undersigned, at any time as hereinbefore provided.

8. The undersigned will at all times maintain margins for said accounts, as required by you from time to time.

9. The undersigned undertakes, at any time upon your demand, to discharge obligations of the undersigned to you, or, in the event of a closing of any account of the undersigned in whole or in part, to pay you the deficiency, if any, and no oral agreement or instructions to the contrary shall be recognized or enforceable.

10. In case of the sale of any security, commodity, or other property by you at the direction of the undersigned and your inability to deliver the same to the purchaser by reason of failure of the undersigned to supply you therewith, then and in such event, the undersigned authorizes you to borrow any security, commodity, or other property necessary to make delivery thereof, and the undersigned hereby agrees to be responsible

for any loss which you may sustain thereby and any premiums which you may be required to pay thereon, and for any loss which you may sustain by reason of your inability to borrow the security, commodity, or other property sold.

11. At any time and from time to time, in your discretion, you may without notice to the undersigned, apply and/or transfer any or all monies, securities, commodities and/or other property of the undersigned interchangeably between any accounts of the undersigned (other than from Regulated Commodity Accounts).

12. It is understood and agreed that the undersigned, when placing with you any sell order for short account, will designate it as such and hereby authorizes you to mark such order as being "short", and when placing with you any order for long account, will designate it as such and hereby authorizes you to mark such order as being "long". Any sell order which the undersigned shall designate as being for long account as above provided, is for securities then owned by the undersigned and, if such securities are not then deliverable by you from any account of the undersigned, the placing of such order shall constitute a representation by the undersigned that it is impracticable for him then to deliver such securities to you but that he will deliver them as soon as it is possible for him to do so without undue inconvenience or expense.

13. In all transactions between you and the undersigned, the undersigned understands that you are acting as the brokers of the undersigned, except when you disclose to the undersigned in writing at or before the completion of a particular transaction that you are acting, with respect to such transaction, as dealers for your own account or as brokers for some other person.

14. Reports of the execution of orders and statements of the accounts of the undersigned shall be conclusive if not objected to in writing, the former within two days, and the latter within ten days, after forwarding by you to the undersigned by mail or otherwise.

15. Communications may be sent to the undersigned at the address of the undersigned given below, or at such other address as the undersigned may hereafter give you in writing, and all communications so sent, whether by mail, telegraph, messenger or otherwise, shall be deemed given to the undersigned personally, whether actually received or not.

16. Any controversy between you and the undersigned arising out of or relating to this contract or the breach thereof, shall be settled by arbitration, in accordance with the rules, then obtaining, of either the Arbitration Committee of the Chamber of Commerce of the State of New York, or the American Arbitration Association, or the Board of Arbitration of the New York Stock Exchange, as the undersigned may elect. If the undersigned does not make such election by registered mail addressed to you at your main office within five (5) days after receipt of notification from you requesting such election, then the undersigned authorizes you to make such election in behalf of the undersigned. Any arbitration hereunder shall be before at least three arbitrators and the award of the arbitrators, or of a majority of them, shall be final, and judgment upon the award rendered may be entered in any court, state or federal, having jurisdiction.

17. This agreement and its enforcement shall be governed by the laws of the State of New York and its provisions shall be continuous; shall cover individually and collectively all accounts which the undersigned may open or re-open with you, and shall enure to the benefit of your present organization, and any successor organization, irrespective of any change or changes at any time in the personnel thereof, for any cause whatsoever, and of the assigns of your present organization or any successor organization, and shall be binding upon the undersigned, and/or the estate, executors, administrators and assigns of the undersigned.

18. The undersigned, if an individual, represents that the undersigned is of full age, that the undersigned is not an employee of any exchange, or of any corporation of which any exchange owns a majority of the capital stock, or of a member of any exchange, or of a member firm or member corporation registered on any exchange, or of a bank, trust company, insurance company or of any corporation, firm or individual engaged in the business of dealing, either as broker or as principal, in securities, bills of exchange, acceptances or other forms or commercial paper. The undersigned further represents that no one except the undersigned has an interest in the account or accounts of the undersigned with you.

Very truly yours,

Witness, ______________________ ______________________

Dated, ______________________ ______________________

______________________ ______________________
(City) (State)

CUSTOMER'S LOAN CONSENT

Until you receive written notice of revocation from the undersigned, you are hereby authorized to lend, to yourselves as brokers or to others, any securities held by you on margin for the account of, or under the control of, the undersigned.

Dated, ______________________ ______________________

______________________ ______________________
(City) (State)

Witness, ______________________ ______________________

months when the movement is sharper, but of the same general character. According to the theory, a chart of business extending over several years will show continual fluctuations corresponding to the Short-Term Cycle and alternating like pulse-beats up or down on a gradually ascending or descending scale, within the Minor Cycle, which in itself is part of the broad, over-all trend or Major Cycle that moves either upward or downward. The best known of these is the 8 to 11 year Minor Cycle, whose fluctuations visibly influence the national economy and often produce, or retard, prosperity.

D

D. The TICKER abbreviation for Douglas Aircraft Company, Inc.

DATE OF TRADE. The day on which an order to buy or sell is executed. See SETTLEMENT DATE.

DAY ORDER. An order to buy or sell at a stated price that is good only through the close of business on the day it is entered. The opposite of G.T.C. ORDER or OPEN ORDER.

DEAD ASSETS. Assets which produce no income of any kind.

DEAD BEAT. A slang expression meaning one who is notorious for non-payment of debts.

DEAD MARKET. A market characterized by low volume and few significant price changes.

DEALER. An individual, or firm, who deals in securities as a principal, rather than as a broker. A dealer buys from, or sells to, a client at a net price; whereas a broker buys and sells for the account of a client and charges a stipulated commission.

DEAR MONEY. Money difficult to borrow and obtainable usually at high interest rates. See TIGHT MONEY.

DEBENTURE. An unsecured, long-term certificate of debt; a corporate IOU. It represents a company's promise to pay and is not backed by a mortgage or pledge of specified assets. However, many debentures today have special protective features, such as a "covenant of equal coverage," which means that if the company later issues a mortgage or other unsecured obligation, the debentures automatically get equal rights. Debentures are most popular with industrial corporations, generally because mortgages on factories supply relatively little for huge capital needs.

DEBIT BALANCE. The balance due to a broker. The excess of debits over credits in a brokerage account which a client must pay in order to withdraw securities. See MARGIN.

DEBT. Money, goods or services owed by one party to another as evidenced by a contract. See FIXED DEBT; FLOATING DEBT.

DECLARE A DIVIDEND. Action taken by the directors of a corporation in voting (declaring) a dividend for its shareholders out of SURPLUS.

DEFAULT. Failure to perform a contract obligation, such as payment of a bond or note at maturity or payment of the interest due thereon at the stipulated date.

DEFENSIVE PORTFOLIO. A portfolio consisting mainly of bonds, preferred stocks, or other securities which are unlikely to fluctuate much in either direction. See AGGRESSIVE PORTFOLIO.

DEFENSIVE STOCKS. The equities of seasoned companies which emphasize stability over growth. The fact that these equities are generally slow moving and therefore relatively unattractive to in-and-out traders and speculators nevertheless represents a kind of built-in safety feature in that they are also better able to withstand selling pressure in a declining market. They are sometimes called "protective stocks."

DEFERRED BOND. See EXTENDED BOND.

DEFERRED CHARGES. Costs or expenses accepted for benefits expected in a later period or periods, which a company will charge against future operations. Included would be land development costs, promotional expenses or the costs of organizing a company.

DEFERRED STOCK. A stock on which dividends are not payable until a certain date has been reached or certain conditions have been met.

DEFICIT. The excess of liabilities over assets at a specific moment of time. It is the opposite of SURPLUS or NET WORTH.

DEFICIT FINANCING. The raising of money by the U.S. Treasury to meet expenditures which tax revenues do not cover.

DEFINITIVE BOND. A bond complete in every detail, which represents final evidence of indebtedness and is exchangeable for temporary certificates.

DEFLATION. A phase of the BUSINESS CYCLE during which consumer spending is seriously curtailed, bank loans contract and the amount of money in circulation is reduced. It is the opposite of INFLATION.

DELAYED DELIVERY. The delivery of securities which were sold with the understanding that such delivery would not be made on the regular clearance date. See CLEARED; CLEARING.

DELAYED OPENING. A situation caused by an overnight accumulation of large buy or sell, orders in a stock. If the stock were left alone, its opening price might differ substantially from the previous night's close. The SPECIALIST, therefore, consults with one or more floor officers and the opening is *delayed* while efforts are made to attract more counter-balancing orders. This is done by informing individuals and institutions known to have an interest in the stock that it will probably open sharply higher or lower. If the imbalance between immediate supply and demand is still large, the Specialist may sell some of his own stock, or even "go short" of it, to arrange a reasonable opening price. See SHORT SALE.

DELIST. To suspend or cancel all privileges accorded a LISTED SECURITY. This may take place on the New York Stock Exchange if an issue is held by less than 300 "stockholders of record" (see HOLDER OF RECORD; RECORD DATE) after substantially discounting ODD-LOTS; if shares OUTSTANDING, exclusive of concentrated family holdings, total less than 100,000; or, if the total market value of common shares outstanding, exclusive of concentrated or family holdings, is less than $1 million. Delistings are infrequent.

DELIVERY. The transfer of possession from one individual or firm to another of securities in fulfillment of contracts made on an exchange and which meet all requirements of that exchange. See CASH SALE; REGULAR WAY DELIVERY; SELLER'S OPTION.

DENOMINATION. The FACE VALUE of paper money, coins, notes, coupons, bonds, stocks.

DEPLETION. The tendency of the natural assets of such industries as mining and oil to become exhausted. See EXTRACTIVE INDUSTRY.

DEPLETION ALLOWANCE. An amount which is deductible from taxable income to compensate for the loss in value caused by DEPLETION.

DEPRECIATION. A decrease in the value of an asset owing to wear and tear, obsolescence, or action of the elements. The purpose of depreciation is to conserve the capital invested in long-lived production facilities which wear out, or become obsolete. It differs from deterioration which means loss of quality or substance, and from DEPLETION, which means loss in quantity. A taxpayer may deduct each year from current income a reasonable allowance for depreciation of his business or income-producing property. This enables him to recover the cost (or other basis) over its estimated useful life. The shorter the life, the larger is the annual deduction for depreciation.

There are several methods of figuring depreciation. The simplest allows the cost to be written off in equal yearly amounts. Other so-called "rapid" methods allow a bigger deduction in the early years of use when the decline in value is greatest. Thus, how much depreciation can be deducted during the year depends on (A) how long the useful life of the property is and (B) which method is used to write off the cost.

To be depreciable, a property must be used by the taxpayer in his trade or business, or held for the production of income (business buildings, machinery, office furniture, rental real estate). If property is used partly for business and partly for pleasure, depreciation write offs can be taken on the business uses. See ACCELERATED DEPRECIATION.

DEPRECIATION RESERVE. An amount set aside annually or at the end of certain periods to cover DEPRECIATION of certain assets. It is designed to reclaim the original cost of the asset concerned and is not intended to cover the cost of replacement.

DEPRESSION. A phase of the BUSINESS CYCLE featured by subnormal prices and activity, drastically curtailed production, lower purchasing power, a declining stock market, widespread pessimism and unemployment. The opposite of PROSPERITY.

DIFFERENTIAL. See ODD-LOT DIFFERENTIAL.

DIGESTED SECURITIES. Securities held firmly by investors on a cash basis, after the speculators have sold their holdings and a settled price has been established.

DILUTION. Weakening, or changing; virtually the same as "watering down," as when a pie is cut into twelve slices instead of the usual eight. In a corporate sense, dilution occurs when a company issues new shares faster than its total earnings grow. The slices are growing faster than the pie. Dilution may come about also through a STOCK DIVIDEND, a STOCK SPLIT, an offer of subscription RIGHTS at a low price. It often reflects a management more interested in growing for the sake of sheer size, than in making money for its stockholders.

DIP. A mild setback, or reaction, in price.

DIRECT FINANCING. The solicitation of funds by a corporation, made by appealing directly to investors without recourse to "underwriting." See UNDERWRITE; UNDERWRITER.

DIRECTORATE. Term referring to the Board of Directors of a corporation.

DIRECTORS. Elected individuals, who are responsible for the welfare and management of a corporation.

DISBURSEMENT. Generally, an expenditure or cash payment made by a corporation such as a dividend.

DISCONTINUOUS MARKET. The market existing for UNLISTED SECURITIES, as contrasted with the New York Stock Exchange which provides a continuous market for LISTED issues.

DISCOUNT. 1. The difference between the original offering price of a security and the price to which it may fall in the "after offering" market. See PREMIUM.

2. The amount by which a security sells below its FACE VALUE (PAR VALUE). A $1,000 par value bond selling at 95 (worth $950) would be selling at a $5.00 or 5% discount. The opposite of PREMIUM.

3. See DISCOUNTING THE NEWS.

DISCOUNT FROM ASSET VALUE. The price of a stock divided by the value of its assets; generally expressed in terms of a percentage. See DISCOUNT.

DISCOUNTING THE NEWS. The reevaluation of stock prices to conform with anticipated news events, or developments, or corporate earnings and dividend prospects three to six months hence. For example: on January 10, 1962, Ford Motor Co. stock opened 1½ points lower and then closed down four points on the day, after a 2-for-1 split and an increase in the dividend were announced. Reason: the market had already *discounted* the favorable news.

DISCOUNT RATE. The interest rate the Federal Reserve Bank charges to member banks for loans. To a commercial bank, this is one of the most important advantages of Federal Reserve membership. There is a close correlation between increases or decreases in the volume of member bank discounts and a condition of tightening or easement in the credit market. Also, higher interest rates often lead to lower securities prices. See EASY MONEY; TIGHT MONEY.

DISCRETIONARY ACCOUNT. An account in which the selection of securities and the price and timing of purchases or sales are left to the broker's discretion. He is not obligated to consult with the customer. See DISCRETIONARY ORDER. Following is a sample trading authorization permitting money and/or securities to be withdrawn from an account.

DISCRETIONARY ORDER. An order given to a broker, or to one person acting as agent for another, to buy or sell at his discretion; that is, to use his own judgment over the execution of an order. The words *Not Held* might be included in such an order. For example: "Sell 1,000 QRS at the market—*not held,*" or "Buy 1,000 QRS at 50, with ⅛ point *discretion.*" See DISCRETIONARY ACCOUNT.

DISCRETIONARY POOL. A combination of individuals given authority to act for others, on their own motion, to buy and sell securities or commodities.

DISPOSABLE PERSONAL INCOME. The amount available to individuals for spending in any given year. It represents PERSONAL INCOME, minus personal taxes.

DISTRESS SELLING. Enforced liquidation caused by the failure of the owner of securities held on MARGIN to maintain sufficient EQUITY in his account. See EXHAUST PRICE; FORCED SALE.

DISTRIBUTION. 1. A period marking the top of a speculative market cycle when so-called insiders, or well-informed investors, begin to dispose of their security holdings. The opposite of AC-

Form 107

FULL TRADING AUTHORIZATION WITH PRIVILEGE TO WITHDRAW MONEY AND/OR SECURITIES

DOE, ROE & CO.,
WALL STREET,
NEW YORK, N. Y.

Gentlemen:

The undersigned hereby authorizes ______________________ (whose signature appears below) as his agent and attorney in fact to buy, sell (including short sales) and trade in stocks, bonds and any other securities and/or commodities and/or contracts relating to the same on margin or otherwise in accordance with your terms and conditions for the undersigned's account and risk and in the undersigned's name, or number on your books. The undersigned hereby agrees to indemnify and hold you harmless from and to pay you promptly on demand any and all losses arising therefrom or debit balance due thereon.

You are authorized to follow instructions of ______________________ in every respect concerning the undersigned's account with you, and make deliveries of securities and payment of moneys to him or as he may order and direct. In all matters and things aforementioned, as well as in all other things necessary or incidental to the furtherance or conduct of the account of the undersigned, the aforesaid agent and attorney in fact is authorized to act for the undersigned and in the undersigned's behalf in the same manner and with the same force and effect as the undersigned might or could do.

The undersigned hereby ratifies and confirms any and all transactions with you heretofore or hereafter made by the aforesaid agent or for the undersigned's account.

This authorization and indemnity is in addition to (and in no way limits or restricts) any rights which you may have under any other agreement or agreements between the undersigned and your firm.

This authorization and indemnity is also a continuing one and shall remain in full force and effect until revoked by the undersigned by a written notice addressed to you and delivered to your office at ____________________, but such revocation shall not affect any liability in any way resulting from transactions initiated prior to such revocation. This authorization and indemnity shall enure to the benefit of your present organization and of any successor organization or organizations irrespective of any change or changes at any time in the personnel thereof for any cause whatsoever, and of the assigns of your present organization or any successor organization.

Very truly yours,

Dated, ____________________ ____________________

____
(City) (State)

Signature of Authorized Agent

____

CUMULATION. Indications that distribution is taking place include: fast movements up and down with the market CHURNING on large volume; many stock and cash dividend increases; failure of the market to respond to good news.

2. Term describing a dividend paid in the form of cash or stock.

DIVERSIFICATION. 1. The spreading of investment funds among classes of securities and localities in order to distribute the risk. It favors the maxim: "Don't put all your eggs in one basket."

2. As it relates to corporate activity, the term means to participate in another line (or lines) of business, which is not generally associated with the company's normal line of work. For example: U.S. Tobacco is diversified in specialty nut foods and ballpoint pen lines; Ronson Corp. also manufactures rare earth products, aerospace components, electrical appliances.

DIVIDEND. The proportion of net earnings paid to its stockholders by a corporation. The longest consecutive dividend payer on the New York Stock Exchange is the Pennsylvania Railroad Co., which began payments in 1848. The longest consecutive payer on the American Stock Exchange is Providence Gas Co., which initiated dividends in 1850. See CASH DIVIDEND; CUMULATIVE DIVIDEND; EXTRA DIVIDEND; INTERIM DIVIDEND; LIQUIDATING DIVIDEND; OPTIONAL DIVIDEND; PHONY DIVIDEND; PROPERTY DIVIDEND; REGULAR DIVIDEND; SCRIP DIVIDEND; SEAT DIVIDEND; SPECIAL DIVIDEND; STOCK DIVIDEND.

DIVIDEND, DECLARE A. Action taken by the directors of a corporation in voting a dividend for its shareholders out of SURPLUS.

DIVIDEND ON. When a stock is sold with the understanding that the buyer will receive the next dividend, the dividend is said to be *on*. If the stock has already sold EX-DIVIDEND, it will be accompanied by a DUE BILL, stating the right of the new owner to receive the dividend.

DIVIDEND PAY-OUT RATIO. A ratio obtained by dividing the total of cash dividends declared for the calendar or fiscal year, plus any payments on the preferred stock, by cash earnings for the year.

DOLLAR COST AVERAGING. A formula which provides for the regular purchase of equal dollar amounts of the same stock or group of stocks at fixed intervals, regardless of the prevailing market price. Temporary reactions are beneficial, in that more shares may be acquired when prices are low. Assuming that the stock selected for dollar averaging is not always in a declining trend, purchases will be made at a better-than-average price over the long run. The system is most appealing to small investors, who wish to lay the cornerstone of a new portfolio or add methodically to existing holdings. See MONTHLY INVESTMENT PLAN. Dollar Cost Averaging is sometimes called "actuarial buying" or "fluctuation harnessing."

DON'T KNOW (D.K.). Term used to deny knowledge of a securities transaction which another firm may be attempting to confirm or compare. In such cases, the COMPARISON is marked "D.K." and returned. The member, or member organization, which attempted to compare must, not later than the opening of the exchange on the second business day following the day of the transaction, report the fact to the executing broker for investigation, and the FLOOR BROKER concerned must investigate such item immediately.

DORMANT ACCOUNT. An account in which virtually no transactions have been made over an extended period of time.

DOUBLE BOTTOM (TOP). A technical expression indicating that the general market or an individual stock has twice declined to, but failed to penetrate, the approximate lowest level reached during the preceding reaction. This is sometimes construed to mean that the INTERMEDIATE TREND downward has been concluded. The reverse holds true of a *double top* and the same principle may be applied to TRIPLE BOTTOMS and TRIPLE TOPS.

DOUBLE OPTION. A SPREAD, or STRADDLE. See OPTION.

DOUBTFUL ASSETS. Various assets for which the original value might not be realized in the event of sale.

DOW-JONES AVERAGES. A popular gauge of the stock market based on the average closing prices of active representative stocks, as published by Dow-Jones & Co. since July 3, 1884. Nine of the original eleven stocks were rails.

The *D-J Averages* currently consist of 65 stocks (30 Industrials, 20 Rails, 15 Utilities). They include only high quality, common stocks LISTED on the New York Stock Exchange. While hourly and intra-day high and low prices are recorded, the averages are based on closing prices. If a particular stock fails to sell during the day, the last previous closing price is used. The practice of "flashing" the Dow Averages 11 times daily at half hour intervals, instead of 5 times on an hourly basis was started July 8, 1963.

The average price of stocks comprising the Dow-Jones Industrials was originally obtained by dividing the total of the daily closing prices of stocks in the Average by the number of issues included; but, in 1928, a new method was introduced, to eliminate occasional distortions caused by complex stock changes and to maintain the sequence of the Average. This method is still used and is founded on an artificial divisor for each of the averages. For example, instead of dividing the sum of thirty Industrials and their multiples by thirty, the total of these stocks is divided by a constant divisor, which remains unchanged until a stock in the Average is split, reduced substantially in price by a STOCK DIVIDEND, or until another stock is substituted. When any of these occur a new divisor is computed; and the same procedure applies to all averages compiled by Dow-Jones & Co., including bond averages, which were started in 1915. The Utility Average has been computed since January 1, 1929. See DOW THEORY; STANDARD & POOR'S 500-STOCK PRICE INDEX.

Components of the Dow-Jones Averages:

Thirty Industrials:

Allied Chemical
Aluminum Co.
American Can
American Tel. & Tel.
American Tobacco
Anaconda Co.
Bethlehem Steel
Chrysler
du Pont
Eastman Kodak
General Electric
General Foods
General Motors
Goodyear
Int'l Harvester
Int'l Nickel
Int'l Paper
Johns-Manville
Owens-Ill. Glass
Procter & Gamble
Sears, Roebuck
Standard Oil of Calif.
Standard Oil of N.J.
Swift & Co.
Texaco
Union Carbide
United Aircraft
U.S. Steel
Westinghouse Elec.
Woolworth (F.W.)

Twenty Railroads:

Atchison
Atl. Coast Line
Baltimore & Ohio
Canadian Pacific
Chesapeake & Ohio
Chicago & N.W.
Chicago Rk. Is. & Pac.
Del. & Hudson

Erie-Lackawanna
Great No. Railway
Illinois Central
Kansas City Sou.
Louisville & Nash.
New York Central
N.Y. Chicago & St. Louis
Norfolk & Western
Pennsylvania RR
Southern Pacific
Southern Railway
Union Pacific

Fifteen Utilities:

Amer. Electric Power
Cleveland Elec. Ill.
Columbia Gas Syst.
Commonwealth Edison
Consolidated Edison
Consolidated Nat. Gas
Detroit Edison
Houston Light & Power
Niag. Mohawk Power
Pacific Gas & Elect.
Panhandle E. Pipe Line
Peoples Gas
Philadelphia Elec.
Public Serv. E & G
South. Cal., Edison

DOWN GAP. A formation appearing on a stock chart caused by the low price of any market day holding above the highest price of the succeeding day with sufficient margin to form an open space or gap.

DOW THEORY. A theory of stock market analysis originated by the late Charles H. Dow, founder of the *Wall Street Journal,* and based on the price performance of the Dow-Jones Industrial and Railroad Averages. The theory originated from a series of editorials, which Dow wrote about speculation between 1900 and 1902; but it was formulated by William Peter Hamilton, his associate on the paper.

According to Mr. Hamilton, three movements are underway simultaneously in the stock market: (A) The major, or PRIMARY MOVEMENT, which tends to run for at least a year and represents the basic trend of the market—BULL or BEAR. (B) Running coincidentally with it is the SECONDARY MOVEMENT, which represents sharp rallies in a primary bear market or sharp declines in a primary bull market (Example: the sharp setback caused by President Eisenhower's heart attack on September 26, 1955); (C) Finally, the TERTIARY MOVEMENT, which runs conjunctively with the primary and secondary movements and consists of day-to-day fluctuations.

The Dow Theory includes many implications, yet the one best tested is that the Industrial and Railroad averages confirm each other, and that there is never a primary movement and rarely a secondary movement where they fail to agree. When the two averages advance together on heavier volume, carrying above the previous highest level attained, the implication is strongly bullish. However, if both averages break through the lower level they are said to be "in gear," and may be signalling a secondary bear movement in a bull market, or the start of a primary bear market.

A bull market remains in force as long as new highs reached during the secondary movements exceed the previous highest levels achieved. Bear periods are in effect when the lowest points attained continue to carry below the previous low points. The crux of the Dow Theory rests, of course, on the price action of various stocks which make up the Dow Averages.

DOWN TICK. Term designating a securities transaction made at a price that is lower than the last different price. It is also called *Minus Tick*. See UP TICK; ZERO PLUS TICK.

DRIED UP. Ceased, came to a halt. "The selling *dried up* around noon today, and the market recovered sharply."

DRIVE. A concerted downward or upward movement in prices.

DUAL LISTING. The listing of a stock on more than one exchange. About 80% of the securities traded outside of New York are also listed on the New York Stock Exchange. Dual listings actually split the overall market for an issue. See LISTED SECURITIES, LISTING REQUIREMENTS.

DUE BILL. A promise to pay a dividend which has been declared, but not yet paid by the company.

DUE DATE. The maturity date; the date when a bond, note, or other evidence of debt becomes payable or legally demandable.

DUMP. To offer stock for sale AT THE MARKET, regardless of prices obtained. To unload stock in a hurry.

DUTIES OF BROKER. A broker's duties to his customer include: (A) Advancing whatever funds are necessary above the required MARGIN to fill a client's order (See MARGIN REQUIREMENTS); (B) Executing all orders efficiently and as soon as possible after they are received; (C) Advising the client when additional margin is necessary and that the account will be closed upon failure to meet the demand; (D) Retaining the stock as the client's property, at his risk and subject to his order; (E) Selling securities at the client's order and, if requested, forwarding the amount due him from the sale. A statement of all transactions must always be remitted to the customer; (F) Delivering securities to the client upon receipt of the DEBIT BALANCE on his account, and crediting or forwarding all dividends, or interest payments received, to him.

DUTIES OF CUSTOMER. A customer's duties to his broker include: (A) Paying promptly for securities purchased and maintaining sufficient MARGIN in his account at all times; (B) Informing the broker of any change of address and whether securities purchased in a CASH ACCOUNT are to be transferred and shipped or held for the customer's credit in a STREET NAME.

DYNAMITER. Slang expression meaning a high-pressure, fly-by-night salesman who sells fraudulent securities by telephone.

E

E. The TICKER abbreviation for Erie-Lackawanna R. R. Company. See SCARLET WOMAN OF WALL STREET.

EACH WAY. Refers to the commission a broker charges to execute both sides of a transaction. The commission for buying is one way; the commission for selling is the other way. See ROUND TRIP TRADE.

EARNED INCOME. Income resulting from personal effort such as salary, or wages, received for work actually done. From a corporate standpoint, it would include income received for services rendered from trading or some other comparable business operation.

EARNED SURPLUS. The undistributed profits of a corporation.

EARNING POWER. The ability of a corporation to consistently maintain earnings and operations at a high and satisfactory level or to return to profitable operations after a period of earnings drought.

EARNINGS. The compensation derived from labor, service, or performance. For corporations, the term is generally synonymous with INCOME. See GROSS EARNINGS; NET EARNINGS.

EARNINGS PER COMMON SHARE. A figure obtained by deducting taxes and all charges, including dividends on any PREFERRED STOCK, from the net income of a corporation and dividing the remainder by the number of common shares "outstanding." See OUTSTANDING SECURITIES.

EARNINGS PER PREFERRED SHARE. A figure obtained by deducting taxes and all charges, including dividends on any PRIOR PREFERRED STOCK, from the net income of a corporation and dividing the remainder by the number of preferred shares "outstanding." See OUTSTANDING SECURITIES.

EARNINGS REPORT. A formal statement issued by a corporation in which are set forth its profits or losses for a given period of time. See PROFIT AND LOSS STATEMENT.

EASED OFF. Term indicating that security prices have eased or receded moderately without much selling pressure.

EASY MONEY. 1. Money obtainable at low interest rates and without much difficulty.

2. A condition existing when the supply of funds available for loans equals or exceeds the demand. Also called "cheap money." See TIGHT MONEY.

EIGHTH STOCKS. Stocks in which ODD-LOT ORDERS will be executed at one-eighth of a point above (when buying), or one-eighth of a point below (when selling), the next price of a ROUND-LOT sale. Stocks selling at 39⅞, or below, in which the unit of trading is 100 shares, are in this category. See ODD-LOT DIFFERENTIAL; QUARTER STOCKS.

ENFORCED LIQUIDATION. See DISTRESS SELLING; EXHAUST PRICE; FORCED SALE.

EQUIPMENT TRUST. A trust agreement set up to purchase and lease railroad equipment; this represents an actual interest in the ownership of the property and not just a claim as does a MORTGAGE BOND. It virtually enables a railroad to buy equipment on the installment plan. Equipment trusts are not attractive vehicles for capital gain, and are therefore held mostly by INSTITUTIONAL INVESTORS. However, in their earlier maturities they provide better yields than Government bonds of comparable maturities, and in later years many surpass 4% and even the 4.6% paid by some SAVINGS AND LOAN ASSOCIATIONS.

EQUIPMENT TRUST CERTIFICATES. Certificates issued by airlines, railroads and bus companies to finance the purchase of equipment. They represent an actual interest in the ownership of the property, and have won a status second only to U.S. Government obligations. See EQUIPMENT TRUST.

EQUITY. 1. The difference between the market value of securities held in a MARGIN ACCOUNT and the amount owed on them, i.e., the amount borrowed from the broker to make the purchase.

2. The value of a property in excess of all liens and claims against it.

3. Since common stock represents the assets of a corporation after all obligations have been satisfied, it also is referred to as equity.

ERRATIC. A market where the price action is irregular, first moving up, then down or vice versa, with no clearly defined trend.

ERROR ACCOUNT. A form of HOUSE ACCOUNT maintained by most brokerage firms, against which is charged any errors which might be made by the firm's personnel during the course of the business day.

EVENING UP. Realizing a profit to offset a loss. Also, a condition existing when the holders of LONG STOCK sell and the SHORT SELLERS buy back (COVER), so that prevailing supply and demand factors offset one another and price changes are insignificant.

EVEN LOT. Same as FULL LOT, ROUND LOT.

EVEN UP. Term indicating that the buyers and sellers of securities are about equally divided. When used before the market opens, it means that opening prices on that day will show little change from closing prices of the previous day.

EXACT INTEREST. Interest computed on the basis of 365 days to the year. See COMPOUND INTEREST; ORDINARY INTEREST; SIMPLE INTEREST.

EXCESS EQUITY. A condition existing when the cash (liquidating) value of an account exceeds the amount required for MARGIN.

EXCESS PROFITS TAX. A tax primarily intended to reduce corporate profits derived from an abnormal consumer demand. The first *EPT* was enacted in 1917 and expired in 1922. The most recent *EPT* was enacted in 1940 and repealed on December 31, 1946.

EXCHANGE. Generally, a meeting place for buyers and sellers of securities, or commodities. An unincorporated membership association the members of which trade in securities, or commodities, for themselves and for others. See AMERICAN STOCK EXCHANGE; COMMODITY EXCHANGE; NATIONAL STOCK EXCHANGE; NEW YORK STOCK EXCHANGE; REGIONAL EXCHANGE.

EXCHANGE ACQUISITION. Method of filling a large buy order on the trading floor of the Stock Exchange without disturbing the regular auction market. The purchase may be facilitated by a member-broker soliciting sell orders from other member-brokers, then lumping the individual orders together to offset the buy order. Such transactions are designated on the TICKER TAPE with the symbol "ACQ." See SPECIAL BID.

EXCHANGE DISTRIBUTION. Method of disposing of a large block of stock on the trading floor of the Stock Exchange without disturbing the regular auction market. The sale may be facilitated by a member-broker soliciting buy orders from other member-brokers, then lumping such orders together and CROSSING them against the large sell order. No publicity is given to the distribution, except that *DIST* precedes the prints of the transaction on the TICKER TAPE. The seller usually pays a single commission. Exchange distributions exceeded two million shares for the first time in 1962. See SECONDARY DISTRIBUTION; SPECIAL OFFERING.

EXCHANGE OF SECURITIES. A method whereby the securities of one corporation are exchanged for those of another corporation on a mutually agreeable basis—usually the result of a merger, or consolidation.

EX-COUPON. *Without the coupon.* When a security is sold *ex-coupon,* it means that the coupon for the current interest payment is detached.

EX-DIVIDEND. *Without the dividend.* On the day a stock sells *ex-dividend,* the quoted market price of the stock will usually measure a decline which equals the value of the dividend. The buyer of a stock selling ex-dividend is not entitled to the dividend.

EXECUTE AN ORDER. To fulfill an order to buy or sell. When an execution is referred to as "good," it generally means that both the broker and the customer are satisfied that the price obtained was fair. Brokers must submit to their customers a confirmation of every order executed for their account.

EXERCISE. To take advantage of the privilege sometimes given to a stockholder to subscribe to bonds of the same company, to additional stock of the same or another class, or to convert bonds into stock at a stipulated price.

EXHAUST PRICE. The price or level at which the EQUITY (MARGIN) in a brokerage account becomes exhausted. When this level is reached, the customer must furnish additional margin, or the broker will be obliged to sell enough securities from the account to satisfy the MARGIN REQUIREMENTS. See DISTRESS SELLING; FORCED SALE.

EX-INTEREST. Without interest; i.e., FLAT.

EXPIRATION DATE. The date on which RIGHTS, OPTIONS, or other privileges expire. If not exercised on or before the expiration date they become worthless.

EX-RIGHTS. Without RIGHTS. When a stock is traded "ex-rights," it means that the rights have been retained or exercised by the seller.

EXTENDED BOND. A bond which, by mutual consent, has had its maturity date extended.

EXTRACTIVE INDUSTRY. An industry which depletes natural resources such as oil, timber, coal, and gas; or which manufactures or uses extracts in its line of work.

EXTRA DIVIDEND. A dividend paid in cash or in stock which supplements the regular payment.

EX-WARRANTS. Without WARRANTS. When a stock is traded *ex-warrants,* it means that the warrants have been retained (exercised) by the seller.

F

F. 1. The TICKER abbreviation for Ford Motor Company.

2. When printed on the TICKER TAPE following symbols, this letter indicates that the foreign stock the symbol represents has been sold by a foreign owner. This is in accord with a proposed 15 percent tax on foreign equity securities bought from foreigners on the New York Stock Exchange and the American Stock Exchange.

The interest equalization tax proposal is retroactive to July 19, 1963.

FACE VALUE. The nominal value of a security as stated on the face of the security itself; this value is not to be confused with MARKET VALUE. See PAR VALUE.

FAIR RETURN. A reasonable rate of return on invested capital.

FALL OUT OF BED. To decline suddenly and sharply in price for no apparent reason. See SLEEPER.

FANCIES. Nickname for highly priced stocks which usually fluctuate over a wide price range.

FANNIE MAE. Nickname for FNMA (Federal National Mortgage Association), a constituent agency of the Housing and Home Finance Agency, which assists segments of the national population unable to obtain adequate housing under established home financing programs by purchasing eligible mortgages and selling them to INSTITUTIONAL and other investors. FNMA is the only publicly traded, government-controlled common stock on the market.

FEATURE. A stock more active than others in the general list.

FEDERAL RESERVE ACT. The act signed by President Wilson on December 23, 1913, which established the Federal Reserve System. The basic function of the Federal Reserve is to make possible a flow of credit and money that will foster orderly economic growth and a stable dollar.

FEDERAL RESERVE BANK. One of twelve banks created under the Federal Reserve Act, which acts as fiscal agent for the United States in each of the twelve Federal Reserve Districts. Each bank has a number according to the district in which it operates. Following are the twelve Federal Reserve cities and their district numbers. Puerto Rico and the Virgin Islands belong to District 2; Alaska and Hawaii to District 12.

1. Boston
2. New York City
3. Philadelphia
4. Cleveland
5. Richmond
6. Atlanta
7. Chicago
8. St. Louis
9. Minneapolis
10. Kansas City
11. Dallas
12. San Francisco

FEDERAL RESERVE BOARD. The Board of Governors of the Federal Reserve System. A governmental institution located in Washington, D.C. It consists of seven members appointed by the President and confirmed by the Senate. Members devote their full time to the business of the Board and are appointed for terms of fourteen years, with terms so arranged that one expires every two years. No two members of the Board may come from the same Federal Reserve District. The Board's expenses are paid out of assessments upon the Reserve Banks, and its accounts are audited each year by qualified public accountants.

FIDUCIARY. A person or corporation (bank or trust company), who holds property in trust for the benefit of another person. A breach of fiduciary relationship occurs if a partner furthers his own interest at the expense of the partnership.

FIFO. The abbreviation for *First in, First out,* one of two important methods of calculating inventory values. Fifo represents the "lower of cost or market" method, in which the value of each article is computed according to the cost of the most recent acquisitions; the cost of articles sold, or used, is based on the cost of earlier acquisitions. Fifo assumes that the first articles purchased or produced are the first ones sold. See LIFO.

FILL. 1. To fill (complete) an order to buy or sell.

2. To satisfy the demand existing for a security at a certain moment by selling an amount equivalent to the number of shares bid for at the highest QUOTED PRICE. See HIT THE BID.

FILL OR KILL. See IMMEDIATE ORDER.

FINANCE. The science of money and monetary affairs; to raise money for necessary requirements.

FINANCED. A condition existing when sufficient credit or money has been raised to organize, reorganize, or extend, an enterprise or a business; a corporation has *financed* when it has acquired WORKING CAPITAL by selling its securities or procuring an UNDERWRITING for them.

FINANCIAL CONDITION. The actual condition of a corporation's finances as shown on its books.

FINANCIAL SERVICES. See BEST, ALFRED M. CO., INC.; FITCH INVESTOR'S SERVICE, MOODY'S INVESTOR'S SERVICE; STANDARD & POOR'S CORP.

FINANCIAL STATEMENT. Another term for BALANCE SHEET.

FINANCING. Raising credit or money to supply an enterprise with WORKING CAPITAL or to place it in a satisfactory financial condition. This is generally accomplished by the sale of its stocks, bonds, or notes (see RAISING FUNDS) or through bank loans.

FINDER'S FEE. A fee that is usually paid to a third party which helps to bring together two companies that wish to merge. See MERGER.

FIRM. 1. A partnership; a business association of two, or more persons.

2. An expression denoting a market where prices are holding steady with a tendency to advance.

FIRM BID, OR OFFER. A bid to buy or an offer to sell that is entered on a security at a definite price with the understanding that it will hold good for a certain period of time.

FIRM-COMMITMENT OFFERING. An offering of securities wherein the UNDERWRITING brokers assume the risk of selling the entire issue to the public. Less well-known companies must sometimes settle for an underwriting agreement in which the brokers agree to try to sell the securities but assume no risk for doing so.

FIRM PRICE. A stated price which the maker is obligated to meet if accepted within a specified time.

FIRST LIEN. The first claim or right against property. A first mortgage bond, for example, has preference against the earnings and assets of a corporation after any prior claims, such as wages and taxes, have been satisfied.

FIRST PREFERRED STOCK. Stock with dividends which are preferred over those of the common stock. It also ranks ahead of the second or any third, preferred issue.

FISCAL YEAR. Any twelve months period selected as a year in financial operations, which may or may not coincide with the calendar year. The United States Government, for example, and some corporations end their fiscal years on June 30 of each year.

FISHYBACKING. Transporting demountable railroad vans by barge or ship. It gives the railroads a chance to trim costs and recapture lost business and is a time and money saver for shippers and trucking companies. See PIGGYBACKING.

FITCH INVESTOR'S SERVICE. A financial organization started in 1913 by John K. Fitch, which rates securities, publishes investor services and supervises investment funds. Home office: 120 Wall Street, New York, N.Y. See BEST, ALFRED M. & CO.; MOODY'S INVESTOR'S SERVICE; STANDARD & POOR'S CORP.

FIXED ASSETS. Permanent or non-trading assets necessary for operating a business, such as land, machinery, buildings and equipment. As distinguished from CURRENT ASSETS, they are assets that exist forever and will not be converted into cash.

FIXED CAPITAL. The proportion of a corporation's capital which is tied up, or locked up, in permanent assets, such as buildings, land, and machinery. It is the excess of FIXED ASSETS over FIXED LIABILITIES.

FIXED CHARGES. Charges (debt) which remain constant, without regard to the volume of business. They usually include rentals and interest on BONDED DEBT. The term applies especially to railroads where fixed charges equal a relatively large percentage of net earnings.

FIXED DEBT. A permanent debt, such as that represented by bonds, which continues for an extended period. See FIXED CHARGES.

FIXED INCOME. Income which remains constant and does not fluctuate, such as income derived from bonds, annuities, preferred stock, and royalties.

FIXED LIABILITIES. Liabilities for which the debtor is definitely responsible, such as a written agreement, a contract or a MORTGAGE BOND.

FIXED PRICE. The minimum price established by the UNDERWRITER of a new issue of securities below which purchases cannot be made.

FLASH PRICES. The latest prices printed by the TICKER on about 100 stocks, in two groups of 50, and at approximately five-minute intervals, whenever the tape runs five or more minutes late. See LATE TAPE.

FLAT. Without interest. When bonds are dealt in *flat,* it means that the market price is the full price. This applies to bonds on which the interest is defaulted, also it applies to INCOME BONDS, which pay interest only when earned. All other bonds are usually dealt in AND INTEREST. The term also applies to lending stocks. When stocks are loaned *flat,* the lender pays no interest to the borrower.

FLIER. A speculative commitment made recklessly in a stock.

FLOAT. To sell (market) the securities of a company in order to raise capital.

FLOATING ASSETS. Same as CURRENT ASSETS; QUICK ASSETS.

FLOATING CAPITAL. Capital which does not represent a permanent investment, i.e., that which is invested in things produced. It is vaguely equivalent to WORKING CAPITAL and is sometimes known as "circulating capital."

FLOATING DEBT. The aggregate of short-term indebtedness, maturing within a year, as distinguished from FUNDED DEBT or CURRENT LIABILITIES.

FLOATING SUPPLY, OR FLOATING STOCK. The proportion of the LISTED capital stock of a corporation which is available for trading or speculative purposes. Stock which is not held permanently. See STRONG HANDS or WEAK HANDS.

FLOOR. The trading room of an exchange where securities are bought and sold. The *floor* of the New York Stock Exchange is three stories high and about the size of a football field. Some 2,000 men are present each day including members (about 500 Stock Exchange employees and 750 MEMBER FIRM employees). Telephones were first installed on the trading floor November 13, 1878.

FLOOR BROKER. A broker who executes buy and sell orders mainly for others on the trading floor of a stock exchange; he is also sometimes known as TWO-DOLLAR BROKER. A floor broker often walks fifteen miles a day on the job.

FLOOR PARTNER. A partner of a brokerage firm who buys and sells securities for his firm on the trading floor of an exchange of which he is a member.

FLOOR REPORT. A report transmitted from the trading floor of an exchange, which confirms the execution of an order and supplies such details as the number of shares involved in an execution just completed, the name of the security, and the price. See COMPLETES; TO COME—TO GO.

FLOOR TRADER. A member of an organized stock exchange who, while on the trading floor, buys and sells securities for his own account. There are about 40 floor traders on the American Stock Exchange, and between 30 and 35 on the New York Stock Exchange. Floor traders operate under special rules. They may not, for example, "congregate in a particular stock, and individually or as a group, dominate the market in that stock," or "effect such purchases except in a reasonable and orderly manner." In 1962, when total N.Y.S.E. transactions amounted to 1,187,000,000 shares, exchange members traded 484.3 million for their own accounts. Of this amount, about 58% was traded by SPECIALISTS and floor traders.

FLOTATION. The launching of a new issue of securities on the market.

FLUCTUATION HARNESSING. See DOLLAR COST AVERAGING.

FLUCTUATIONS. Variations in the market price of a security up or down. If a stock advances or declines three points, it is said to have experienced a three-point fluctuation.

FLURRIES. Sudden, short-lived price movements caused by unexpected news.

FOR A TURN. A commitment in a security made in the hope of gaining a small, but quick, profit.

FOR CASH. A transaction which demands that the securities sold be delivered to the buyer on the same day.

FORCED SALE. The sale of a security regardless of the owner's wishes; usually due to a lack of sufficient MARGIN. Also called DISTRESS SELLING; ENFORCED LIQUIDATION. See EXHAUST PRICE.

FORMULA INVESTING. An investment method which calls for the automatic sale or purchase of securities under predetermined circumstances. Also, it is the shifting of funds from common stocks into preferred stocks or bonds, or vice versa, when the market, on average, reaches a prescribed level. See DOLLAR COST AVERAGING; MONTHLY INVESTMENT PLAN; SCALE ORDER.

FRACTIONAL LOT. Same as ODD-LOT.

FREE AND OPEN MARKET. A market that is free to all, where prices are determined by open competition between many buyers and sellers.

FREE RIDING. 1. The purchase and rapid subsequent sale of securities, collecting the proceeds from the sale without putting up personal funds for the original purchase.

2. The withholding of offerings by brokerage firms of new securities which are expected to rise beyond the initial public offering price fixed by the UNDERWRITERS.

3. The sale by NASD (National Association of Securities Dealers) member firms of securities to preferred individuals while they still have unfilled orders from the public. NASD rules strictly prohibit this practice.

FROZEN ACCOUNT. An account which has been restricted from further trading.

FROZEN ASSETS. Long-term assets whose cash value can be realized only at some future date.

FULL LOT. Same as EVEN LOT; ROUND LOT.

FUNDAMENTALIST. See STATISTICIAN.

FUNDAMENTALS. Basic underlying economic factors which ascertain the state of business. They include the trend of corporate earnings and dividends, the level of steel production, automobile output, housing starts, railroad carloadings, and the conditions prevailing in credit, investment and banking.

FUNDED DEBT. The long-term indebtedness of a corporation, as contrasted with FLOATING DEBT. It is usually created by the sale of a long-term issue of securities; the proceeds of which are used to finance purchases of tangible assets or to pay off a number of short-term debts.

FUTURES. Term which designates any or all contracts covering the sale of commodities for future delivery made on a commodity exchange and subject to its rules (see SPOT). A futures contract is a right to deliver or receive a specified commodity at a prescribed time in the future. The majority of all commodity trades are in futures.

FUTURES CONTRACT. A contract which requires delivery of a commodity in a stated month in the future—if not liquidated before the contract reaches maturity. Every futures contract for a specific commodity is identical in its provisions for quantity and quality. Thus, as far as the futures trader is concerned "wheat is wheat" and "cotton is cotton." Quantity is identical because every cotton futures contract traded on the New York Cotton Exchange is for 50,000 pounds; every cocoa futures contract traded on the New York Cocoa Exchange is for 30,000 pounds, etc.

Quality is identical in that each commodity futures contract provides for basis grades for actual delivery against contracts. A commodity futures contract has been compared to a share of stock—as units of trading in their respective markets. However, there are certain differences when more explicitly comparing a share of stock with a commodity futures contract involving a specific commodity.

G

G. The TICKER abbreviation for The Greyhound Corporation.

G.T.C. (GOOD 'TIL CANCELLED, OR COUNTERMANDED) ORDER. A order to buy or sell at a specific price limit which remains in effect with the SPECIALIST until it is executed, cancelled, or changed in price. Same as OPEN ORDER. See G.T.M.; G.T.W.; DAY ORDER; LIMIT ORDER; MARKET ORDER.

G.T.M. (GOOD THIS MONTH) ORDER. An order to buy or sell at a specific price limit which remains in effect with the SPECIALIST until the close of business on the last day of the month it is entered unless it is executed, cancelled or changed in price. See G.T.C.; G.T.W.; DAY ORDER; LIMIT ORDER; MARKET ORDER; OPEN ORDER.

G.T.W. (GOOD THIS WEEK) ORDER. An order to buy or sell securities which remains in effect with the SPECIALIST until the close of business on the last day of the week it is entered unless it is executed, cancelled or changed in price. See G.T.C.; G.T.M.; DAY ORDER; LIMIT ORDER; MARKET ORDER; OPEN ORDER.

GAMBLING (STOCK). Buying and selling stocks at random without any intelligent attempt at foresight. See INVESTMENT; SPECULATION.

GARAGE, THE. Brokers' nickname for the annex of the New York Stock Exchange trading floor where 6 of the 18 trading POSTS and POST 30 are located.

GATHER IN THE STOPS. To sell a stock in sufficient quantity in order to drive the price down to a level where many STOP ORDERS are known to be entered. Because such orders automatically become MARKET ORDERS when 100 shares or more of the same stock sell at or below the STOP PRICE, this additional selling may cause a further decline which traders might use to their advantage. The practice could involve manipulation and is therefore closely supervised. The term is synonymous with UNCOVER THE STOPS. See SNOWBALLING.

GENERAL MORTGAGE BOND. A bond secured by a general mortgage upon property which is already subject to one or more prior mortgages.

GENERAL PARTNER. One who shares in the profits and is liable for the debts of a partnership. See ACTIVE PARTNER; LIMITED PARTNERSHIP; SILENT PARTNER; SPECIAL PARTNER.

GILT-EDGED. Premier quality; top grade; first class. A security of superior merit, which is generally considered safer than other securities.

GIVE AN INDICATION. To show definite interest toward a new issue of securities by entering a firm buy order for a stated amount.

GIVE AN ORDER. To instruct a broker to buy or sell a stated number of shares of a certain security with, or without, specifying price or time limit. See G.T.C.; G.T.M.; G.T.W.; DAY ORDER; DISCRETIONARY ORDER; LIMIT ORDER; MARKET ORDER; OPEN ORDER.

GIVE-UP ORDER. 1. An order executed on the trading floor of an exchange by Broker A on behalf of Broker B. In reporting to Broker C from whom he buys, or to whom he sells, Broker A gives the name of Broker B for whom he is acting. He is said to *Give-up* the latter, who receives the stock and completes the transaction.

2. Term referring to securities which a participating UNDERWRITER will not accept for direct sale. See TAKE UP.

GOING CONCERN. A business in operation, as opposed to one which is defunct or being liquidated.

GO LONG. To buy for investment or as a speculation. The opposite of "selling short." See SHORT SALE.

GOOD DELIVERY. A security which is physically genuine and properly in accord with specific regulations respecting days, hours, assignments, and powers of attorney. One which is considered valid or "good" for transfer to the buyer.

GOOD THROUGH. An order to buy or sell at a stipulated price limit which remains valid for only a specified period of time, unless it is executed, cancelled, or changed as to price. Such an order may be entered G.T.W. (Good This Week), G.T.M. (Good This Month), or Good Through the close of business on some definite future date.

GOOD WILL. An INTANGIBLE ASSET representing the advantage in earning power enjoyed by one company over another in terms of reputation, business connections, individuality, locality, superior management, good labor relations, and efficiency.

GO PUBLIC. To offer securities for public sale, usually to raise money for the company concerned, but also they may be offered if the major stockholders wish to diversify their holdings or get a market valuation for them.

In most cases if a company wants to raise $300,000, or more, the offering must be registered with the SECURITIES & EXCHANGE COMMISSION. If stockholders are the sellers and the issue involves $100,000, or more, it must also be registered with the S.E.C. See REGISTRATION OF SECURITIES.

GO SHORT. To sell a security "short." The opposite of buy, or GO LONG. See SHORT SALE.

GOVERNING COMMITTEE. A title accorded the governing body of the New York Stock Exchange, the American Stock Exchange, or any other recognized exchange. The first Governing Committee of the New York Stock Exchange was elected in 1868. See BOARD OF GOVERNORS.

GRANGER ROAD. A railroad whose earnings depend largely upon the transportation of grain and farm produce.

GRAVELLED. The London Stock Exchange equivalent of BOTTOM OUT.

GRAVEYARD MARKET. A type of market in which those who are in it can't get out, and those who are out of it don't want to get in.

GREENBACKS. United States notes or scrip issued during the Civil War, and so-named because they were the first to be engraved with green backs. They were also known as "legal tender."

GROSS EARNINGS. The total operating receipts of a corporation before any deductions are made.

GROSS INCOME. Total receipts from which no deductions have been made; includes income from other sources such as securities, rentals, and interest, sales of capital assets.

GROSS NATIONAL PRODUCT. The total market value of the output of all goods and services in the nation, as reported periodically by the U.S. Department of Commerce. It is a gauge of the nation's business activity that measures at prevailing market prices the value of all contributions made to the economy, "before deducting depreciation charges and other allowances for business and institutional consumption of durable CAPITAL GOODS." It includes: the number of persons employed (civilians and armed forces); the length of the work week; the price level; consumer expenditures; gross private domestic investments; net foreign investments and goods and services purchased by the government.

GROSS PROFITS. Profits accruing to a company after deducting the cost of goods sold from the selling price but before allowing for general administrative and selling expenses which, when deducted, will determine NET PROFITS.

GROSS RECEIPTS. The total receipts of a corporation before deducting expenses.

GROSS SALES. A corporation's total volume of sales.

GROUND FLOOR. The lowest price, or opportunity, available to the originators of a financial operation. "He got in on the ground floor," meaning that he was one of the favored few to participate in the original UNDERWRITING.

GROWTH STOCK. The stock of a corporation whose earnings have increased consistently over a number of years and show every indication of considerable further expansion. Most growth stocks provide a relatively low dividend yield. They are primarily attractive for price appreciation potential, especially from a long range standpoint. Growth companies should have the following characteristics:

1. A young and aggressive management team.
2. Strong emphasis on research and development.
3. A favorable record of sales and earnings.
4. A line of essential products that seems destined to increase in popularity over the years, while new ones are being constantly introduced.

GUARANTEED BOND. A bond on which the principal or interest, or both, have been guaranteed by other than the original debtor.

GUARANTEED STOCK. A stock on which the payment of principal or dividends, or both, are guaranteed by another corporation. However, there is no such thing as a stock that is guaranteed to advance in price.

GUTTER MARKET. The outdoor securities market that was conducted on New Street near the New York Stock Exchange building, when the Exchange was closed in 1914 because of war.

H

H. The TICKER abbreviation for Hupp Corporation.

HAND SIGNALS. Signals used by some of the old-time American Stock Exchange FLOOR BROKERS to communicate with their clerks. They are an offshoot of the open-air "Curb Market," which existed for many years on Broad Street, where each broker and the firm he represented was identified by a novel hat or colored jacket. The reports of executions and quotations which he flashed by hand signals to his clerk, watching from a window above the street, were relayed immediately back to the headquarters of the firm.

HARD MONEY. Metallic money, as distinguished from paper money.

HARD SPOT IN THE MARKET. A stock or group of stocks which is prominently strong in a generally weak market.

HEART ATTACK MARKET. The sharp sell-off on Monday, September 26, 1955, caused by President Eisenhower's heart attack. The Dow-Jones Industrial Average dropped 6.5%, or 31.89 points on volume of 7.7 million shares, their greatest one-day decline since October 28, 1929.

HEAVY INDUSTRY. An industry engaged in manufacturing basic products or equipment such as metals and machines.

HEAVY MARKET. A market where the bids entered to buy stocks are insufficient to absorb the offerings entered to sell them, and prices decline.

HEDGING. An operation intended to protect against loss in another operation. It involves selling short to nullify a previous purchase, or buying LONG to offset a previous SHORT SALE. The operator is in a neutral position since profits made on one side of the market cancel losses showing on the other side. See SELLING AGAINST THE BOX.

HIDDEN ASSETS. Term used to differentiate between the true value of assets and that which appears in public reports. The practice of hiding assets, values, or reserves, not only is morally improper, but any corporation doing so incurs the risk of a tax penalty.

HIGH GRADE BOND. A bond of superior merit upon which the principal and interest will be paid under any conceivable circumstances, as with U.S. Government obligations.

HIGH GRADE STOCK. A security of a leading railroad, utility, or industrial corporation which enjoys the highest investment rating.

HI-LO INDEX. A moving average of the individual stocks that reach new highs and new lows each day. It reveals many things about the main body of stocks that the DOW-JONES AVERAGES do not show.

In a broad, aggressive market many stocks reach new highs every day, compared with very few new lows. In the late stages of a BULL MARKET, however, while outstanding strength among various BLUE CHIP issues may carry the D-J Averages higher, the majority of other stocks may be selling too far below their previous highs to make new highs. A low average of the highs taken at such times would indicate that the market is deteriorating internally, and its TECHNICAL POSITION is worsening. The way in which the average of new lows performs in a BEAR MARKET would signal the opposite.

HIT THE BID. To sell at the highest BID PRICE quoted for a security, before the bid may be filled, changed, or cancelled. After a person has become discouraged from trying to sell at 15⅛, one hundred shares of a stock in which the BEST BID showing is 15, he may instruct his broker to *Hit the Bid,* or "Sell 100 shares at 15, cancelling 15⅛."

HOLDER OF RECORD. The individual or organization whose name appears on the transfer books of a corporation as the owner of securities in that corporation at a certain date. Such an owner is therefore entitled to receive any benefits or dividends declared. See RECORD DATE.

HOLDING COMPANY. A corporation which owns all or the majority of the stock of one or more SUBSIDIARY companies, or owns enough of the VOTING STOCK to have working control. A holding company may be, but usually is not, an operating company. Its principal purpose is either to consolidate a group of competing organizations in order to curtail competition and still meet with legal requirements or to centralize management and operating methods so as to effect economies. See PARENT COMPANY.

HOLDING THE MARKET. Supporting the market for a particular stock by buying enough of it, as offered, to prevent a decline in price.

HOLIDAYS. The New York Stock Exchange has been closed on Saturday since September 29, 1952—and, subject to an affirmative vote, on the following legal holidays in New York State: New Year's Day, Washington's Birthday, Memorial Day, Independence Day, Labor Day, Election Day, Thanksgiving Day, Christmas Day. The Exchange has also been closed on every Good Friday since 1900, except in 1906 and 1907.

HONEYCOMBED WITH STOPS. Refers to a market where numerous STOP ORDERS have been entered.

HOT ISSUE. A security which meets heavy demand on being sold publicly for the first time. The stock is said to be *hot*. In such cases, the price usually rises sharply after it comes on the market, and the original buyers are in a position to turn a quick profit.

HOT MONEY. Short-term capital which is shifted from country to country in search of high interest rates and quick profits. It is a major factor in this country's losses of gold and BALANCE OF PAYMENTS problem.

HOT STUFF. Slang expression for literature pertaining to a stock issue that embodies good selling propaganda, regardless of the truth.

HOURS OF BUSINESS. Hours of business on the New York Stock Exchange and the American Stock Exchange are 10 A.M. to 3:30 P.M. on weekdays. MEMBER FIRMS must remain open on every full business day during these hours, which have been in force since September 29, 1952. See HOLIDAYS.

HOUSE. Term virtually synonymous with FIRM, but also used occasionally where business is conducted under the name of one person only. *The House* is also a recognized name for the London Stock Exchange.

HOUSE ACCOUNT. An account maintained by a brokerage firm for its own use, as when the partners or officers wish to take a position in a security in the name of the firm itself.

HOUSE OF ISSUE. A firm of investment bankers which UNDERWRITES a new issue of securities and offers it for public sale.

HUNG UP. The plight of an investor when his capital is tied up in a stock which has declined below his original purchase price so that he cannot dispose of it without taking a loss.

HYPOTHECATE. To pledge negotiable securities or other property as collateral for a loan while still retaining title to them.

HYPOTHECATED STOCK. Stock which has been pawned or pledged as collateral against a loan.

I

IMMEDIATE ORDER. An order entered on the TRADING FLOOR of a stock exchange, which demands a prompt execution at a stipulated price. If the order cannot be executed at that price, it is cancelled automatically, and the broker must report back with a fresh QUOTATION on the stock concerned. Also known as *Fill, or Kill.*

INACTIVE POST. See POST 30.

INACTIVE STOCK. A stock which is traded infrequently—as for example, where the UNIT OF TRADING is less than 100 shares. Also, any stock for which it may be difficult to find a market or for which the existing market is unusually "thin." See MAKING A MARKET; ODD-LOT; POST 30; ROUND-LOT; THIN MARKET.

IN-AND-OUT. A transaction of short duration; a stock bought and sold on the same day would be an *in-and-out* transaction. The London Stock Exchange term for an in-and-outer is *Punter.*

INCOME. Revenue; the money received annually by a person, a firm, or a corporation, from investments. See DISPOSABLE PER-

SONAL INCOME; EARNED INCOME; FIXED INCOME; GROSS INCOME; OPERATING INCOME; OTHER INCOME; UNEARNED INCOME.

INCOME ACCOUNT. See PROFIT AND LOSS STATEMENT.

INCOME BOND. A bond on which the payment of interest is contingent upon earnings. Income bonds usually result from reorganizations and are not generally regarded as high-grade investments.

INCOME PORTFOLIO. A portfolio consisting of securities whose principal attractiveness lies in the steady income they provide.

INCOME STATEMENT. See PROFIT AND LOSS STATEMENT.

INCREASE IN NUMBER OF INVESTORS. Approximately 19 million persons in the United States owned securities in 1963 and their number is increasing steadily, while the number of shares held per person has decreased. In 1912, the average holding of American Telephone & Telegraph's 50,000 stockholders was 66 shares. In 1925, the Company's 345,000 stockholders held an average of 26.2 shares. At the end of 1960, seventeen percent, or 321,000, of the Company's 1.9 million shareowners held 10 shares or less.

INDENTURE. A formal contract or written agreement between two or more parties; an example would be a document under which corporate bonds are issued. The name stems from the former custom of drawing the agreement with the edge indented, or zigzagged, for better identification and security purposes.

INDICATED INTEREST. The degree of public interest shown toward a new issue of securities, as evidenced by the number of orders received by the UNDERWRITER. Same as OPEN INTEREST. See HOT ISSUE.

INDICATED MARKET. The price at which a trader believes a security might be bought or sold since there is no FIRM BID OR OFFER showing on which to base a more definite opinion.

INDICATED YIELD. The annual income (YIELD) it is estimated a stock will provide on the basis of projected earnings.

INDUSTRIAL STOCK. The stock of a corporation engaged in the production or sale of goods or services as distinguished from railroad, public utility, bank, or insurance companies.

INFLATION. A phase of the BUSINESS CYCLE characterized by abnormally high prices, a decrease in the purchasing power of money, and spiraling costs and wage rates. Inflation may occur when purchasing power is in excess of goods and services for sale, and/or buyers stampede to convert money into commodities; or when production costs and prices advance to consecutively higher levels. See DEFLATION.

INITIATION FEE. An amount levied on all newly elected members to an exchange. In 1962, the initiation fee on the New York Stock Exchange was increased from $4,000 to $7,500—the first change since 1920. See MEMBERSHIP DUES.

INSIDER REPORTS. The Securities and Exchange Commission requires the directors and officers of any company whose stock is LISTED on a national securities exchange to file a monthly report showing: (A) all purchases or sales made during the previous month; (B) the total number of shares held at the end of the month. A similar report must be filed by the beneficial owners of more than 10% of a stock registered on any exchange, and all indirect holdings must also be made known. Together with information published regularly by various funds, showing what positions in securities have been initiated, augmented or eliminated entirely, it is possible to know what market action the directors, officers and other large stockholders of various companies have been taking and what specific stocks and groups of stocks have gained or lost favor with the INSIDERS.

INSIDERS. Those who have knowledge of corporate developments before they are made public. Included among these are: (A) Bankers, corporation directors and executives, trust officers, managers of large portfolios and pension funds and others who help to formulate economic policy; (B) Big individual operators, who generally are not members of any exchange, but are apt to take a major position in one, or several stocks when their sources of information suggest that the moment is timely; (C) The so-called professionals—thoroughly experienced individuals, operating as floor or office traders—who base their market commitments on a variety of FUNDAMENTAL and TECHNICAL factors such as tape action, volume, sponsorship, earnings, yields, and changing economic and international conditions; (D) The semi-professionals—not necessarily members of the brokerage fraternity—who concentrate their full-time efforts on buying low and selling high. Also referred to as "They." See INSIDER REPORTS.

INSTALLMENT BOND. A bond with PRINCIPAL that is paid off at intervals, or installments, rather than on a single maturity date.

INSTALLMENT PURCHASES. Purchases of selected stocks made at certain time intervals; usually monthly, quarterly, or semi-annually. See DOLLAR COST AVERAGING; MONTHLY INVESTMENT PLAN.

INSTITUTIONS. See INSTITUTIONAL INVESTORS.

INSTITUTIONAL INVESTORS. Institutions whose investments constitute a highly important part of their over-all operations, although they are formed primarily for purposes other than investments. Included among these are: savings and commercial banks, life insurance companies, investment associations, mutual and pension funds, charitable institutions, churches, and hospitals.

Institutions held $82.4 billion (market value) of stocks LISTED on the New York Stock Exchange—approximately 20% of the total—at the end of 1963, compared with 18.7% as of December 31, 1961. The volume of securities business carried on by such institutions has grown so large over the past few years that several brokerage firms have set up or expanded special institutional departments which emphasize tailor-made reports that take up to three months to prepare.

INTANGIBLE ASSETS. Assets which have a value, but represent no material substance. They include copyrights, good will, patents, claims, discoveries, trademarks. See TANGIBLE ASSETS.

INTEGRATED COMPANY. A company which has been completed by unifying its various parts in order to widen the marketing area and achieve better control over costs, efficiencies and raw material sources.

An important provision of the Public Utility Holding Company

Act of 1935 is its requirements for the physical integration and corporate simplification of holding company systems. An integrated system under this provision is one capable of economic operation as a single coordinated system confined to a single area or region in one or more states, and not so large as to impair the advantages of localized management, efficient operation and effectiveness of regulation.

INTERCHANGEABLE BOND. A COUPON BOND which may become a REGISTERED BOND, or vice-versa.

INTEREST. Money paid for the use of capital, such as the interest paid by a corporation to its bondholders. See ACCRUED INTEREST; ACCUMULATED INTEREST; COMPOUND INTEREST; EXACT INTEREST; LONG INTEREST; ORDINARY INTEREST; SHORT INTEREST; SIMPLE INTEREST.

INTEREST CHARGES. See CARRYING CHARGES.

INTERIM BOND. A bond issued to raise funds to tide a corporation over temporary financial difficulties and which may be exchanged eventually for a permanent bond. Since bonds may take as long as six months to be prepared, engraved and printed, a company may issue interim bonds or temporary certificates until the final product is available.

INTERIM DIVIDEND. A dividend paid in advance of the full (regular) dividend.

INTERIM REPORT. A report submitted quarterly or semi-annually by a corporation to its stockholders to keep them informed about earnings progress or special developments which have taken place since the ANNUAL REPORT was published.

INTERMEDIATE TREND. The tendency of an individual stock or the general market to run from ten to thirty points in one direction and then in another while remaining within the framework of the long-term, MAJOR TREND. It consists of many small movements which may last for several days and which determine the short-term or MINOR TREND of the market. It is virtually the same as SECONDARY MOVEMENT.

INTER-SYMPATHY BETWEEN STOCKS. The tendency of a stock to advance or decline in line with the action of another stock or other stocks in the same group.

IN THE BLACK (RED). To operate at a profit. A profitable business is said to be *in the black*. It is the opposite of *in the red,* which is synonymous with a loss.

INTRADAY HIGH AND LOW. The highest and lowest price level attained by a stock or the general market averages for any particular day under discussion. For example: the price range on a stock for a particular market session is opening-57, High-58¼, Low-56¾ and Close (Last Sale)-57½. Its intraday high and low prices are said to be 58¼ and 56¾, respectively.

INTRASTATE SECURITIES. OVER-THE-COUNTER stocks issued and distributed solely within a state. They are generally issued by companies just getting into business. Large securities houses usually will not UNDERWRITE a stock issue without a proven earnings record. But smaller brokers will often handle the issue on a "best efforts" basis—the company receives its money as the stock is sold, instead of in a lump sum as it is traditionally handled by underwriters.

INTRINSIC VALUE. The actual money value which an object possesses in itself; its value in relation to unsatisfied wants. As applied to securities, it means value as an investment—the basic worth of a corporation, as calculated by its past record, potential earning power, and underlying equities. The intrinsic value of a stock may be above or below its MARKET VALUE and should not be related to it.

INVENTORY. A detailed listing of property owned by an individual or a corporation showing the value of each item.

INVESTMENT. The placing of capital more or less permanently in real property, a business, securities, or something where the element of risk is low, with the expectation of obtaining income or profits from its ownership or use. The first consideration is always safety of principal. As one writer expressed it: "Planting good seed in fertile soil is investment; betting on how many melons the seed will produce is speculation." See GAMBLING; SPECULATION.

INVESTMENT ADVISERS ACT OF 1940. As amended in 1960, a law which establishes a pattern of regulation of investment advisers and is similar in many respects to Securities Exchange Act provisions governing the conduct of brokers and dealers.

It requires, with certain exceptions, that persons or firms who engage for compensation in the business of advising others with respect to their securities transactions shall register with the commission and conform their activities to statutory standards designed to protect the interests of investors.

The registration of investment advisers may be denied, suspended or revoked by the Commission if, after notice and hearing, it finds that a statutory disqualification exists and that such action is in the public interest. Disqualifications include a conviction for certain financial crimes or securities violations, the existence of injunctions based on such activities, a conviction for violation of the Mail Fraud Statute, the willful filing of false reports with the Commission, and willful violations of this Act, the Securities Act or the Securities Exchange Act. In addition to the administrative sanction of denial, suspension or revocation, the Commission may obtain injunctions restraining violations of this law and may recommend prosecution by the Department of Justice for fraudulent misconduct or willful violation of the law or rules of the Commission thereunder.

The law contains anti-fraud provisions; it empowers the Commission to adopt rules defining fraudulent, deceptive or manipulative acts and practices; and it is designed to prevent such activities. It also requires that investment advisers disclose the nature of their interest in transactions executed for their clients; and in effect, it prevents the assignment of investment advisory contracts without the client's consent. The law also imposes on investment advisers subject to the registration requirement the duty to maintain books and records in accordance with such rules as may be prescribed by the Commission, and it authorizes the Commission to conduct inspection of such books and records.

INVESTMENT BANKER. A merchandiser of marketable securities, who buys all of a securities issue, or large portions thereof, for resale to others—generally in smaller amounts.

INVESTMENT CLUB. An informal group of neighbors, friends or business associates, who get together to invest relatively small sums of money in jointly selected securities. The average club has about fourteen members and usually meets monthly on an informal basis to collect payments, discuss securities and plan future action.

The financial interest which each member holds in an investment club depends upon the number of shares of club assets he owns. An article of agreement for an investment club is usually obtainable at the office of any leading brokerage firm.

INVESTMENT COMPANY. 1. A company engaged in retailing securities.

2. A company which invests the combined funds of many participants in a varied list of securities. See CLOSED-END FUND; MUTUAL FUND.

INVESTMENT COMPANY ACT OF 1940. A federal statute enacted in 1940 under which the activities of companies engaged primarily in the business of investing, reinvesting, and trading in securities and whose own securities are held by the investing public, are subject to statutory limitations and to SECURITIES AND EXCHANGE COMMISSION regulation, in accordance with prescribed standards deemed necessary to protect the interests of investors and the public. The Commission does not supervise the investment activities of these companies and regulation by the Commission does not imply safety of investment in such companies.

In addition to a requirement that such companies register with the SEC, the law (A) Requires disclosure of their financial condition and investment policies so as to afford investors full and complete information as to their activities; (B) Prohibits such companies from changing the nature of their business or their investment policies without the approval of the stockholders; (C)

Bars persons guilty of security frauds from serving as officers and directors; (D) Prevents underwriters, investment bankers or brokers from constituting more than a minority of the directors of such companies; (E) Requires management contracts (and material changes therein) to be submitted to security holders for their approval; (F) Prohibits transactions between such companies and their directors, officers, or affiliated companies, except upon approval by the Commission as being fair and involving no overreaching; (G) Forbids the issuance of SENIOR SECURITIES by such companies except under specified conditions and upon specified terms; and (H) Prohibits pyramiding of such companies and cross ownership of their securities.

INVESTMENT COUNSELOR. One who manages securities portfolios and provides investment advice and services to others for a fee.

INVESTMENT INCOME. Income derived from capital invested in securities or other property.

INVESTMENT PORTFOLIO. A securities portfolio in which is held securities whose principal is considered relatively safe and which provides a fair return.

INVESTMENT PROGRAM. The course of action (stated policy) followed by an individual or an institution in investment matters.

INVESTOR. An individual who buys and holds securities for steady income, safety of principal and, secondarily, for capital gain.

INVOLUNTARY INVESTOR. One who normally trades in stocks but, having bought near the top of a rise, cannot sell without taking a loss; hence he becomes an *investor*. See LOCKED IN; TRADER.

IRREGULAR MARKET. A market where the price action is uneven, some stocks moving erratically higher, others moving lower.

ISSUE. 1. To put forth for sale or delivery an issue of corporate bonds or stocks.

2. A block of securities issued by a corporation.

ISSUED CAPITAL STOCK. That part of a corporation's stock which is held by stockholders or has been repurchased and held as TREASURY STOCK. It represents the difference between AUTHORIZED and UNISSUED capital stock. See OUTSTANDING SECURITIES.

ISSUE PRICE. The price at which an "underwriting syndicate" offers a new issue of securities to the public. See SYNDICATE; UNDERWRITER.

J

J. The TICKER abbreviation for Standard Oil Company (New Jersey).

JOBBER. One of two classes of London Stock Exchange members; jobbers differ from brokers in that they may not deal with the public. Their business involves MAKING A MARKET in various securities for fellow members, and they act as dealers for their own account. The term *stock jobber* dates back to 1688.

JOINT ACCOUNT. 1. A method of titling securities in more than one name. This method is often utilized by a husband and wife in effecting securities transactions.

2. Any business or securities venture undertaken by two or more individuals for their mutual benefit and risk.

JOINT STOCK COMPANY. A form of business organization in which the capital contributions of the partners are represented by shares of transferable stock. It is similar to a corporation in that management is vested in a governing board and death or the transfer of membership does not dissolve the company. However, where the shareholders of a company have only a limited liability, members of a joint stock company are held fully responsible for the company's debts.

JOINT VENTURE. A new company set up by two established concerns to launch an enterprise which the individual owners cannot, or dare not, try alone. The first joint ventures were formed in sailing-ship days to spread the risks of far-flung trading voyages.

JOURNAL. See BLOTTER.

JUNIOR SECURITIES. Securities which are preceded by another issue and, in the event of foreclosure, have claim against the property only after all prior claims by the SENIOR SECURITIES have been settled. For example, the common stock of a corporation is *junior* to any preferred stock outstanding, just as both the preferred stock and the common stock are considered *junior* to any bonds.

ASEF—Form 103—Revised May, 1955

JOINT ACCOUNT AGREEMENT

DOE, ROE & CO.,
WALL STREET,
NEW YORK, N. Y.

Gentlemen:

In consideration of your carrying a joint account for the undersigned, the undersigned jointly and severally agree that each of them shall have authority on behalf of the joint account to buy, sell (including short sales), and otherwise deal in, through you as brokers, stocks, bonds and other securities and commodities, on margin or otherwise; to receive on behalf of the joint account demands, notices, confirmations, reports, statements of account and communications of every kind; to receive on behalf of the joint account money, securities and property of every kind and to dispose of same; to make on behalf of the joint account agreements relating to any of the foregoing matters and to terminate or modify same or waive any of the provisions thereof; and generally to deal with you on behalf of the joint account as fully and completely as if he alone were interested in said account, all without notice to the other or others interested in said account. You are authorized to follow the instructions of any of the undersigned in every respect concerning the said joint account with you and to make deliveries to any of the undersigned, or upon his instructions, of any or all securities in the said joint account, and to make payments to any of the undersigned, or upon his order, of any or all monies at any time or from time to time in the said joint account as he may order and direct, even if such deliveries and/or payments shall be made to him personally, and not for the joint account of the undersigned. In the event of any such deliveries of securities or payments of monies to any of the undersigned as aforesaid, you shall be under no duty or obligation to inquire into the purpose or propriety of any such demand for delivery of securities or payment of monies, and you shall not be bound to see to the application or disposition of the said securities and/or monies so delivered or paid to any of the undersigned or upon his order. The authority hereby conferred shall remain in force until written notice of the revocation addressed to you is delivered at your main office.

The liability of the undersigned with respect to said account shall be joint and several. The undersigned further agree jointly and severally that all property you may at any time be holding or carrying for any one or more of the undersigned shall be subject to a lien in your favor for the discharge of the obligations of the joint account to you, such lien to be in addition to and not in substitution of the rights and remedies you otherwise would have.

It is further agreed that in the event of the death of either or any of the undersigned, the survivor or survivors shall immediately give you written notice thereof, and you may, before or after receiving such notice, take such proceeding, require such papers and inheritance or estate tax waivers, retain such portion of and/or restrict transactions in the account as you may deem advisable to protect you against any tax, liability, penalty or loss under any present or future laws or otherwise. The estate of any of the undersigned who shall have died shall be liable and each survivor shall continue liable jointly and severally, to you for any net debit balance or loss in said account in any way resulting from the completion of transactions initiated prior to the receipt by you of the written notice of the death of the decedent or incurred in the liquidation of the account or the adjustment of the interests of the respective parties.

*(a) It is the express intention of the undersigned to create an estate or account as joint tenants with rights of survivorship and not as tenants in common. In the event of the death of either or any of the undersigned, the entire interest in the joint account shall be vested in the survivor or survivors on the same terms and conditions as theretofore held, without in any manner releasing the decedent's estate from the liability provided for in the next preceding paragraph.

*(b) In the event of the death of either or any of the undersigned the interests in the account as of the close of business on the date of the death of the decedent (or on the next following business day if the date of death is not a business day), shall be as follows:

____________________ or his or her estate ________________ %
Name of Participant

____________________ or his or her estate ________________ %
Name of Participant

____________________ or his or her estate ________________ %
Name of Participant

but any taxes, costs, expenses or other charges becoming a lien against or being payable out of the account as the result of the death of the decedent, or through the exercise by his or her estate or representatives of any rights in the account shall, so far as possible, be deducted from the interest of the estate of such decedent. This provision shall not release the decedent's estate from the liability provided for in the paragraph next preceding "(a)" above.

The undersigned request you to open the joint account under the following designation:

____

Subject to the provisions hereof, all notices or communications for the undersigned in respect of the joint account are to be directed to

Name __________________________________

Address ....

City ....Zone (if any)..............State ....

Each of the undersigned has signed the Customer's Agreement and Consent to Loan of Securities which are intended to cover, in addition to the provisions hereof, the terms upon which the joint account is to be carried.

Dated, ... Very truly yours,

....
(City) (State)

....

....

....

*Strike out paragraph (a) or (b) whichever is inapplicable, and if paragraph (b) is retained, fill in the names and percentage amounts of the interests of the respective parties.

K

K. The TICKER abbreviation for Kellogg Company.

KAFFIRS. Term applied to South African mining securities on the London Stock Exchange.

KANGAROOS. Term referring to Australian land, tobacco and mining securities on the London Stock Exchange.

"KATY". Nickname for the Missouri, Kansas & Texas Railway Co.

KEY INDUSTRY. An industry whose position is dominant in the field in which it operates or in the general economy.

KILLING. Expression used by speculators to denote an unusually large trading profit.

KITING. 1. Pushing stock prices to unwarranted high levels.

2. Writing checks against a bank account where the funds are insufficient to cover them, hoping that before they are presented for payment, the necessary funds will be deposited.

L

L. The TICKER abbreviation for Sinclair Oil Corporation.

LAMB. A beginner at speculation; one who is inexperienced at operating in stocks. He follows the flock, buying or selling blindly on tips and rumors because others do so.

LAST SALE. The last price at which a transaction in a security took place on a certain day or a particular time during a trading session.

LATE TAPE. A condition existing when trading is so heavy that the TICKER is unable to print sales fast enough to keep pace with transactions on the TRADING FLOOR. Except for a 160-minute *late tape* by the old, slow-speed tickers in 1929, the 143-minute lag of May 23, 1962, was the greatest ever. See FLASH PRICES.

LEADERS. Individual stocks or groups of stocks which set the pace and tone of the market for other stocks to follow.

LEGAL SECURITIES. Securities which are legal for investment by savings banks, trust funds, insurance companies and other

Institutional investors. State and Federal laws vary as to what is permissible for legal investment, but they usually emphasize safety of principal and are intended to protect the individual by making such investments as "fool proof" as possible.

LEVERAGE. Ratio of common stock to total Capitalization; a kind of built-in reflector of good times and bad. If a company's earnings remain at a given level and large amounts must be paid for bond interest and preferred stock dividends, the amount available for dividends on the common stock will be lower. If common stock constitutes the sole capitalization, there is no leverage factor; it applies mostly where large fixed obligations are present. Leverage in itself, like debt, is neither favorable nor unfavorable. But in a highly profitable and expanding business, leverage can be very beneficial in returns on the common stock. When a relatively small change in operating earnings can cause a big change in net profits per share, a company is said to be *leveraged.* It is a good thing to have in times of boom and inflation because it makes the dollar go further, but it is dangerous in times of depression and deflation because it increases risk.

LIABILITIES. Debts; obligations. Something owed which must be paid in money or the equivalent. The opposite of assets in a Balance sheet. See Accrued liabilities; Capital liabilities; Contingent liabilities; Current liabilities; Fixed liabilities; Long-term liabilities.

LIEN. A claim on property given by law to secure the satisfaction of some demand, or payment of some debt.

LIFO. The abbreviation for *Last in, First out;* a method for calculating inventory values and cost-of-sales in which the value of each item is computed according to the cost of the earliest acquisitions, and the cost of goods sold, or used, is based on the cost of the latest acquisitions. Lifo assumes that the articles sold, or used, are those most recently acquired, and that articles remaining in the inventory are those that were first acquired. See FIFO.

LIMITED PARTNERSHIP. A PARTNERSHIP consisting of GENERAL and SPECIAL partners, with at least one member being fully responsible for all debts who is also the manager of the firm.

LIMIT ORDER. An order instructing a broker to buy or sell at a specified price. The broker must not exceed or go below the stated limit without the knowledge and consent of the person who entered the order, unless he can execute it at a price more favorable to the customer. The opposite of MARKET ORDER.

LINE CHART. A piece of graph paper on which is recorded daily, weekly, or monthly, the price range of a particular stock, or the MARKET AVERAGES, with attendant trading volume. The pattern thus formed over a period of time helps the chartist formulate an opinion regarding the future price action of the stock. Also sometimes called BAR AND LINE chart. See POINT AND FIGURE. The chart reproduced on page 150, through the courtesy of F. W. Stephens, New York, N.Y., shows the monthly price action of Woodall Industries.

LINE OF STOCKS. A large amount of stock which has been bought or sold systematically—such as on a "scale." See SCALE ORDER.

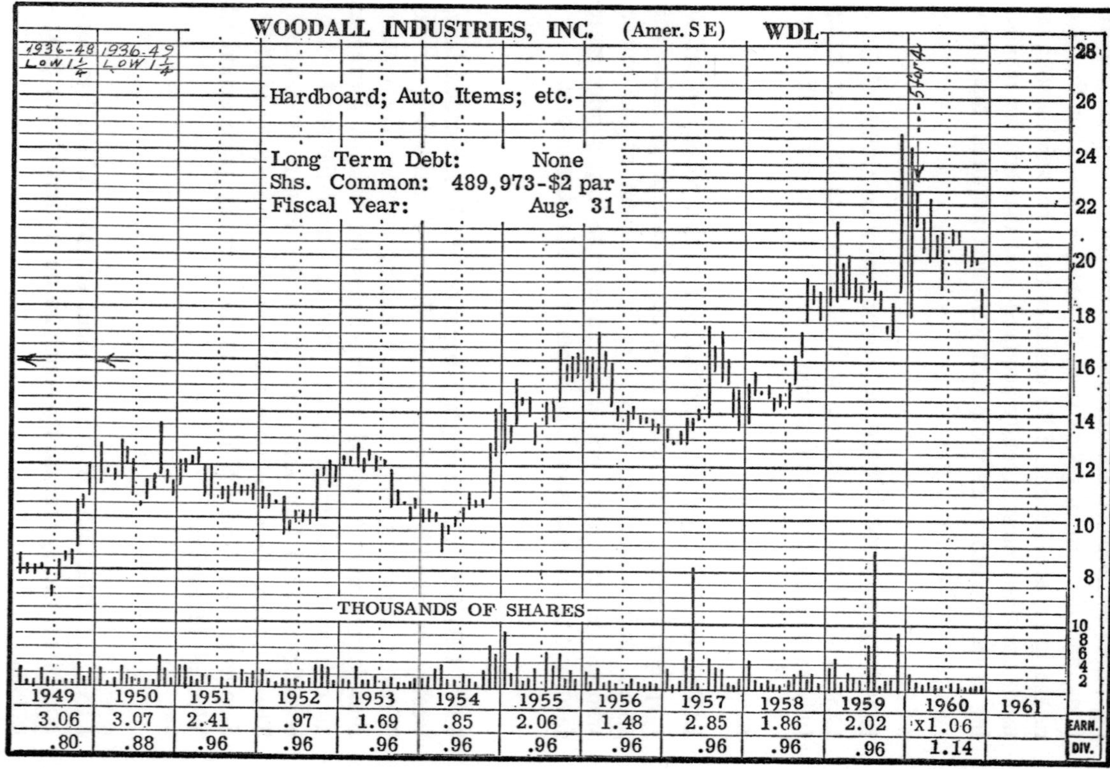

WOODALL INDUSTRIES, INC. (Amer. SE) WDL
1936-48 LOW 1 1/4
1936-49 LOW 1 1/4
Hardboard; Auto Items; etc.
Long Term Debt: None
Shs. Common: 489,973-$2 par
Fiscal Year: Aug. 31
5 for 4
THOUSANDS OF SHARES
28
26
24
22
20
18
16
14
12
10
8
10
8
6
4
2
1949
1950
1951
1952
1953
1954
1955
1956
1957
1958
1959
1960
1961
EARN.
3.06
3.07
2.41
.97
1.69
.85
2.06
1.48
2.85
1.86
2.02
x1.06
DIV.
.80
.88
.96
.96
.96
.96
.96
.96
.96
.96
.96
1.14

LIQUID ASSETS. Assets consisting of cash or other property which can be readily converted into money. Virtually the same as QUICK ASSETS.

LIQUIDATING DIVIDEND. A pro rata distribution of property paid to the owners, creditors, depositors and other lawful claimants when a corporation is being settled or liquidated.

LIQUIDATING MARKET. A market in which the selling is aggressive at lower prices.

LIQUIDATION. 1. Panic-type selling on heavy volume with most stocks moving sharply lower.

2. The termination of a business and the conversion of its assets into cash. Liquidation may be forced or voluntary.

LIQUIDITY. A condition existing when an investor or a business holds largely cash or other assets which can be readily converted into cash with little loss in value.

LISTED SECURITIES. Securities which have passed the LISTING REQUIREMENTS and have been accorded the right of being traded on a stock exchange. Listing is no guaranty of a security's worth (market value) and does not mean it will pay dividends or maintain its current rate of payment. However, the stockholder has complete knowledge of the price of his holdings at all times; he receives complete and frequent (usually quarterly) reports of earnings and activities of the company, and he can find a ready market for his stock should he wish to sell. Listing also increases the collateral value of securities.

LISTING REQUIREMENTS. To have its securities listed on the New York Stock Exchange, a corporation must have: (A) a minimum of 500,000 common shares OUTSTANDING, exclusive of concentrated or family holdings; (B) a total market value of $10 million for the outstanding common shares, or net TANGIBLE ASSETS applicable to the common stock; (C) at least 1,500 ROUND-LOT holders and demonstrated earning power under competitive conditions of $1 million annually after all charges and taxes.

Other general guides for consideration of companies for listing include the requirement that they be GOING CONCERNS, or successors to going concerns; that there be a degree of national interest in these companies; that they have a relatively good position and some stability in the industry, and that they are engaged in an expanding industry with prospects of at least maintaining their relative position. These companies must also agree to report earnings at frequent intervals to shareholders and to the public. See DELIST.

LIST, THE. The total of securities listed for trading on a specific stock exchange. See LISTED SECURITIES.

LITTLE BOARD. Another name for the American Stock Exchange; the term *Big Board* is synonymous with the New York Stock Exchange.

LOAD CHARGE. A commission charged to the buyer of most MUTUAL FUND shares, which takes care of sales, promotion and distribution costs. Mutual fund shares are sold at net asset value plus commission. The average commission runs about 7½ percent. See NO LOAD FUND.

LOAD UP. To buy securities to the limit of one's financial capacity, usually for speculative purposes.

LOAN CROWD. The aggregate of brokers which meets intermittently throughout the day on the trading floor of the Stock Exchange to borrow or lend stocks to other brokers.

LOANED FLAT. Term referring to stock which has been loaned without interest. The lender normally pays interest to the borrower, but if the stock becomes scarce, the lender will pay a lower rate or none at all (FLAT), or even exact a daily PREMIUM rate from the borrower.

LOANED STOCK. Stock which has been loaned to a SHORT SELLER or the broker acting for him in order to fulfill the terms of a short selling contract. The borrower gives the lender the market value of the stock in money. Unless the stock is LOANED FLAT, or at a PREMIUM, the lender pays to the borrower interest on the money the borrower used to pay for the stock. See BORROWED STOCK; SHORT COVERING; SHORT SALE.

LOCKED IN. An investor is said to be *locked in* when he is reluctant to accept a large PAPER PROFIT on a security because of the tax penalty, or when he cannot sell without incurring an expensive loss.

LOCK UP. To withdraw from circulation; to deposit in a strong box for safekeeping, securities which have been bought and transferred into the owner's name for long-term investment purposes.

LONG. The market position of one who has bought securities for a rise. The opposite of this term is "short," and he who is short of stocks is a BEAR. See SHORT SALE.

LONG ACCOUNT. 1. The aggregate of securities held by traders and investors in expectation of rising prices.

2. Specific securities held by a broker for his client, either for cash or on MARGIN.

LONG INTEREST. The collective holding of an individual stock, or particular group of stocks. "The long interest in metal stocks is reported to be very large."

LONG POSITION. The market attitude assumed by one who owns securities.

LONG PULL. The purchase, or SHORT SALE, of a security. It is made with the intention of holding position for some time in expectation of a substantial profit.

LONG SIDE. The side of the market which attracts purchases by those who believe that prices will rise. The opposite of SHORT SIDE.

LONG STOCK. Securities which have been purchased in expectation of rising prices.

LONG TERM. A period of six months or more. Long-term profits made in the sale of securities are accorded more favorable tax treatment than are short-term profits (less than six months). News and rumor mostly govern the short-term trend; long-term is determined more by basic fundamentals and intrinsic value. The opposite of NEAR-TERM or SHORT-TERM.

LONG-TERM LIABILITIES. Debts or obligations which are not due for at least a year from the time they are incurred. See FIXED LIABILITIES.

LONG-TERM TREND. The basic direction in which market prices seem likely to move over the foreseeable future.

LOST CERTIFICATES. Before 1936, the New York Stock Exchange printed information concerning lost certificates on the TICKER TAPE. But this practice has been discontinued and the Exchange now advises that owners of destroyed or misplaced securities make contact directly with the TRANSFER AGENT of the company concerned. The requirements for issuing a new certificate and the cost of the perpetual security bond the owner must furnish differ with each company. However, positive identification is always imperative, as is a complete rundown of facts surrounding the loss. See CARE OF SECURITIES.

LOT. A unit of trading. See ODD-LOT; ROUND LOT.

LOWEST OFFER. The lowest price that anyone will accept in the sale of a security at a specific moment. The opposite of BEST BID.

M

M. The TICKER abbreviation for Montgomery Ward & Company, Inc.

MAINTENANCE. The total of cash or securities deposited in a brokerage account to meet the broker's MARGIN REQUIREMENTS.

MAJORITY STOCKHOLDERS. Stockholders who own or control the majority of stock in a corporation. They represent the controlling interest.

MAJOR TREND. The basic direction in which stock prices move over a period of time, regardless of temporary setbacks and rallies. Virtually the same as PRIMARY MOVEMENT. See INTERMEDIATE TREND, MINOR TREND.

MAKING A LINE. Term referring to the action of a stock which has remained within a narrow price range for some time. In such cases, *making a line* can indicate that the stock is being accumulated or distributed. If the *line* shows ACCUMULATION, the stock is considered a good buy. If DISTRIBUTION is indicated it is a sale.

Market TECHNICIANS, or CHARTISTS, will watch such a stock closely for a clue to the direction of the move that may be pending.

MAKING A MARKET. 1. Creating or stimulating an interest toward a stock by publicity in the press or by listing it on a recognized stock exchange. This increases its MARKETABILITY, which is especially desirable if the issue is new, or relatively unknown. See LISTED SECURITIES.

2. When one broker names a price at which he will buy a certain security and another broker a price at which he will sell, they are said to be *making a market* in it.

3. One of the principal functions of a dealer in OVER-THE-COUNTER securities is to aid in creating or maintaining a market in a security which has been publicly distributed for the first time. To make a market, the dealer must know where he can acquire the security or dispose of it quickly, and he must stand ready to "take a position" (acquire an inventory in that security, using his own money) against which he can sell. His profit is derived usually from the difference or "spread" between what he pays for the security and the price for which he sells it, either to the public or another dealer. Sometimes his profit comes from the improvement in market value of his inventory position. See SPREAD.

MANIPULATION. Stimulating or depressing the movements of stock prices by artificial methods. It is a criminal offense to furnish false information about a stock to influence its price, punishable by 2–5 years in jail. The New York Stock Exchange has a "stock watching" department whose function is to detect any unusual activity and price movement in specific issues. A formula is used to determine just when an issue merits closer inspection and possibly a follow-up examination.

The first of the great market manipulators was Jacob Little, who failed for $10 million in 1856. He is credited with inventing "short selling" as it applies to securities. See SHORT SALE.

MARGIN. The amount of money and/or securities deposited by a client with his broker to finance part of the cost of purchasing LISTED SECURITIES. The broker advances the necessary balance, holds the purchased stock as collateral in his client's name and charges him interest on the money loaned. Margin rates are set by the Federal Reserve Board. A 50% rate means that $1,000 worth of stock can be purchased for $500 down; a 75% rate would call for $750 to buy the same amount of stock, etc. See MARGIN REQUIREMENTS. In its public transaction study of September 13, 1961, the New York Stock Exchange said that margin transactions by public individuals accounted for 16.3% of the total share volume. In the years over which these studies have been carried out, the figure has never moved above 27%.

MARGIN ACCOUNT. A brokerage account wherein LISTED SECURITIES may be purchased with the aid of credit provided by the buyer's broker.

MARGIN CALL. A demand made by a broker upon his client to advance money or securities—either to finance an initial purchase or to maintain the minimum MARGIN REQUIREMENTS set by the Stock Exchange or the brokerage firm or both.

MARGINED SECURITIES. Securities bought on credit or held as collateral in a MARGIN ACCOUNT which cannot be withdrawn until the debit balance owing in the account has been paid in full.

MARGIN OF SAFETY. 1. The excess of average earnings over dividend or interest requirements.

2. The excess value of COLLATERAL over the amount borrowed against it. If a $1,000 loan is placed against collateral worth $2,000, the margin of safety is $1,000.

MARGIN REQUIREMENTS. The downpayment necessary to buy LISTED SECURITIES on credit or margin as regulated by the Board of Governors of the Federal Reserve System under the Securities Act of 1934. Margin requirements have ranged from a low of 45% in the 1937–1945 era to a high of 100% (all cash) following World War II. Prior to 1934, margins were negotiated by brokers and their clients. They sometimes dropped as low as 10% before the crash in 1929, when stock market credit exceeded $8.5 billion, a figure never closely approached since. A 50% margin means that $100 worth of a listed stock can be bought for $50 down.

The New York Stock Exchange also has its own margin requirements in addition to those set by the Federal Reserve: (A) A margin account may not be opened with a MEMBER FIRM, unless a minimum of $1,000 or its equivalent in securities is deposited; (B) In general, the EQUITY in an account may never be less than 25% of the market value of securities held in the account. If the equity declines below 25%, the client must put up more margin, or be sold out by the broker. Brokerage firms may also have their own margin rules, supplementing those of the Stock Exchange and the Federal Reserve.

MARKET. A place where buyers and sellers meet to deal in securities or commodities for their own account or for others.

MARKETABILITY. Term synonymous with salability and meaning the degree of investment or speculative interest which underlies any security; the ease with which it can be sold. This is an important factor to consider in the event an emergency should arise, requiring an immediate need for cash. LISTED SECURITIES usually have the greatest marketability.

MARKETABLE SECURITIES. Securities for which there is always a ready market available, such as active, LISTED SECURITIES.

MARKET AVERAGES. One of the principal barometers studied by speculators and investors for determining the trend and condition of the market. None of the averages is perfect, but they nevertheless help to give market students a good picture of the action of a cross section of the market. The DOW-JONES AVERAGES, New York *Herald Tribune* Averages, New York *Times* Averages and STANDARD & POOR'S 500-STOCK PRICE INDEX are the most popular averages in use today.

MARKET CYCLE. A period of rising security prices comprising ACCUMULATION and advance followed by a period of lower prices consisting of DISTRIBUTION and decline. It coincides roughly with periods of recovery, prosperity, recession and depression in a normal BUSINESS CYCLE.

MARKET INSTINCT. The ability to interpret with reasonable accuracy, the true meaning and significance of price movements and volume changes and their relationship.

MARKET LEADERS. Prominent individual stocks or groups of stocks which have a large investment or speculative following.

MARKET LETTER. A report published daily, weekly, or monthly, by many brokerage firms giving their current opinions of the market and usually including advice regarding what stocks to buy, sell, or avoid entirely. Its primary purpose is to create and stimulate business by attracting new clients to the firm and supplying the older clients with new ideas.

Both the New York Stock Exchange and the American Stock Exchange have been doing their best to police "mailed tipping" and advertising by their members. Says the New York Stock Exchange on the subject: "Each market letter and all sales literature prepared and issued by a member or member organization for general distribution to customers or the public shall be approved by such member or by a partner of such firm, or by an officer who is a holder of voting stock in such corporation. Each market letter and piece of sales literature which refers to the market or to specific companies or securities, listed or unlisted, shall be retained by the issuing member or member organization for at least three years. The copies retained shall contain the name of the member, partner, or holder of voting stock approving its issuance, and shall be subject to delivery, upon request, to the Exchange and shall at all times within the three-year period be readily available."

MARKET OFF. Refers to a market that is selling lower for the day in terms of which set of MARKET AVERAGES a person happens to follow, and, psychologically, also in terms of which stocks a person happens to own.

MARKET ORDER. An order to buy or sell a stipulated amount of a certain security *at the market,* i.e., the best price obtainable after the order is received by the broker on the trading floor. The opposite of LIMIT ORDER.

MARKET PRICE. The last sale or the best price that can be realized for a security or commodity at a specific moment of time. Market prices are primarily a reflection of public opinion.

MARKET REPORT. 1. A verbal or written report submitted by a broker from the trading floor of an exchange which states that a buy or sell order previously entered has been executed at the price named in the report.

2. Term referring to a news report of the action or condition of the general market.

MARKET SECURITIES. To offer (bring out) securities for sale on the market. Also, these are securities which are traded publicly in a market, as opposed to those with limited or local salability.

MARKET SENTIMENT. The mass psychology which affects the trend of stock prices. Market sentiment may be pessimistic, optimistic, or mixed, on a particular day, week, or month.

MARKET VALUE. The value of a security based on its prevailing market price. See INTRINSIC VALUE.

MARK TO THE MARKET. To check the last sales prevailing for securities held in a MARGIN ACCOUNT, in order to determine if the value of the account meets the minimum MARGIN REQUIREMENTS set by the Stock Exchange and/or the brokerage firm concerned.

With respect to the determination of value for margin purposes, the rules of the New York Stock Exchange state: "Active securities dealt in on a recognized exchange shall, for margin purposes, be valued at current market prices. Other securities shall be valued conservatively in the light of current market prices and the amount which might be realized upon liquidation. Substantial additional margin must be required in all cases where the securities carried are subject to unusually rapid or violent changes in value, or do not have an active market on a recognized exchange, or where the amount carried is such that it cannot be liquidated promptly."

MATCHED AND LOST. Term used on the trading floor of an exchange to indicate that one broker has lost in flipping a coin with another broker to decide which of them is the seller. This is necessary sometimes if two offers to sell the same stock are made at the same time. When simultaneous offering prices are equal to, or larger than, the number of shares bid for, both offers are considered equal.

MATCHED ORDERS. 1. Orders to buy or sell a particular stock that are placed simultaneously with different brokers by the same person; the intention of the orders is to distribute or accumulate stock as high or as low as possible. This is a form of manipulation and is strictly prohibited.

2. Buy and sell orders *matched* legitimately by the SPECIALIST in a stock in order to arrange an opening price as closely as possible to the previous close. In doing so he takes into consideration general market conditions plus any special circumstances surrounding the stock.

MATURITY. A fixed moment of time when a bond or a loan becomes due and payable.

MELON. Slang expression referring to the sum total of extraordinary profits waiting to be divided.

MEMBER. One who has been accepted as a member of an organized stock exchange and granted all the privileges of membership.

Persons admitted to membership or allied membership on the New York Stock Exchange are required to pass tests covering general and specific areas of securities industry practice before engaging in activities on the trading floor or in MEMBER FIRM offices. The testing system centers on a basic examination concerning general knowledge of the securities business and its ethics and regulations. Members planning to be active on the floor are tested in depth on their knowledge and understanding of Exchange trading rules and floor procedures and related federal regulations. Office members and allied members are tested on their knowledge of Exchange rules and regulations, and federal regulations governing the conduct and operations of member organizations.

MEMBER CORPORATION. "A corporation, transacting business as a broker or dealer in securities, approved by the Board of Governors as a member corporation, having at least one member of the Exchange who is a director thereof and a holder of voting stock therein. A corporation shall cease to be a member corporation if the approval of the Board of Governors is withdrawn, or if it shall cease to transact business as a broker or dealer in securities or to have a member of the Exchange as a director thereof and holder of voting stock therein, unless the corporation has the status of a member corporation by virtue of permission given to it by the Board of Governors" (New York Stock Exchange Constitution).

MEMBER FIRM. "A firm transacting business as a broker or dealer in securities, at least one of whose general partners is a member of the Exchange, or who has the status of a member firm by virtue of permission given to it by the Board of Governors"

(Constitution of the New York Stock Exchange). The N.Y.S.E. has over 660 member firms, which operated some 3,400 offices in 722 cities throughout the United States on July 1, 1963.

MEMBERSHIP DUES. The annual fee paid by 1,366 members of the New York Stock Exchange. In 1962, membership dues were increased from $1,000 a year to $1,500—the first change since 1942. See INITIATION FEE.

MERGER. A combination or amalgamation of two or more corporations into a single business unit, usually to offset competition by (1) cutting costs and increasing profits through a stronger market position; (2) financing expansion; (3) acquiring modern research facilities; (4) keeping the business going; (5) diversifying or filling out the product line; (6) branching out into new territories and getting supplies more easily.

MIDDLE OF THE ROAD POLICY. Noncommittal; to be neither optimistic nor pessimistic on the future trend of stock prices.

MINORITY STOCKHOLDERS. Term referring to the interest of those who hold less than 50% of a corporation's stock. The majority of stock in a corporation is sometimes held by another corporation, or by certain individuals who comprise the "controlling group" by reason of the voting power of the stock they own.

MINOR TREND. Day-to-day fluctuations which have virtually no influence on the INTERMEDIATE or MAJOR TREND. Virtually the same as TERTIARY MOVEMENT.

MISCELLANEOUS STOCKS. Stocks which do not belong to any particular industry group.

MISCONCEPTIONS OF THE PUBLIC. General misunderstanding of the purpose and functions of the security exchanges. Following are a few of them: Prices are set by the exchanges, who also recommend what to buy or sell; secret transactions are permitted; the large buyer gets more consideration than the small buyer; the exchanges make a profit from public losses; the exchanges may buy and sell for their own account; manipulation and creating artificial prices are permitted; the SECURITIES AND EXCHANGE COMMISSION determines the value of securities. All of the above are positively false.

MISS THE MARKET. To allow any particularly advantageous opportunity to buy or sell securities to slip by.

MIXED COLLATERAL. Securities of different kinds pledged against the payment of borrowed money.

MONEY BROKER. One who acts as intermediary between the lenders and borrowers of money.

MONTHLY INVESTMENT PLAN (MIP). An income investing technique introduced to the public early in 1954 by MEMBER FIRMS of the New York Stock Exchange. It enables an investor to acquire stock on a regular convenient basis, with payments as small as $40 every three months or as large as $1,000 a month. See DOLLAR COST AVERAGING.

MONTHLY STATEMENT. A posted record, usually issued monthly by brokerage firms to their clients, in which is set forth the date, amount, name of company, price and money involved in any securities transactions made during the past month. All dividends, interest and securities received or delivered from the account are also listed, as is the credit or debit balance existing at the month's end. Sometimes called *Statement of Account.*

MOOCH. Slang expression for one who buys securities without investigating on the lure of big profits.

MOODY'S INVESTOR'S SERVICE. A subsidiary of Dun & Bradstreet, Inc. and a publisher of some of the statistical bibles of Wall Street, which delivers to subscribers more than 19,000 pages a year. Founded in 1900 by security analyst John Moody, the first analyst to rate the investment quality and character of bonds. The company has expanded in many directions within the industry. Home office: 99 Church Street, New York, N.Y. See BEST, ALFRED M. CO., INC.; FITCH INVESTOR'S SERVICE; STANDARD & POOR'S CORPORATION.

"MOP." Nickname for Missouri Pacific R.R. Co.

MORTGAGE BOND. A bond secured by a mortgage on certain real property and usually classified according to its priority of claim against the property. If interest or principal is defaulted it may be sold to satisfy the debt. This is probably the most popular type of bond—especially for individually owned businesses, partnerships and small corporations.

MUNICIPAL BOND. A bond issued by a town, city, county or state for such things as highway improvement, schools and equipment, irrigation, public buildings, and sewers. Municipal bonds are generally exempt from federal taxes and regarded as ranking next in safety to U.S. Government bonds. Payment of interest and principal is based on the willingness of citizens of the issuing municipality to pledge future taxes.

MUTUAL FUND. An INVESTMENT COMPANY which raises money by selling its own stock to the public and invests the proceeds in other securities. Also known as *Open-end Fund;* the name being derived from the fact that the CAPITALIZATION is not fixed—more shares may be issued to satisfy the demand. See CLOSED-END FUND. The idea is that the fund's professional management can handle investments better than the average individual and that the owners of mutual fund shares have the benefit of diversification because of their indirect ownership of many different securities. There are some 200 mutual funds in the United States with assets in excess of $25 billion.

N

N. The TICKER abbreviation for International Nickel Co. of Canada, Ltd.

NARROW MARKET. A market characterized by low volume and small price changes.

NATIONAL ASSOCIATION OF SECURITIES DEALERS. A voluntary association of brokers and dealers handling OVER-THE-COUNTER securities. The Association resulted from special legislation passed by Congress in 1938 (*Maloney Act*), for the purpose of regulating the *Over-the-Counter* Market. The loss of NASD membership would severely restrict a securities firm's operations, since nonmembers are not entitled to reduced commissions from NASD members and cannot participate with members in "underwritings." See UNDERWRITER.

NATIONAL INCOME. The total net earnings which may be ascribed to factors used in producing goods and services in the nation for any given period. It differs slightly from GROSS NATIONAL PRODUCT because it excludes costs which do not represent payments to individuals or corporations. For example, the cost of wear and tear on machinery (DEPRECIATION) is not included in national income, nor are excise taxes on products such as liquor and cigarettes. These taxes go directly to the government and are not counted in the individual's, or manufacturer's income.

NATIONAL STOCK EXCHANGE. A stock-trading subsidiary of the New York Mercantile Exchange which became New York's third securities exchange when it opened for business March 7, 1962, with eight "listings." The NSE's current appeal is to the small company that seeks wider ownership. Requirements for listing include a minimum of 500 shareholders, 100,000 shares in public hands and net worth of at least $500,000.

NATURAL RESOURCES. The wealth which nature provides, such as oil reserves, minerals, and timber.

NEAR-TERM. Over the near future; usually a period of two months, or less. Synonymous with SHORT-TERM and the opposite of LONG-TERM.

NEGOTIABLE SECURITIES. Securities which permit a transfer of title by assignment or delivery.

NET. 1. That which is left over after all possible deductions and allowances have been made.

2. A fixed price at which a person agrees to deliver or receive a security.

NET ASSETS. The excess value of the total property of a corporation over liabilities.

NET ASSET VALUE PER SHARE. A figure computed once or twice daily by INVESTMENT COMPANIES, and considered to be a most reliable indicator of investment progress. It is obtained by subtracting all liabilities from the current asset value of securities held in the portfolio; then dividing this result by the number of shares OUTSTANDING. Most MUTUAL FUND shares are sold at net asset value plus commission, usually called a LOAD CHARGE.

NET CHANGE. The variation in market value between the closing price of a security one day and its closing price on the next day that it is traded.

NET EARNINGS. Term referring to that which is left available for dividends and surplus after deducting all operating costs, fixed charges, rentals, and interest from gross revenues. A distinction is usually made as to whether earnings are pre-tax or after-tax.

NET PROFITS. Term virtually synonymous with net earnings but used more in an industrial and commercial sense. It refers to the sum which may be applied to dividends and surplus after deducting the cost of goods sold and all general administrative and selling expenses from gross profits. It often includes non-recurring profits derived from sources outside the company's normal operating area, such as from investments in securities.

NET SALES. The actual dollar value received for sales after deducting for allowances, returns, and cash discounts taken by customers.

NET SURPLUS. The profits or earnings left available to a corporation after all operating expenses, taxes, insurance, interest and dividends have been paid. Surplus would be before deducting for dividends and net surplus after deducting dividends.

NET WORKING CAPITAL. The excess of CURRENT ASSETS over CURRENT LIABILITIES, or the result obtained by subtracting current liabilities from current assets. Working capital is the yardstick of a corporation's ability to conduct a normal business without monetary stress and to take possible emergencies, or losses, in stride. The amount of working capital suited to a corporation depends upon its volume of sales and type of business. However, the main point of comparison is how much working capital is available per dollar of sales. Companies doing a cash business have a fast inventory turnover and, consequently, high sales per dollar of working capital; while other companies require large working capital relative to sales because the nature of the business compels them to hold their inventory for longer periods.

NET WORTH. The difference between that which a concern owns or has due it, and that which it owes others. It is the owner's equity in a business (determined by subtracting all liabilities from the BOOK VALUE of assets). In the case of a corporation CAPITAL STOCK plus SURPLUS equals net worth.

NEW HIGH. The highest price reached by an individual security or the general market during a particular phase of action, or the highest level ever attained in history.

NEW ISSUE. A corporate security which is sold publicly for the first time.

NEWS TICKER. See BROAD TAPE.

NEW YORK CURB EXCHANGE. Former title of the AMERICAN STOCK EXCHANGE.

NEW YORK STOCK EXCHANGE. An unincorporated, voluntary association founded in 1792 and existing under a written constitution and by-laws. Membership must be approved by a Committee on Admissions and is obtained by purchasing a SEAT from a retiring, deceased, or expelled member. Privileges include the right to buy and sell securities on the trading floor of the Exchange for one's own account or for others. The name, New York Stock Exchange, was formally adopted January 29, 1863. Until then, the Exchange had been known as the New York Stock and Exchange Board. See BUTTONWOOD TREE. The present building located at 18 Broad Street, New York, N.Y., was opened April 23, 1903, and the office building addition on October 2, 1922.

NICKNAMES OF STOCKS. Familiar names by which certain leading stocks are known, and usually derived from their TICKER SYMBOLS. Thus *Bessie* for Bethlehem Steel (symbol BS); *Navy* for North American Aviation (symbol NV); *Molly* for Molybdenum Corp. (symbol MLY); *Sputnik* for Standard Packing Corp. (symbol SPK); *Yellow Belly* for Youngstown Sheet & Tube (symbol YB) and others.

NO LIMIT ORDER. A buy or sell order entered on the floor of a stock exchange with no stipulation as to price. It is the same as MARKET ORDER and the opposite of LIMIT ORDER.

NO LOAD FUND. A MUTUAL FUND which charges little or no commission (LOAD CHARGE) to the buyer of its shares. No sales organization is involved. The shares are sold directly to the public by the sponsoring firm.

NOMINAL PRICE. An estimated price quoted in lieu of an actual price and used most frequently in commodities. In determining the price of a stock for a particular day when no actual sale took place, an average price between the closing BID AND ASKED quotation is often used and is referred to as the nominal price.

NON-ASSESSABLE STOCK. A stock which is fully paid for and cannot be assessed in the event of insolvency or failure. Practically all stocks are non-assessable, i.e., assessment cannot be levied against the holder thereof.

NON-CALLABLE SECURITIES. Securities which cannot be paid off before maturity, even if the company can afford to do so. They are NOT SUBJECT TO CALL. The opposite of CALLABLE or SUBJECT TO CALL.

NON-CUMULATIVE PREFERRED STOCK. A type of preferred stock on which dividends do not accrue if payment is omitted at the regular time. The corporation is not obligated to make up the amount at a later date. See ARREARS; CUMULATIVE PREFERRED STOCK.

NO NEAR BID—OFFER. Term meaning that the highest bid or lowest offer quoted for a security is a long way below or above the price of the last sale.

NONE OFFERED. Term indicating a current lack of stock being offered for sale; the condition usually occurs in the OVER-THE-COUNTER MARKET.

NON-RECURRING EXPENSE. An unusual expense or loss that is unlikely to be repeated, such as that caused by fire or theft. See START-UP COSTS.

NON-VOTING STOCK. Stock of any class in a corporation other than VOTING STOCK. The New York Stock Exchange has refused to "list" non-voting stock since 1926. See LISTING REQUIREMENTS.

NO-PAR STOCK. See PAR VALUE.

NOT A DELIVERY. Term referring to a security which is not in proper deliverable form and is unacceptable for deposit with a bank, a broker as collateral, or a sale.

NOTE. A written promise of the maker to pay a specified amount of money on demand, or at some future date, to the person named as payee. Notes may be issued by individuals, corporations and governments. A note has various advantages: the payee can discount it at his bank; it is good evidence of debt and virtually eliminates argument over the account; it demands prompt payment.

NOTES PAYABLE. A liability item meaning the aggregate of notes, acceptances, and IOUs held by others which must be repaid at some future date. The opposite of NOTES RECEIVABLE.

NOTES RECEIVABLE. A business asset referring to all notes and acceptances, which are charged to others and are due to be paid in future. The opposite of NOTES PAYABLE.

NOT HELD. Term which sometimes accompanies a MARKET ORDER to buy or sell. It gives the broker some discretion over the execution and indicates that he will not be held responsible if he temporarily "misses" the market. See DISCRETIONARY ORDER; MISS THE MARKET.

NOT SUBJECT TO CALL. Term designating bonds or notes which cannot be paid off and retired before their date of maturity. The opposite of CALLABLE (SUBJECT TO CALL).

O

O. When printed on the lower line of the TICKER TAPE, preceding prices, this letter means *offered.*

OBLIGATION. Indebtedness in any form. An enforceable liability, such as a bond, contract, or note.

OBSOLETE SECURITIES. The securities of an abandoned, or defunct, corporation. A bond which has matured or been retired.

ODD-LOT. A number of shares which is less than the accepted trading unit: below $1,000 FACE VALUE of bonds or less than 100 shares in most stocks. Sometimes called BROKEN LOT; FRACTIONAL LOT; UNEVEN LOT. See ROUND-LOT; TEN SHARE UNIT STOCK. Not until 1874 were arrangements made to trade in *odd-lots*. Certain members of the New York Stock Exchange set themselves up as dealers in odd-lots to service brokers who had buy or sell orders in less than 100 shares.

ODD-LOT BROKER. A member of a stock exchange who specializes in executing orders in ODD-LOTS for other brokers and has no contact with the public. See ODD-LOT DIFFERENTIAL.

ODD-LOT DIFFERENTIAL. The compensation received for his services by an ODD-LOT BROKER. It is added to the price of the effective ROUND-LOT sale on buy orders and subtracted from the price on sell orders. On 100-share unit stocks, the differential amounts to 12½-cents per share (⅛ point) on stocks selling below $40, and 25-cents per share (¼ point) on stocks selling at $40, or above.

ODD-LOT HOUSE. A brokerage firm which specializes in handling orders from investors who wish to buy or sell securities in lots of less than 100 shares. Two firms handle 99% of the business in odd-lots. They are dealers rather than brokers in that the nature of their business obliges them to take positions in the market. They draw on their own inventory to satisfy the demand for securities.

ODD-LOT INDEX. A measurement of public psychology toward the market, and computed by dividing total ODD-LOT sales by odd-lot purchases on a ten-day moving average. When sales outnumber purchases, it indicates the public is reluctant to buy and this is interpreted as favorable. When purchases outnumber sales, the reverse holds true.

ODD-LOT ORDER. An order to buy or sell a security in an amount that is less than the established trading unit, i.e., below 100 shares for the majority of stocks and less than $1,000 FACE VALUE of bonds.

ODD-LOT TRADER. One who buys and sells securities in lots of less than 100 shares, as distinguished from professional investors and people of substantial means who deal in larger amounts.

OFF. 1. Term indicating lower prices; i.e., "The market is *off* today," meaning it is selling lower than yesterday.

2. Also denotes without. "Dividend *off*" means without the dividend.

OFFER. 1. To offer or put up for sale. See FIRM OFFER.

2. Synonymous with ASKED in a market price QUOTATION.

OFFERED AHEAD. A condition existing, sometimes, when a person who has entered an order to sell at a stipulated price finds that similar or lower offers have been previously submitted on the same stock; these naturally take precedence over his.

OFFERED DOWN. Offered for sale at levels that are continually lower than the last sale or quoted price of the same security.

OFFERING PRICE. The stated price at which anyone is willing to sell a security at a specific moment.

OFFER WANTED. Request made by a willing buyer of a security for which there is no apparent market. He is anxious to find a seller with whom he can trade.

OFF-THE-BOARD. Term referring to a transaction made OVER-THE-COUNTER or that which involves a block of LISTED SECURITIES that was not executed on an organized exchange. See SECONDARY DISTRIBUTION.

ON A SCALE. See AVERAGING; BUY ON SCALE; SELL ON SCALE.

ON BALANCE. The excess over previous sales or purchases. If a trader, who has sold 1,500 shares of a stock, turns around and buys 2,500 shares of the same stock, he is said to have bought 1,000 shares *on balance.*

ON BID, OR OFFER. A method whereby an ODD-LOT trader can operate in a LISTED STOCK without having to wait for an actual trade in 100 shares or more of the same stock to take place. He can buy at the OFFERING PRICE or sell at the BID PRICE.

ONE-EIGHTH RULE. A rule governing "short selling." See SHORT SALE. According to the *Securities Exchange Act of 1934,* a stock may be sold short, only if the selling price is at least ⅛ point higher than the last REGULAR WAY SALE or if the selling price is the same as the last sale, if such sale is higher than the last different price of a Regular Way Sale.

At 1:30 P.M., a client instructs his broker to sell 100 shares of PDQ stock "At the market—short" for his account. The stock is quoted "49⅝ bid, offered at 50." The last sale was 50, at 1:25 P.M. Following is a possible sequence of ROUND-LOT sales, about the time the order was entered:

Example One		*Example Two*	
Time	*Price*	*Time*	*Price*
1:25	50	1:25	50
1:35	49 ¾	1:28	49 ⅝
1:40	49 ⅝	1:30	49 ¾
1:43	49 ¾	1:35	49 ¾

Shortly before two o'clock, it is reported to the client that he has "sold 100 PDQ at 49¾—short." In example one, this was possible because 49¾, the effective sale, was higher than 49⅝, the last Regular Way Sale. In example two, the short sale was possible, because 49¾, the effective sale, was identical with the previous sale, which, in turn, was at least ⅛ higher than the last different sale (49⅝, at 1:28 P.M.).

ON MARGIN. Term referring to purchased securities which have not been fully paid for. They are held *on margin,* part of the purchase price having been borrowed from the broker. See MARGIN.

OPEN AN ACCOUNT. To make oneself known to a broker and to establish enough credit with him to substantiate the purchase or sale of securities or commodities.

OPEN CONTRACT. 1. An oral or written contract between two or more parties, the terms, or duration, of which remain unfulfilled.

2. In the commodity markets, it means a transaction which has not yet been completed by the sale or repurchase of a contract previously bought or sold, or by the actual delivery or receipt of the commodity. Also called *Open Trade.*

OPEN-END FUND. See MUTUAL FUND.

OPENING OF THE EXCHANGE. See HOURS OF BUSINESS.

OPENING PRICE. The first price at which a transaction in a security takes place each day. Also refers to the first quoted price of a new issue of securities.

OPEN INTEREST. 1. The number of commodity contracts remaining *open*. See OPEN CONTRACT. It means unliquidated purchases or sales—not their combined total.

2. The interest shown toward a new securities issue, as evidenced by the number and size of buying orders entered. The potential buyer is said to be showing an interest, or "giving an indication" of willingness to buy. See INDICATED INTEREST.

OPEN ORDER. An order to buy or sell at a stipulated price which remains effective until it is executed, cancelled or changed to a different price. It is the same as G.T.C. ORDER, meaning Good 'Til Cancelled or Countermanded. See DAY ORDER.

OPEN TRADE. A trade (transaction) which has not yet been closed.

1. When a stock is "sold short" the *trade* remains open until a COVERING purchase of the same stock is made. See SHORT SALE.

2. See OPEN CONTRACT—Part 2.

OPERATING EXPENSES. The costs involved in operating a business: manufacturing expenses, selling and general administrative expenses and maintenance and repair costs; but not including FIXED CHARGES (interest on funded debt, taxes, insurance).

OPERATING INCOME. The gross profit on sales less all costs, administrative, advertising, selling and general expenses. DEPRECIATION is sometimes deducted by industrial companies before determining operating income and sometimes after. Public utility companies nearly always first deduct depreciation, maintenance and taxes.

OPERATING SURPLUS. The profit remaining after deducting all costs of operating a business for a given period of time. Such things as interest on capital and indebtedness should not be deducted before determining the operating surplus; whether or not taxes and insurance should be deducted depends upon the system of bookkeeping.

OPERATOR. Term referring to a large and frequent buyer and seller of securities for his own account, a professional speculator, for example.

OPTION. 1. An agreement, or privilege, which conveys the right to buy (receive) or sell (deliver) a specific security or property at a stipulated price and within a stated period of time. If not exercised during that time, the money paid for the option (but no more than that amount) is forfeited. Also known as a *paper* or *privilege*. See STOCK OPTION CONTRACT.

2. See STOCK OPTIONS.

OPTIONAL BOND. A bond which may be redeemed (paid or cancelled) before its maturity date at the option of the issuing company.

OPTIONAL DIVIDEND. A dividend payable either in cash or additional shares of stock of the distributing company at the option of the securities holder.

OPTION WRITER. A person—usually an investor with a large portfolio—who supplies STOCK OPTION CONTRACTS to PUT AND CALL BROKERS for resale to the investing and trading public. The primary purpose of the option writer is to obtain capital gain or income or to purchase stock at lower-than-market prices. In recent years large financial institutions have been showing more interest in writing options against their portfolios as a way of earning more and establishing the prices at which they will buy or sell stocks.

ORDER ROOM. The department in a brokerage firm which facilitates and is solely responsible for the flow of buy and sell orders and the reports of executions of them to and from the trading floor of a stock exchange.

ORDERS. Verbal or written, instructions to a broker to buy, or sell, securities or commodities. See CONTINGENT ORDER; DAY ORDER; DISCRETIONARY ORDER; G.T.C. ORDER; G.T.M. ORDER; G.T.W. ORDER; GIVE-UP ORDER; IMMEDIATE ORDER; LIMIT ORDER; MARKET ORDER; MATCHED ORDERS; ODD-LOT ORDER; OPEN ORDER; ROUND-LOT ORDER; SCALE ORDER; SPLIT ORDER; STOP LIMIT ORDER; STOP LOSS ORDER; STOP ORDER; SUPPORTING ORDERS.

ORDINARY INTEREST. Interest computed on the basis of 360 days to the year—12 months of 30 days each. See COMPOUND INTEREST; EXACT INTEREST; SIMPLE INTEREST.

OTHER INCOME. Corporate income derived from sources other than operations; such as rentals, interest, sales of capital assets, increase in inventory and security values.

OUT OF LINE. Term referring to a security whose price is considered to be too far above or below a level that seems warranted considering the general market averages or selling level of other securities in the same group.

OUT OF THE MARKET. A condition describing one who has no market position and is bare of stocks, having closed out all open commitments and taken a sidelines stand.

OUT-OF-TOWN-BUSINESS. The aggregate of orders to buy and sell securities or commodities received from locations outside the town or city in which the main office of a brokerage firm is situated.

OUTSIDE BROKER. A dealer in UNLISTED SECURITIES; not a member of a regular exchange.

OUTSIDE MARKET. OVER-THE-COUNTER. A market where UNLISTED SECURITIES are traded.

OUTSIDERS. The general public. Those who speculate or invest occasionally, usually on the basis of surface factors and without much prior investigation.

OUTSIDE SECURITIES. UNLISTED SECURITIES; those which have no trading privileges on a regular exchange. See LISTED SECURITIES; OVER-THE-COUNTER.

OUTSTANDING DEBTS. The unpaid obligations of an individual or a corporation.

OUTSTANDING SECURITIES. That part of the AUTHORIZED CAPITAL STOCK of a corporation which has actually been issued and sold to the public and is still in public hands. Term does not apply to stock that was issued and later cancelled or reacquired by the corporation.

OUT-THE-WINDOW. Term usually describing a new issue of stocks or bonds which moves out immediately or is quickly sold to investors.

OVERBOUGHT. A TECHNICAL market condition which develops after aggressive purchases made by a large number of speculators have carried a security, or the general market, to unjustifiably high levels. An overbought (top heavy) market is said to be *technically weak* and due for a price correction. See OVERSOLD.

OVERCAPITALIZED. A company which is unable to earn profits large enough to provide a fair return on its capital. According to E. S. Meade in *Trust Finance:* "Overcapitalization is that condition in which the par value of the securities of a company exceeds their actual value based on profits." See CAPITALIZATION.

OVERSOLD. The reverse of OVERBOUGHT and referring to a market which has declined sharply under heavy selling pressure to a level where many stocks seem unusually cheap. Such a market is said to be "technically strong" and likely to stage a recovery.

OVERSTAY THE MARKET. To hold a position in securities for too long a time; such as after a sustained advance when the market seems OVERBOUGHT and due for a price correction.

OVERSUBSCRIBED. A condition existing when the applications received to buy a new issue of securities exceed the amount being offered for sale.

OVER-THE-COUNTER. The world's oldest and largest securities market where UNLISTED securities (and many LISTED securities) are traded. Any transactions not made on an organized stock exchange take place in the Over-the-Counter market, whose operations are both local and national in scope. The term probably originated from the counters in private banking houses over which investors transacted their securities business in an earlier period.

O-T-C differs from the New York Stock Exchange in that it is primarily a *negotiation* market, rather than an *auction* market. It is not located in any one spot and buyers must find the sellers, or vice versa, and negotiate prices on the best basis they can arrange, over a vast communications network in a market consisting of about 4,000 securities houses and 3,000 branch offices. A large amount of business is carried out by dealers acting solely as agents for their client.

O-T-C is primarily a seasoning ground for untried companies, yet it also has its share of old-line, blue chip issues. It is the sole market for the initial distribution of new issues, including U.S. Government bonds, municipal, corporate and foreign bonds; bank and insurance stocks, and investment trust shares. It is often a vehicle for liquidating large blocks of listed or unlisted securities.

Among other important functions, the market is constantly determining and adjusting the level of long-term interest rates. This is done in the Government bond market, the largest single segment of the bond market. More than 95% of the trading in such bonds is conducted over-the-counter. The securities of more than 13,000 commercial banks and 1,400 life insurance companies (excluding mutuals) are also traded here. The market is closely regulated both by state and federal laws, and is also supervised constantly by the NATIONAL ASSOCIATION OF SECURITIES DEALERS, which sets high standards for its members and handles disciplinary action.

OVERTRADING. Buying and selling speculative stocks frequently in the hope of scalping quick profits. One of the greatest causes of loss in Wall Street.

OWNER OF RECORD. See HOLDER OF RECORD.

P

P. The TICKER abbreviation for Phillips Petroleum Company.

PACKET. The London Stock Exchange equivalent of BLOCK.

PAINTING THE TAPE. 1. Causing a stock to appear frequently on the TICKER TAPE by trading constantly in it. Such advertising—intended to excite the curiosity (and the buying interest) of traders and BOARD ROOM watchers—is a form of manipulation currently outlawed.

2. Refers to a condition existing when a particular stock is the object of unusual public interest; such interest causes it to be traded frequently.

PANIC. A severe financial disturbance of relatively short duration, usually preceded by over-speculation, inflation and/or stringent credit conditions. Securities are thrown overboard recklessly at great sacrifice. The collapse of the South Sea Company in England and John Law's Mississippi Company in France caused the world's first great financial panic (1720–1724).

PAPER PROFIT. A profit in a security which has not yet been closed (realized). All profits are *paper* until they are actually taken by selling a LONG POSITION, or "buying-in" (COVERING) a SHORT POSITION.

PARENT COMPANY. A corporation which owns or controls another company or companies. Income stems from dividends, interest, royalties, and rents, and if also an operating company, from sales. The term is sometimes used for HOLDING COMPANY.

PARIS BOURSE. The Stock Exchange in Paris, France, whose full title is Company of the Paris Bank, Exchange, Trade and Finance Brokers. A market in shares has existed in Paris since 1138, but laws regulating the Paris exchange were not passed until 1808. There are only seventy broker-members of the *Bourse.* They cannot trade for their own account, but serve the several hundred "curb brokers" who deal for investors.

PARITY. 1. The equivalent price for a given security in a different currency.

2. On the New York Stock Exchange, a term meaning an equality of bids or offers at a given price. In other words, an absence of any clear preference or sequence of orders. Bids arc on *Parity* most frequently after an execution has cleared the trading floor and several orders are reentered simultaneously. Parity may also occur when several brokers arrive at a trading POST at the same time and call out their orders so close to one another that their time priority is not clear. It also occurs at the opening of the Exchange, especially in stocks with competing SPECIALISTS. Most frequently, however, parity situations occur in markets so busy that a dozen or more brokers are executing orders in rapid sequence. See PRECEDENCE OF ORDERS.

3. Term referring to the prices a farmer should receive for his commodities so that he may buy the same amount of goods and services that these commodities purchased in some "base period." For most commodities the base period is the average of 60 months from August, 1909 to July, 1914—a period when prices paid and received by farmers were in good balance. Thus, if five bushels of corn were required to buy a pair of shoes during the base period, it would take the same amount of corn to buy the shoes today if prices were at 100% parity.

The Government's price support program is designed to prevent farm income from declining sharply during periods of agricultural surpluses. Since the support levels differ each year, a basic relationship should exist between the minimum prices farmers receive for their commodities and the prices they pay for other goods and services. That is, an attempt is made to maintain a parity between prices for agricultural commodities and other prices.

PARTICIPANT. A bank, investment house, or brokerage firm, which has accepted membership in a SYNDICATE organized to sell an issue of securities to the public.

PARTICIPATING BOND. A bond which bears a fixed minimum rate of interest and, because it is entitled to share in excess profits of the issuing corporation, is also known sometimes as a *profit-sharing bond.* Unlike INCOME BONDS, where the maximum interest rate is fixed but is contingent upon earnings, the interest on participating bonds is an enforceable obligation. The conditions governing participation are carefully stipulated and such bonds are seldom used.

PARTICIPATING PREFERRED STOCK. A relatively rare class of stock which entitles the holder to a stated rate of dividends, and also the right to participate in earnings above the fixed rate. The holder is thus enabled to share in extreme prosperity along with the common stockholders but without relinquishing any of his priority rights. A provision for participation is generally intended to make a stock more salable.

PARTICIPATION. 1. The interest held by each individual in a JOINT ACCOUNT.

2. The amount of securities allotted to each member of a SYNDICATE by the syndicate manager.

PARTLY PAID. Securities which have been paid for only in part and on which a liability still exists, such as those held in a MARGIN ACCOUNT.

PARTNERSHIP. A business organization in which two or more persons are associated, each member being personally responsible for all liabilities of the partnership. See ACTIVE PARTNER; GENERAL PARTNER; LIMITED PARTNERSHIP; SILENT PARTNER; SPECIAL PARTNER.

PAR VALUE. The FACE VALUE of a security, regardless of its denomination; usually $1,000 in the case of bonds and $100 per share in the case of stocks. Par is also the basis on which dividends are paid on preferred stocks. It should not be confused with MARKET PRICE or BOOK VALUE. A "No-Par" stock is one with no designated par value. The first law permitting shares to be issued without par value was passed in New York in 1912.

PASS A DIVIDEND. Failure to declare a dividend at the regular expected time.

PEGGED PRICE. 1. The price at which any commodity has been fixed (pegged) by agreement, custom, or law.

2. A price level at which buying support always seems to materialize for a security, causing it to be said that the security is "pegged" at or about that price.

PENNY STOCKS. Stocks selling below $1 and therefore quoted in cents.

PERIODIC PAYMENT PLAN. See MONTHLY INVESTMENT PLAN—MIP.

PERPETUAL BOND. A bond bearing no fixed date of maturity, and also sometimes referred to as an annuity bond. It entitles the purchaser to income during the period while he holds the bond, but it is actually a contradiction of the term *bond,* because a bond represents a promise to pay the interest and principal thereon at a stipulated date.

Perpetual bonds are quite rare in the United States. The West Shore Railroad 4's of 2361 and the Elmira & Williamsport 5's of 2862 bear fixed maturity dates, but since such dates are years away, the bonds should really be considered as perpetual. Foreign perpetuals include: Canadian Pacific Railway Perpetual 4's (bear interest, but have no fixed maturity date), French *rentes,* and British Consolidateds, or *consols.*

PERSONAL INCOME. The financial return or material benefits accruing to an individual from the use of his wealth or services. It is that part of NATIONAL INCOME that goes to individuals as opposed to corporations. It does not include profits retained by business or taxes paid by business. Added to personal income are payments by the government to individuals which are not wages for current labor. These include social security benefits and veteran's pensions and are called *transfer payments.* Business profits are subtracted from national income to obtain personal income, but transfer payments from the government to individuals are added. See DISPOSABLE PERSONAL INCOME.

PHONY DIVIDENDS. Illegal dividends paid immediately out of part of the money that comes in for purchasing a new stock. They are a big factor in promoting more sales of the stock. But the investor is actually being paid out of his own money which he has just put into the company.

PIGGYBACKING. Hauling truck trailers on railroad flat cars. See FISHYBACKING.

PINK SHEETS. Quotation lists of various OVER-THE-COUNTER securities published daily on pink paper by the National Quotation Bureau, Inc., a private corporation founded in October, 1913. The publishing company has its own requirements for firms wishing to subscribe to or list in the service.

BELMAR WALL NATL BK	FIRST NEW JERSEY SEC CO INC A PK	212 DI9 0268		OW		10 1/2
BELMONT IRON WKS	STROUD &CO PH	212 WA5 1990		9 1/2		10 3/4
	E W SMITH CO PH	212 RE2 0037		10		10 1/4
	G C HAAS&CO NY	212 BO9 7060		9 1/2		10 1/4
	SUPLEE YEATMAN MOSLEY CO PH	212 CA6 7207		9 1/2		10 1/2
BELMONT SAVINGS& LOAN	DOYLE O'CONNOR &C OINCNY	212 HA5 5780		14		14 1/2
BELTONE RECORDING	LAPHAM &CO NY	212 WH3 1975	500	OW	500	BW

PIT. An octagonal structure where wheat, corn, oats, and other futures are traded on the floor of a commodity exchange. One commodity is dealt in at each pit, which corresponds to a POST on a stock exchange.

PIVOTAL STOCK. A stock which is generally considered the leader of its group and whose performance in the market often influences the action of other stocks.

PLACE. To find a market for a stock; to sell it. The term applies especially to the successful marketing or *placement* of a large amount of stock, such as by a PRIMARY DISTRIBUTION, SECONDARY DISTRIBUTION, or SPECIAL OFFERING. It may also refer to a *private placement,* where a block of securities is sold to INSTITUTIONAL INVESTORS rather than to the public. See PRIVATE FINANCING.

PLANT. The tools, machinery, equipment, fixtures and buildings belonging to a corporation and usually including the ground on which they stand.

PLOW BACK. To reinvest profits in a business rather than pay them out in the form of dividends.

PLUNGER. One who speculates wildly with little or no prior investigation.

PLUS TICK. See UP TICK.

POINT. 1. The unit in which market price fluctuations are measured. In stocks, a point is $1.00 a share; in bonds, a point is $10 per bond. Quotations in stocks were originally all in percentages. Not until October 13, 1915, did the Stock Exchange rule that stocks sell on a dollar-share basis.

2. A fact, or tip, on which a speculative commitment is based.

POINT AND FIGURE CHART. A piece of graph paper, or chart, which indicates price changes of a stock or the market averages. These changes are indicated only when they equal or exceed the number of points (or fractions of points), on which the chart is based. For example: A one-point chart will only show price changes that equal or exceed one point in either direction. However, there is no set rule governing the number of points, or fractions of a point, on which a chart should be based. If the stock being charted on a one-point chart advances from 50 to 51, a mark is put in the square representing 50–51. Should it continue advancing to 60, the action is recorded by a mark in each of the corresponding vertical squares in the same column.

Conversely, any decline of a point or more from the 60 level will be recorded by descending marks in the next vertical column to the right. When the advance resumes, the next adjacent column is used. The extent of the move, when the stock breaks out of an established trading range in either direction, is supposed to coincide with the number of horizontal units it leaves behind within the ACCUMULATION or DISTRIBUTION area as the case may be. Thus, if the stock has formed eight units within the horizontal BREAKOUT area, the point and figure chartist assumes that the advance or decline from that area will approximate eight points. See LINE CHART. Following is a sample one-point chart showing the market action of Kennecott Copper Corp.

POOL. Nearly the same as CLIQUE and meaning a combination of persons organized under an individual manager for the purpose of influencing the price of a certain stock or stocks. A form of manipulation currently outlawed. See BLIND POOL; BOBTAIL POOL; DISCRETIONARY POOL. The first recognizable Wall Street pool was organized in 1791 to "corner" the stock of the United States Bank. See CORNER.

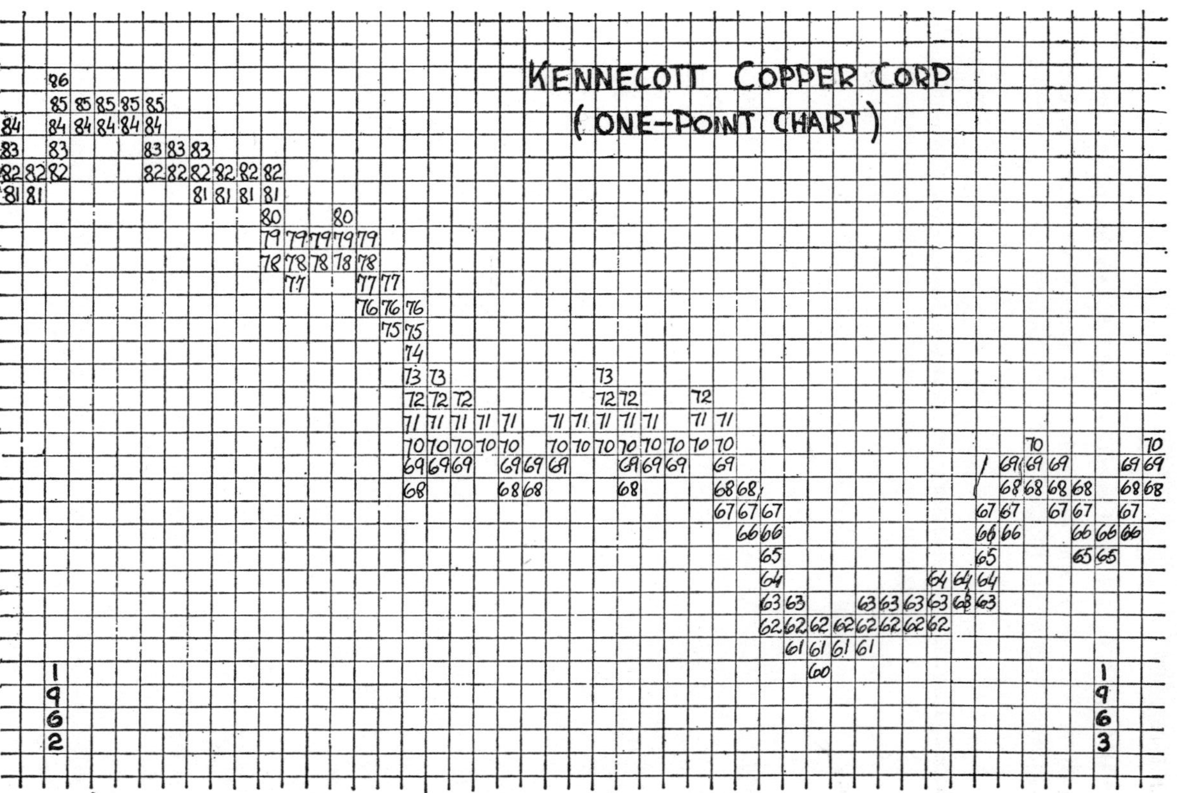

KENNECOTT COPPER CORP
(ONE-POINT CHART)
1962
1963

PORTFOLIO. The total securities held by an institution, or a private individual, for investment, or speculative purposes. See AGGRESSIVE PORTFOLIO; DEFENSIVE PORTFOLIO.

POSITION. 1. An inventory of securities held LONG or SHORT.

2. The prevailing status of a brokerage account, as determined by the market price of all the securities held in the account and by the credit, or debit, balance. See MARK TO THE MARKET.

POST. A horseshoe-shaped structure located on the New York Stock Exchange trading floor where 100-share unit stocks and active 10-share unit stocks are traded. They are eighteen in number—twelve on the main floor and six in the annex (GARAGE), plus Post 30. Each LISTED stock is assigned to a specific post, about 75 stocks per post. The stock's TICKER SYMBOL, the price of the last sale and whether it is above, or below, the previous sale are displayed on the exterior of the post where that stock is traded. The practice of dealing in active stocks at specific locations on the trading floor was first started around 1868. See POST 30

POST 30. A special POST located in the GARAGE annex of the New York Stock Exchange where 10-share unit stocks are traded, i.e., ten shares are an accepted unit of trading at POST 30, and no ODD-LOT DIFFERENTIAL is involved on purchases or sales.

PRECEDENCE OF ORDERS. The priority which one order to buy or sell securities has over another order. According to the Constitution and Rules of the New York Stock Exchange, where bids are made at the same price, the priority and precedence shall be determined as follows:

"Priority of first bid: a) When a bid is clearly established as the

first made at a particular price, the maker shall be entitled to priority and shall have precedence on the next sale at that price, up to the number of shares of stock or principal amount of bonds specified in the bid, irrespective of the number of shares of stock or principal amount of bonds specified in such bid.

"Precedence of bids equaling or exceeding amount offered: b) When no bid is entitled to priority under paragraph (a) hereof, (or when a bid entitled to, priority or precedence has been filled and a balance of the offer remains unfilled), all bids for a number of shares of stock or principal amount of bonds equaling or exceeding the number of shares of stock or principal amount of bonds in the offer or balance, shall be on a parity and entitled to precedence over bids for less than the number of shares of stock or principal amount of bonds in such offer or balance, subject to the condition that if it is possible to determine clearly the order of time in which the bids so entitled to precedence were made, such bids shall be filled in that order.

"Precedence of bids for amounts less than amount offered: c) When no bid is entitled to priority under paragraph (a) hereof (or when a bid entitled to priority or precedence has been filled and a balance of the offer remains unfilled) and no bid has been made for a number of shares of stock or principal amount of bonds equaling or exceeding the number of shares of stock or principal amount of bonds in the offer or balance, the bid for the largest number of shares of stock or the greatest principal amount of bonds shall have precedence, subject to the condition that if two or more such bids for the same number of shares of stock or principal amount of bonds have been made, and it is possible to determine clearly the order of time in which they were made, such bids shall be filled in that order.

"Simultaneous bids: d) When bids are made simultaneously, or when it is impossible to determine clearly the order of time in which they were made, all such bids shall be on a parity subject only to precedence based on the size of the bid under the provisions of paragraphs (b) and (c) hereof.

"Sale removes bids from floor: e) A sale shall remove all bids from the Floor except that if the number of shares of stock or principal amount of bonds offered exceeds the number of shares or principal amount specified in the bid having priority or precedence, a sale of the unfilled balance to other bidders shall be governed by the provisions of these Rules as though no sales had been made to the bidders having priority or precedence.

"Subsequent bids: f) After bids have been removed from the Floor under the provisions of paragraph (e) hereof, priority and precedence shall be determined, in accordance with these Rules, by subsequent bids.

"Bids on called securities: g) . . . the Exchange may, when all or any part of an issue of securities is called for redemption, require that all bids at the same price in the called securities shall be on a parity and that no bidder shall be entitled to more than the amount of his bid.

"Transfer of priority, parity and preference: h) A bid may be transferred from one member to another and as long as that bid is continued for the same account, it shall retain the same priority, parity and precedence it had at the time it was transferred.

"Offers: Where offers are at the same price the priority, parity and precedence shall be determined in the same manner as specified in the case of bids. An offer may be transferred from one member to another and, as long as that offer is continued for the same account, it shall retain the same priority, parity and precedence it had at the time it was transferred."

Concerning bids and offers made by Exchange members, the Constitution states: "a) No bid or offer made by a member or made on an order for stock originated by a member while on the Floor to establish or increase a position in such stock for an account in which such member has an interest shall be entitled to parity with a bid or offer made on an order originated off the Floor; b) No bid or offer made by a member or made on an order for stock originated by a member while on the Floor to establish or increase a position in such stock for an account in which such member has an interest shall be entitled to precedence based on size over a bid or offer made on an order originated off the Floor."

PREFERRED STOCK. A portion of the capital stock of a corporation which ranks after all bonds or other debt but has certain preferences over the common stock. Dividends may be CUMULATIVE or NON-CUMULATIVE; but they are usually at a fixed rate and are payable before distributions can be made on the common stock. There are about 400 preferred stocks LISTED on the New York Stock Exchange. See CUMULATIVE PREFERRED; FIRST PREFERRED; NON-CUMULATIVE PREFERRED; PARTICIPATING PREFERRED; PRIOR PREFERRED; SECOND PREFERRED.

PRELIMINARY PROSPECTUS. See RED HERRING.

PREMIUM. 1. The difference between the original offering price of a security and the price to which it may rise in the "after-offering" market.

2. The amount by which a security sells over its FACE (PAR VALUE). A $1,000 par value bond selling at 105 (worth $1,050) would be selling at a $5.00 or 5%, premium. The opposite of DISCOUNT. The premium is also that part of an investment paid at the time of purchase that will not be returned at maturity.

3. The amount charged sometimes for borrowing stock to make delivery on a SHORT SALE.

PREMIUM STOCK. A stock which lends at a *premium.* See PREMIUM—PART 3. Also, a superior stock; an established leader; one far above-average.

PREPAYMENT. Payment made before the date it is due.

PRE-TAX EARNINGS. Income which is subject to federal income taxes.

PRICE. The market value of anything being offered for sale. See ACTUAL PRICE; ASKED PRICE; BID PRICE; CLOSING PRICE; EXHAUST PRICE; FIRM PRICE; FIXED PRICE; FLASH PRICES; ISSUE PRICE; MARKET PRICE; NOMINAL PRICE; OFFERING PRICE; OPENING PRICE; QUOTED PRICE.

PRICE CHANGES. Fluctuating securities values caused by the personal judgment of thousands of people who, by their bids to buy and their offers to sell, indicate their opinion of a stock's worth. Changing business and economic trends, the need for money, or a desire to put money to work are among the factors influencing their decisions and actions.

PRICE-EARNINGS RATIO. A popular yardstick for evaluating market prices. If a company earns $10 a share for each share of its common stock OUTSTANDING and the prevailing price of the stock is 100, the price-earnings ratio is 10-to-1. In other words, it is said to be "selling at 10 times earnings." When stock prices are high, P-E ratios are also high. GROWTH STOCKS normally have higher ratios than conservative stocks because the market prices for such stocks are pushed up by eager buyers who prefer to purchase those stocks on the basis of future anticipated earnings, rather than on the basis of current earnings.

PRICE LIMIT. The stipulated price at which an order to buy or sell is entered on the trading floor of an Exchange. See LIMIT ORDER; MARKET ORDER.

PRICE RANGE. A combination of the highest price and the lowest price reached by a certain security, or the general market, during any specific day, week, month or year under discussion.

PRIMARY DISTRIBUTION. The first time the securities of a company are publicly offered for sale, either directly or through INVESTMENT BANKERS, in order to acquire new funds. Also called PRIMARY OFFERING. See SECONDARY DISTRIBUTION.

PRIMARY MARKET. A firm, trading market maintained in a security by a trader or his firm who perform the functions of SPECIALIST by standing ready to execute orders in that security.

PRIMARY MOVEMENT. One of the classifications of price movements developed by Charles H. Dow (founder of the *Wall Street Journal* and originator of the *Dow Theory*) which holds that in the long run prices are controlled by the intrinsic value of the security. The primary or basic movement is ultimately the controlling factor in investment and speculation. This movement tends to run for at least a year and usually much longer. See DOW THEORY; SECONDARY MOVEMENT; TERTIARY MOVEMENT.

PRIMARY OFFERING. Same as PRIMARY DISTRIBUTION.

PRIME INVESTMENT. A first class, gilt-edged, high grade investment; one considered so safe, conservative and sound, dividends or interest payments are unquestioned.

PRIME RATE. The minimum rate on bank loans set by commercial banks and granted only to top business borrowers. It is affected by overall business conditions, the availability of reserves, the general level of money rates, and it may vary geographically. Lending rates are also greatly influenced by the size of the loan: the largest loans naturally command the lowest rates.

PRINCIPAL. 1. The sum of money upon which interest is paid, such as funds that have been loaned, borrowed, or invested in a business.

2. The face amount, or PAR VALUE, of a bond or stock.
3. A person who employs a broker or other agent.

PRIOR PREFERRED STOCK. A class of stock which has preference as to dividends over other preferred issues or common stock of the same company.

PRIVATE FINANCING. The raising of capital through private placement or the sale of new securities to a limited number of "institutional" investors like insurance companies rather than with the public. See INSTITUTIONAL INVESTORS. Since no public offering is involved, the securities do not necessarily have to be registered with the SECURITIES AND EXCHANGE COMMISSION. Most public offerings of new securities must be cleared first by the Commission, under the Securities Act of 1933. See REGISTRATION OF SECURITIES. The institutional investor is thus able to acquire a large amount of a securities issue without much expense and difficulty and often at a higher yield than in the public market. The issuer benefits also, since the expenses involved are smaller than in a public offering, considerable time is saved, the corporation's credit status is enhanced, and it can time its financing program more accurately. The major buyers in private placements are life insurance companies.

PRIVATE WIRE. A wire connection leased to a broker for his exclusive use. See WIRE HOUSE. The New York Stock Exchange recently rescinded its ruling that a MEMBER FIRM needed to seek approval in order to establish a private wire service with a non-member firm.

PRIVILEGE. Another name for STOCK OPTION CONTRACT, such as a CALL or PUT, which permits one of the parties to exercise some right or privilege, during the time period stated by the contract. In any kind of privilege the purchaser is not liable for loss beyond the amount actually paid for the privilege. Dealings in options or privileges are conducted through PUT AND CALL BROKERS.

PROFESSIONAL. One who makes a regular business of buying and selling securities for his own account or for others in contrast to amateurs who trade occasionally, or frequently, but more as an avocation than as a business.

PROFIT AND LOSS STATEMENT. A detailed summary of the income and expenses of a business over a period of time (usually quarterly, semi-annually or annually) showing the net income or loss incurred. Also known as *Income Account* or *Income Statement.*

PROFIT TAKING. The conversion of PAPER PROFITS into cash —either by selling a LONG position or COVERING a SHORT position. Profit taking should occur, for example, after a stock has performed in accordance with prior expectations and has reached a level where it has lost most of its former investment or speculative appeal.

PRO FORMA. For form's sake. A specimen financial statement showing the effect that new financing, a merger, or other contemplated changes, will have on a corporation or corporations. It portrays something that does not exist but is expected to exist after contemplated or planned financial transactions have taken place. It is also called an *as if* or *giving effect* statement.

PROMOTER. A person who especially assists the formation of a company, industry or enterprise by securing the necessary capital from bankers or moneyed interests. He is a type of middleman between a company needing capital and those who can supply it.

In the words of the SECURITIES AND EXCHANGE COMMISSION, a promoter includes "(A) any person who, acting alone or in conjunction with one or more persons, directly or indirectly, takes the initiative in founding and organizing a business or enterprise of an issuer; (B) any person, who in connection with the founding or organizing of the business or enterprise of an issuer, directly receives in consideration of services or property, or both services and property, 10 percent or more of any class of securities of the issuer, or 10 percent or more of the proceeds from the sale of any class of securities. However, a person who receives such securities or proceeds either solely as underwriting commission or solely in consideration of property shall not be deemed a promoter within the meaning of this paragraph if such person does not otherwise take part in founding and organizing the enterprise."

PROPERTY DIVIDENDS. Dividends paid by one corporation in the form of securities of another corporation, which the former may have acquired by purchase or received from the sale of property.

PROSPECTUS. A selling circular containing the salient data set forth in the Registration Statement of an issue of securities being offered for public sale, which will enable investors to evaluate the securities and make informed and discriminatory decisions regarding them. The Registration Statement and Prospectus become public immediately upon filing with the SECURITIES AND EXCHANGE COMMISSION, but it is unlawful to sell the securities until the effective date. In general they both call for the disclosure of information such as: (1) a description of the registrant's property and business; (2) a description of the significant provisions of the security to be offered for sale and its relationship to the registrant's other capital securities; (3) information concerning the management of the registrant; (4) certified financial statements. Also known as RED HERRING. See REGISTRATION OF SECURITIES.

PROSPERITY. A phase of a normal BUSINESS CYCLE characterized by high wage and profit levels, full employment and the maximum use of available production facilities. The opposite of DEPRESSION.

PROTECTIVE STOCKS. Same as DEFENSIVE STOCKS.

PROVISION FOR CONTINGENCIES. See CONTINGENT FUND.

PROXY. A legal appointment in writing giving one person authority to vote for another and represent him at a shareholder's meeting.

In 1957, the New York Stock Exchange tightened its rules on the participation of members, allied members, member firms or corporations and their employees in "proxy fights." (A) Members taking part in proxy battles of unlisted companies must make the same disclosures as required by the SECURITIES AND EXCHANGE COMMISSION in the case of listed companies; (B) If the Exchange member participates with a non-member in an unlisted company proxy contest, the non-member must agree to supply the same information required of a member—otherwise the member cannot take part; (C) A SPECIALIST on the Exchange is barred from participating in a proxy contest involving a company in whose stock he specializes. Nor may a specialist, or any of his partners and employees, serve as a director of such company.

PUBLIC UTILITY. A provider of essential services to the consuming public, such as electric light and power, gas, water, transportation, and communications. Because these services are so important to the public, the prices charged and the activities themselves are supervised closely by regulatory bodies found in most states. Since public utilities require large capital investments in plant and equipment and are therefore suited to monopolistic organization, they are also regulated on a federal level by the SECURITIES AND EXCHANGE COMMISSION under legislation passed in 1935 concerning gas and utility holding companies (*Public Utility Holding Company Act*). Among the more significant abuses which Congress sought to eliminate through passage of this law were:

1. Inadequate disclosure to investors of the information necessary to appraise the financial position and earning power of the companies whose securities they purchase; 2. issuance of securities against fictitious and unsound values; 3. overloading of the operating companies with debt and fixed charges, thus tending to prevent voluntary rate reductions; 4. imposition of excessive charges upon operating companies for various services (management, construction work, and the purchase of supplies and equipment); 5. the control by holding companies of the accounting practices and rate, dividend and other policies of their operating subsidiaries, to complicate or obstruct State obligations; 6. the control of holding companies and subsidiaries through disproportionately small investment; and 7. the extension of holding company systems without

relation to economy of operations or to the integration and co-ordination of related properties.

Gas and power companies that are operating interstate are regulated by the Federal Power Commission, which also authorizes power projects on navigable waters of the U.S. Railroad, bus and trucking companies, and other common carriers are supervised by the Interstate Commerce Commission, and interstate telephone and telegraph companies by the Federal Communications Commission.

The earnings of utility companies are relatively stable; hence, their securities are generally considered suitable for portfolios stressing defensive qualities and moderate income with some growth potential. The first public utility traded on the New York Stock Exchange was New York Gas Light Corp. in 1827.

PULL. To lower the BID PRICE for a security or raise the OFFERING PRICE or cancel entirely.

PULL THE PLUG ON THE MARKET. To cancel or remove supporting bids which had previously been entered just below the market prices prevailing for certain leading issues.

PUP. A low-priced, inactive stock.

PURCHASE OUTRIGHT. To pay the full amount in cash for securities purchased.

PURCHASING POWER. The cash or credit available in a brokerage account which can be utilized for purchasing securities.

THOMAS, HAAB & BOTTS
Member Put and Call Brokers and Dealers Association, Inc.
PUT AND CALL OPTIONS
GUARANTEED BY MEMBERS N. Y. STOCK EXCHANGE
50 BROADWAY, N. Y. C. 4 BOWLING GREEN 9-8470-5

New York, N. Y.____________19____

For Value Received, the BEARER may DELIVER to the endorser ONE HUNDRED (100) shares of the____________

stock of the____________

at____________Dollars ($____________) per share

ANY TIME WITHIN____________days from date.

THIS STOCK OPTION CONTRACT MUST BE PRESENTED, AS SPECIFIED BELOW, TO THE ENDORSING FIRM BEFORE THE EXPIRATION OF THE EXACT TIME LIMIT. IT CANNOT BE EXERCISED BY TELEPHONE.

DURING THE LIFE OF THIS OPTION:

1. (a) — the contract price hereof shall be reduced by the value of any cash dividend on the day the stock goes ex-dividend; (b) — where the Option is entitled to rights and/or warrants the contract price shall be reduced by the value of same as fixed by the opening sale thereof on the day the stock sells ex-rights and/or warrants.

2. (a) — in the event of stock splits, reverse splits or other similar action by the above-mentioned corporation, this Option shall become an Option for the equivalent in new securities when duly listed for trading and the total contract price shall not be reduced; (b) — stock dividends or the equivalent due-bills shall be attached to the stock covered hereby, when and if this Option is exercised, and the total contract price shall not be reduced.

Upon presentation to the endorser of this Option attached to a comparison ticket in the manner and time specified, the endorser agrees to accept notice of the Bearer's exercise by stamping the comparison, and this acknowledgment shall constitute a contract and shall be controlling with respect to delivery of the stock and settlement in accordance with New York Stock Exchange usage.

EXPIRES____________19____
3:15 P. M.

PUT AND CALL BROKERS AND DEALERS ASSOCIATION
CORPORATE SEAL
SOLD BY MEMBER
1934
PUT & CALL
BROKERS & DEALERS
ASSOCIATION, INC.

The undersigned acts as intermediary only, without obligation other than to obtain a New York Stock Exchange firm as Endorser.

____

I No. 651

PUT OPTION

PUT. A STOCK OPTION CONTRACT which obligates the writer, or the seller, to accept delivery of 100 shares of a particular stock at a set price within a specified period of time. The opposite of CALL.

PUT AND CALL. A double OPTION such as a SPREAD or STRADDLE.

PUT AND CALL BROKER. One who deals in OPTIONS or PRIVILEGES. Put and Call brokers are not permitted on the New York Stock Exchange trading floor. See CALL; PUT; SPREAD; STRADDLE.

PUT OUT A LINE. To SELL SHORT a substantial amount of the stock of one or more companies and usually over a period of time in expectation of declining prices. The opposite of TAKE ON A LINE. See SHORT SALE.

PYRAMIDING. Purchasing additional securities or commodities by putting up unrealized PAPER PROFITS as additional MARGIN. A very common practice in commodities, but more difficult with stocks—even if the margin rate is 50%.

Q

Q. When printed on the TICKER TAPE preceding the symbol (abbreviation) for a stock, this letter denotes receivership or bankruptcy proceedings. See TICKER SYMBOLS.

QUALITY STOCK. A high grade stock of superior merit; a BLUE CHIP; representing the elite of American industry whose dividends and earning power are unquestioned.

QUARTER STOCKS. 1. Stocks with a PAR VALUE of $25 rather than $100.

2. Stocks on which the ODD-LOT DIFFERENTIAL is ¼ point or 25 cents a share; such as any 100 share-unit stock selling at 40 or above. See EIGHTH STOCKS.

QUEENS OF FINANCE. Nickname given to Tennessee Claflin and Victoria Woodhull, who opened the first all-female brokerage office at 44 Broad Street, New York, in 1870.

QUICK ASSETS. Cash or other liquid assets which are quickly convertible into cash, such as U.S. Government notes or obligations.

QUICK RATIO. The ratio of CURRENT or QUICK ASSETS to CURRENT LIABILITIES; obtained by dividing the assets by the liabilities. Useful for revealing the liquid resources of a company and helpful to banks in appraising a credit risk. For example: if current assets are sufficient to offset all the liabilities, the company's position would be considered extremely sound.

QUICK TURN. A speculative transaction involving a purchase and a sale completed in a relatively short time—usually in a matter of hours, or days.

QUOTATION. The same as BID AND ASKED; a statement of the highest price that anyone will pay for a security at a particular moment of time, and the lowest price at which anyone will sell it at the same time.

QUOTATION BOARD. An electrically operated blackboard, which usually covers an entire wall in the BOARD ROOM of a brokerage firm. All leading stocks and many others are represented. Each stock occupies a panel on the board, which bears its TICKER SYMBOL, price range for the year to date and sometimes the indicated rate of dividend payment. The opening, high, low and last sale prices of the stocks included are changed automatically as they occur.

QUOTED PRICE. The price made by the market in a particular stock, at which the last purchase and the last sale took place.

QUOTE WIRE. A direct wire from a brokerage firm to the Quotation Department of the New York Stock Exchange. A quotation may be obtained during regular business hours on any LISTED STOCK merely by dialing the number assigned to that stock. The Quotation Department is in continuous touch with special clerks stationed at all POSTS on the trading floor. A quote on U.S. Steel, for example, might be stated as "47 to 47¼." This means that 47 is the highest BID PRICE showing at that particular time and 47¼ is the LOWEST OFFERING price available at the same time. See QUOTATION. The Exchange currently has under consideration proposals to automate bid and asked quotations for all stocks directly from the trading floor, by voice announcement, in much the same way as the 300 most active stocks are now handled.

R

R. The TICKER abbreviation for United States Rubber Company.

RAID. A unified effort made by market BEARS to depress the price of a single stock, or the general market. Currently impossible because of the ONE-EIGHTH RULE restricting short selling and also outlawed as a form of manipulation. See SHORT SALE.

RAISING FUNDS. FINANCING. Acquiring money or credit from any of the following sources: surplus earnings of the corporation; the stockholders; the investing, or speculating public; creditors; customers; employees.

RALLY. A price recovery staged by an individual stock or the general market following a period of decline.

RATE. The ratio of interest earned to the principal during a period of time. It is generally expressed as a percentage and is one of the factors used in computing interest. See RATE OF INTEREST.

RATE OF INTEREST. The charge made by a borrower to a lender for use of the latter's money, expressed as a percentage upon the principal and usually in terms of one year's charges—unless otherwise stated. Thus, if the interest rate is five percent, $5.00 is paid for the annual use of $100.

RATIO. The relationship between one number to another, obtained by dividing the first by the second. The ratio will be described as a fraction, such as ⅓ or 1:3.

REACTION. A temporary reversal of an upward price trend, usually caused by the influence of some unfavorable news development upon a single stock or the general market.

READ THE TAPE. 1. To follow the price changes of various stocks as printed on the TICKER TAPE.

2. To judge and forecast the probable action of stocks over the near-term by studying volume and price changes as printed on the ticker tape.

REALIZE. To sell and accept profits in a stock which appears to have carried as high as can be reasonably expected. Conversely, those who are "short" (see SHORT SALE) may BUY IN or COVER to close out their contracts if they show a profit. "There was substantial *realizing* in the market today"; meaning a good deal of profit taking occurred. The term usually applies more to selling a LONG POSITION, than to "covering" a SHORT POSITION.

RECAPITALIZATION. A form of reorganization in which the OUTSTANDING capital stock may be replaced by a new issue in order to change the amount and priority of different stock issues and/or to reduce the amount, or change the character, of bonds outstanding. See REVERSE SPLIT.

RECEIVER. A representative appointed by the court to take charge and carry on a business that has become insolvent until it is reorganized or liquidated.

RECEIVERSHIP. 1. The state of being in a RECEIVER's hands. 2. The aggregate of duties, or the office held, by a receiver.

RECESSION. The downward phase of a normal BUSINESS CYCLE which follows prosperity and precedes a depression. It is the opposite of RECOVERY which follows a depression and precedes prosperity.

RECIPROCAL BUSINESS. An order to buy or sell securities given by one person to another in return for a more or less equivalent order, or business favor, previously granted.

RECOGNIZED QUOTATIONS. Statements which may be obtained during regular business hours over a direct wire to the quotation department of an organized stock exchange which give the highest prevailing BID PRICE and lowest OFFERING PRICE of stocks traded on that exchange.

RECORD DATE. The date on which a stockholder's name must appear on the books of a corporation; indicating that he is a stockholder and entitled to receive a dividend declared or to vote upon corporate matters. See Ex-dividend; Holder of record.

RECOVERY. 1. The upward phase of a normal Business cycle which follows a depression and precedes a return to prosperity. The opposite of Recession.

2. A rally in the market following a decline.

REDEEMABLE BOND. A bond which may be called or redeemed with prior notice to the holders thereof. Same as Callable bond.

REDEMPTIONS. Cash-ins made of Investment company shares.

REDEMPTION VALUE. The price at which a bond is redeemed; sometimes the same as Par value, especially with old bond issues. Also, the cash-in value of Investment company shares.

RED HERRING. An advance (preliminary) Prospectus which gives the details of an expected offering of corporate securities. Term derived from the fact that it carries in red ink a statement that the issue is in the process of being registered and cannot be sold until cleared by the Securities and exchange commission. See Registration of securities.

RED, IN THE. The opposite of In the black and meaning to show a loss.

REFINANCING. Employing funds received from the sale of a new issue of securities to retire an existing issue.

REFUNDING. Replacing an issue of securities about to fall due with a new issue.

REGIONAL EXCHANGE. An organized securities exchange located outside of New York City. Major ones are the Philadelphia-Baltimore-Washington Stock Exchange, the Midwest Stock Exchange, the Pacific Coast Exchange. Regional exchanges account for less than 10% of all stock trading. See DUAL LISTING.

REGISTERED BOND. A bond issued in the name of the owner in any multiple of $1,000. Interest thereon is paid by check in the same way that dividends are paid on stocks.

Unlike a COUPON BOND, which can be cashed by anyone who gets possession of it, a registered bond is transferable only when properly endorsed. Also, if a registered bond is redeemed, the owner receives a redemption notice in the mail; whereas a coupon bondholder must rely on newspapers, or other sources, for the calling of his bonds.

Most bonds are issued in coupon form, yet coupon bonds may become obsolete as registered bonds gain favor with cost and efficiency-minded bankers and financial men. For example, according to the U.S. Trust Co. of New York, which must set aside a mile and a half of shelf space to keep customers' bonds, some 300 million coupons are clipped every year in the U.S.—a chore that consumes 113,200 man-days and costs $1.8 million. In this connection, the first major corporate debt issue to be made in the form of registered bonds was a $75 million offering by Firestone Tire & Rubber in June, 1963.

REGISTERED REPRESENTATIVE. An employee of a MEMBER FIRM, who has passed certain tests and requirements of the

Stock Exchange and is thereby authorized to serve his own clients or those of his firm. Also known as *customer's man* or *customer's broker*. Every registered representative must sign a statement that he is familiar with the Constitution, rules, regulations and practices of the New York Stock Exchange, and agree to abide by them as they have been amended, or shall from time to time be amended.

One of the major objectives of the Constitution is that "every member, allied member, member firm and member corporation shall at all times adhere to the principles of good business practice in the conduct of his or its business affairs." In addition, no registered employee shall, directly, or indirectly, rebate to any person, firm or corporation, any part of the compensation he may receive as a registered employee . . . or receive a share in the profits of any customer's account, or share in any losses sustained . . . or guarantee the payment of the debit balance in a customer's account . . . or guarantee any customer against losses in his account. . . . Registered representatives are also required "to use due diligence to learn the essential facts relative to every customer, every order, every cash or margin account accepted or carried" . . . such as, for example, residence, occupation, citizenship, reference, and necessary legal documents. As of July 1, 1963, more than 32,000 registered representatives were employed by member firms.

REGISTRAR. A bank or trust company which is responsible for preventing the distribution of more shares of a corporation than have been authorized. No agency can act as TRANSFER AGENT and registrar for the same company simultaneously.

REGISTRATION OF SECURITIES. The preparation and filing with the SECURITIES AND EXCHANGE COMMISSION of a statement applying to securities being offered for public sale by an issuing company or any person in a control relationship to such company.

The objective of registration is the disclosure of facts upon which investors may appraise the merits of the securities. The securities may not be sold until the registration becomes effective—usually 30 days after the filing date (known as the *cooling off period*)—unless the facts justify an earlier date, or the SEC finds any defect in the Registration Statement.

Registration of securities does not insure investors against loss in their purchase, nor does the SEC have the power to disapprove securities for lack of merit—and it is unlawful to represent otherwise in the sale of securities. The only standard that must be met is an adequate and accurate disclosure of the material facts concerning the company and the securities it proposes to sell. The fairness of the terms of securities, the issuing company's prospects for successful operation, and other factors affecting the merits of securities have no bearing on the question of securities registration. See PROSPECTUS.

The first instance of *registering* securities took place in 1869, when the New York Stock Exchange ruled that the shares of active stocks be registered at some satisfactory agency so that the public would know how many shares were outstanding. This was to prevent companies from issuing stock secretly as an aid to manipulation.

REGULAR DIVIDEND. An established dividend rate fixed by a corporation upon its stock and usually paid quarterly or semi-annually.

REGULARITY OF DIVIDENDS. A fixed rate of dividend payments upon which stockholder confidence is based.

REGULAR WAY DELIVERY. Method whereby securities (other than government) sold on the New York Stock Exchange are delivered to the buying broker by the selling broker on the fourth full business day after the transaction takes place. With government bonds, regular way means next day delivery. See DATE OF TRADE; SETTLEMENT DATE.

REGULAR WAY SALE. Term designating a transaction that is not a SHORT SALE.

REGULATION T. Ruling of the Federal Reserve Board which governs the amount of credit that brokers and dealers may advance to their clients for purchasing securities on MARGIN.

REGULATION U. Ruling of the Federal Reserve Board which governs the amount of credit that banks may advance to their clients for purchasing securities. It is intended to prevent the "collateralizing" of securities for the purpose of evading MARGIN REQUIREMENTS. See COLLATERAL.

RELOADER. Slang expression for one who is adept at selling more stock to an individual who has already made a small commitment.

REORGANIZATION. The compulsory financial reconstruction of a company, such as that resulting from receivership and foreclosure. It usually involves installing new management, reducing fixed charges, scaling down upon capital structure and raising new funds—i.e., changing the company's entire previous form, identity and organization. See RECAPITALIZATION.

REPORT. 1. A verbal or written statement transmitted from the trading floor of an exchange concerning the execution of an order to buy or sell securities.

2. A statement made quarterly, semi-annually or annually by a corporation reviewing progress made since the last report and outlining prospects for the future. See ANNUAL REPORT; INTERIM REPORT.

REPORT TO STOCKHOLDERS. A statement made periodically by a corporation to its stockholders which generally includes a BALANCE SHEET and PROFIT AND LOSS STATEMENT, plus any other news or details about corporate affairs which might interest the stockholder.

REQUEST FOR A REPORT. Request made through the ORDER ROOM of a brokerage firm to the broker concerned on the trading floor, asking him to report back on the execution, or current status, of an order previously entered.

RESERVE BANK. See FEDERAL RESERVE BANK.

RESERVE CITY. Any of the twelve cities in which a FEDERAL RESERVE BANK is located.

RESERVES. Certain assets that are set aside periodically for a specific purpose, such as to meet or offset a loss inherent to the business, or one that is expected.

RESISTANCE LEVEL. TECHNICAL MARKET term meaning the price level showing on the chart of an individual stock or the general market, where selling pressure was previously encountered. The more times an advance falters or is turned back around this indicated area, the heavier the resistance becomes on the next attempt at penetration. Same as SUPPLY AREA and the opposite of SUPPORT LEVEL.

RETIREMENT. The redemption or repayment of an obligation on or before its maturity date.

RETURN. The amount of money received annually from an investment, usually expressed as a percentage. Same as YIELD.

REVENUE. Another term for income or cash receipts.

REVENUE BOND. A bond issued to provide immediate funds for current expenses, or to build or acquire facilities such as bridges, highways, and tunnels, until taxes can be collected. Use of these bonds has become widespread in the past several years. Both principal and interest are payable from receipts obtained from operation of the project they finance, rather than general tax monies. The classic example of revenue bonds is the issue secured by earnings of a water revenue system. Water, a necessity, is involved and if revenues are not sufficient, rates can be increased.

REVERSE SPLIT. A reduction in the number of OUTSTANDING shares of a corporation which increases the market price of the fewer remaining shares. A 1-for-3 reverse split, or *split down,* by a company with 3 million shares outstanding would leave 1 million shares outstanding. Splits are usually subject to the approval of stockholders and must be voted upon by directors of the company.

Reverse splits rarely take place unless the market price of the stock concerned is relatively low. See RECAPITALIZATION; STOCK SPLIT.

RIALTO. Term sometimes applied to stock exchanges and other busy centers.

RIGGING THE MARKET. A practice of artificially forcing security prices upward so that the public will be encouraged to buy. A form of manipulation currently prohibited.

RIGHTS. Privileges distributed in certificate form to the stockholders of a company, granting them the right to subscribe to additional shares at a specified price within a stated period of time. The purchase price fixed on the new shares is generally below the prevailing market price. A stockholder thus has two alternatives: (1) Sell the rights in the open market, provided they have a value. (Two firms specialize, or make markets, in rights on the trading floor of the New York Stock Exchange); (2) EXERCISE the rights and buy the new stock at the stipulated price.

If a man owns 100 shares of a stock selling at \$60, and company management gives him rights to buy one share of new stock at \$45 for every four shares he owns of the old stock, what are his rights worth? To figure this, take the \$45 subscription price available to him and subtract it from the market price of \$60, which leaves \$15. Then, because it takes four of the old shares, plus the purchase of one new share, to convert the rights (or five shares in all)—divide the \$15 difference by 5. This equals \$3.00 or the theoretical value of one right.

$$\text{Example: } \frac{\$60 \text{ (old stock) less } \$45 \text{ (new stock)}}{4 \text{ (rights required) plus } 1 \text{ (new share)}} = \frac{\$15}{5} = \$3.00$$

Rights are issued not only for stock but for DEBENTURES, especially convertibles. American Telephone & Telegraph is the largest rights issuer. The biggest rights year in recent history was 1957 when 199,711,000 rights worth $96 million changed hands on the Stock Exchange trading floor.

RIGHTS OFF. Without the RIGHTS.

RIGHTS OF STOCKHOLDERS. The privileges to which stockholders are entitled. Among them are included the right to receive notices of stockholder's meetings; to vote at such meetings or be represented by PROXY; share in all dividends declared and, also, to share proportionately in any assets remaining after creditors have been paid, should the corporation be dissolved.

RIGHTS ON. Term indicating that a stock is selling on a basis and at a price which includes the pro rata of additional stock being offered. The opposite of EX-RIGHTS or RIGHTS OFF. See RIGHTS.

RING. A combination of individuals working together (but each for his own account) which strives to raise or lower the price of a security by buying or selling it simultaneously. A ring is similar to a CLIQUE but differs from a POOL, which acts collectively under a pool manager for the united risk of its members. Such operations constitute manipulation and are banned by the SECURITIES AND EXCHANGE COMMISSION and the New York Stock Exchange.

RISK CAPITAL. Speculative funds employed in a venture which entails a sizable risk. It is also called VENTURE CAPITAL.

ROCK BOTTOM. Term suggesting that prices will fall no further.

ROLLING STOCK. Term referring to railroad cars and to wheeled or mobile equipment such as trucking fleets.

ROUND-LOT. The accepted unit of trading in a security, usually 100 shares, or a multiple thereof, or $1,000 PAR VALUE in the case of bonds. It has been estimated that about 70% of all orders executed on the New York Stock Exchange is in Round-Lots. Synonymous with BOARD LOT; EVEN LOT; FULL LOT and the opposite of ODD-LOT. See POST 30.

ROUND-LOT ORDER. An order to buy or sell a stock in an amount equal to 100 shares, or any multiple thereof, or $1,000 PAR VALUE in the case of bonds. See ODD-LOT; ROUND-LOT.

ROUND TRIP TRADE. A full transaction, consisting of a purchase followed by a sale of the same security, or vice versa. Also known as *Round Turn.*

RUMOR. Hearsay or unfounded gossip intended to cause a rise or fall in stock prices. The Stock Exchange Constitution forbids the spreading of rumors: "The circulation in any manner of rumors of a sensational character by a member, in any case where such action does not constitute fraud, or conduct inconsistent with just and equitable principles of trade, is an act detrimental to the interest and welfare of the Exchange. Members shall report to the Secretary of the Exchange any information which comes to their notice as to the circulation of rumors."

RUNNER. A messenger employed by a brokerage firm or a bank.

RUNNING A BOOK. One of the duties of a person who specializes in certain stocks on the trading floor of a stock exchange. See SPECIALIST; SPECIALIST'S BOOK.

RUNNING IN THE SHORTS. Buying various stocks in which there is known to be a large SHORT POSITION in order to advance the price so that those who are *short* will become anxious and BUY IN, or COVER, their short selling contracts and thereby spark a further advance in price. See SHORT SALE.

RUN OFF. The last sales, or final prices, as printed by the stock TICKER after the market is closed for the day. If volume is especially heavy near the close of a trading session, the ticker may be printing the run off for an hour or more after the last transaction actually took place on the trading floor.

RUN ON BANK. A situation associated with panic, whereby bank depositors become suddenly alarmed about the safety of their money and seek to withdraw it simultaneously.

S

S. The TICKER abbreviation for Sears, Roebuck & Company.

SADDLED. Term describing the position of one who finds himself holding an undesirable stock at a price higher than the prevailing market price. He is *saddled* with it.

SAFETY OF INCOME—PRINCIPAL. A quality associated usually with bonds and preferred stock, as opposed to common stock.

SAG. The tendency of prices to recede moderately.

SALT DOWN STOCK. To buy stocks and hold them, depositing the certificates in a strongbox for an extended period.

SATURATION POINT. A moment which coincides with the peak of a MARKET CYCLE, when the supply of stocks for sale begins to exceed the demand. See DISTRIBUTION; UNDIGESTED SECURITIES.

SAVINGS AND LOAN ASSOCIATION. A private savings institution which facilitates the purchase, construction and repair of homes for its members within a specified radius of the institution. *S&L's* are mutual associations and their depositors are shareholders—part owners. They are considered an excellent aid to periodic savings, and there are about 6,500 of them in the United States.

SAVINGS BANKS. Banks that pay interest on funds deposited. The funds, in turn, are invested by the bank—generally in mortgages, high grade bonds and such securities as are permitted by law. Many commercial banks also have savings departments, but the overall return on their investments is normally lower than savings banks because they must maintain a more liquid position. Savings banks are an attractive means of accumulating savings, and a depositor always has ready access to his funds. See SAVINGS AND LOAN ASSOCIATION.

SCALE ORDER. A mechanical formula plan for AVERAGING cost prices down or selling up. The method involves the purchase or sale of additional shares of the same stock at fixed intervals and to a prescribed point above or below the price of the initial commitment. Scaling differs from AVERAGING because it entails preconceived strategy, the use of standing orders. It is useful for accumulating stocks in a BULL MARKET; or distributing them or SELLING SHORT in a top heavy market. See BUY ON SCALE; SELL ON SCALE.

SCALPERS. In-and-out traders, whose operations are based on a relatively small margin of profit.

SCARLET WOMAN OF WALL STREET. Nickname for Erie-Lackawanna Railroad used during the Civil War era because the stock was manipulated up and down so many times by Daniel Drew—"Speculative Director" of the Company.

SCRIP CERTIFICATE. A certificate representing ownership of a fractional share of stock, which may be converted into a full share when presented in amounts equal to a full share.

SCRIP DIVIDEND. A dividend distributed in the form of a promise to pay some time in the future. It may or may not carry a definite maturity date and may be interest bearing or non-interest bearing.

SEASONAL INFLUENCES. The affect which seasonal weather changes sometimes have on sales and profits of certain industries: soft drink, oil, air conditioning, woolen goods and others.

SEASONED STOCKS. Market bellwethers. The securities of well established companies which represent the elite of American industry and whose dividends and earning power are unquestioned. See SECONDARY STOCKS.

SEAT. Membership on an exchange, which entitles the owner to buy and sell securities on that exchange. The majority of New York Stock Exchange members are partners in brokerage firms, but many individuals own *seats* for their own trading; as members they pay no commissions.

Seats on the New York Stock Exchange were first made salable on October 23, 1868. The highest price paid for a seat was $625,000 in February, 1929. The lowest price since 1900 was $17,000 in 1942. The number of seats is limited to the present

1,366. The only way to acquire one is through purchase from a member or his estate. A new member must prove his solvency and his intention of devoting full time to securities and convince the Committee on Admissions of his good character and knowledge of the business. Membership is limited to males over twenty-one; no woman has ever owned a seat on the New York Stock Exchange. See INITIATION FEE; MEMBERSHIP DUES.

Price Range of Seats Since 1953 and Some Earlier Years

Year	*High*	*Low*	*Year*	*High*	*Low*
1962	$210,000	$115,000	1947	$ 70,000	$ 50,000
1961	225,000	147,000	1942	30,000	17,000
1960	162,000	135,000	1937	134,000	61,000
1959	157,000	110,000	1932	185,000	68,000
1958	127,000	69,000	1929	625,000*	550,000
1957	89,000	65,000	1929	495,000**	350,000
1956	113,000	75,000	1922	100,000	86,000
1955	90,000	80,000	1917	77,000	45,000
1954	88,000	45,000	1911	73,000	65,000
1953	60,000	38,000	1905	85,000	72,000

*—Prior to February 18, 1929.

**—After February 18, 1929, and without "right" to one-quarter of a membership. See SEAT DIVIDEND.

SEAT DIVIDEND. The 25% in the form of RIGHTS, which New York Stock Exchange members voted on the 1,100 memberships (SEATS) existing on February 18, 1929. The rights created 275 new memberships, bringing the total to 1,375—of which nine were retired by the Exchange in 1953, reducing the number to the present 1,366.

SECONDARY DISTRIBUTION. An OFF-THE-BOARD offering of a large block of securities from which the issuing company receives none of the proceeds. The distribution requires methods similar to those used when a new issue is sold publicly for the first time. The owner of the securities agrees to a net price per share, let us say $51.20, which is slightly below the 52¾ closing price on the day the distribution takes place. The brokers handling the distribution (selling group) offer the stock to the public at a net price reflecting the prevailing market level. In other words, the buyer pays 52¾ net, no commission. The cost to the seller is $1.55 per share. The number of *secondaries* tends to decline when stock prices are declining and, conversely, to rise along with advancing stock prices. One of the largest such offerings on record was the more than $650 million of Ford Motor stock sold by the Ford Foundation in 1956. See EXCHANGE DISTRIBUTION; PRIMARY DISTRIBUTION; SPECIAL OFFERING.

SECONDARY MOVEMENT. One of the classifications of price movements developed by Charles H. Dow (founder of the *Wall Street Journal* and originator of the DOW THEORY). It is represented by sharp rallies in a BEAR MARKET and sharp reactions in a primary BULL MARKET. Dow considered it a bull period as long as the highs attained in the secondary movements exceeded the preceding high points, and a bear period when the low points reached on a subsequent reaction were lower than the previous low points. See DOW THEORY; PRIMARY MOVEMENT; TERTIARY MOVEMENT.

SECONDARY STOCKS. The securities of young and growing corporations that have not quite yet demonstrated their ability to withstand competition under certain conditions with the same finesse as older and more established corporations. Sometimes called "pale blue chips." See SEASONED STOCKS.

SECOND PREFERRED STOCK. One of a series of preferred stock issues which ranks behind FIRST PREFERRED STOCK but ahead of any third preferred issue or common stock in dividends or assets.

SECURED BOND. A bond secured by a pledge of assets (plant or equipment), the title to which would be transferred to bondholders in the event of foreclosure.

SECURITIES. Common stock, preferred stock or bonds which are negotiable and have been issued by a corporation as evidence of corporate ownership. See ACTIVE SECURITIES; ASSENTED STOCKS (BONDS); CALLABLE; CORPORATION SECURITIES; DIGESTED SECURITIES; GILT-EDGED, JUNIOR SECURITIES; LEGAL SECURITIES; LISTED SECURITIES; MARGINED SECURITIES; MARKETABLE SECURITIES; NEGOTIABLE SECURITIES; NON-CALLABLE SECURITIES; OBSOLETE SECURITIES; OUTSIDE SECURITIES; OUTSTANDING SECURITIES; SEASONED STOCKS; SECONDARY STOCKS; SENIOR SECURITIES; SHORT-TERM NOTES; STAMPED SECURITY; UNDIGESTED SECURITIES; UNLISTED SECURITIES.

SECURITIES ACTS. Federal laws enforced by the SECURITIES AND EXCHANGE COMMISSION to protect investors; they include the *Investment Advisers Act, Investment Company Act, Securities Act of 1933, Securities Exchange Act of 1934, Trust Indenture Act,* and *Public Utility Holding Company Act.*

SECURITIES AND EXCHANGE COMMISSION. An organization created by an act of Congress, entitled the *Securities Exchange Act of 1934*. The SEC is an independent, bipartisan, quasi-judicial agency of the United States Government.

The laws administered by the Commission relate in general to the field of securities and finance and seek to provide protection for investors and the public in their securities transactions. They include the acts listed under SECURITIES ACTS. The Commission also serves as adviser to federal courts in corporate reorganization proceedings under Chapter X of the *National Bankruptcy Act.*

Organized July 2, 1934, the Commission is composed of five members, not more than three of whom may be members of the same political party. They are appointed by the President with the advice and consent of the Senate, for five-year terms. The terms are staggered so that one expires on June 5 of each year. The chairman is designated by the President.

The Commission's staff is composed of lawyers, accountants, engineers, security analysts and examiners, together with administrative and clerical employees. The staff is divided into Divisions and Offices (including nine Regional Offices), each under charge of officials appointed by the Commission.

The Commission reports annually to Congress. These reports contain a detailed analysis of the Commission's administration of the several laws.

SECURITY PRICE LEVEL. The price level prevailing for a certain security, a group of securities, or the general stock market at a particular time.

SELECTIVITY. The discriminating attitude of speculators and investors, which underlies frequent changes in stock market fashions. In a *selective market,* investors and speculators are more discriminate and cautious in their buying habits; whereas in a broad and aggressive BULL MARKET, they sometimes tend to buy almost anything.

SELL (OR BUY) AT THE CLOSE. An order to be executed at the best price obtainable at the close of the market on the day the order is entered.

SELL (OR BUY) AT THE OPENING. An order to be executed at the best price obtainable immediately after the Stock Exchange opens for business at 10:00 A.M.

SELLER'S (OR BUYER'S) OPTION. 1. A choice or privilege which gives the buyer the right to demand delivery of a specific number of shares of stock at a stated price, or the seller the right to deliver them at any time within the limit fixed. See CALL; PUT; STRADDLE.

2. A privilege which gives the seller of commodities the right to choose the quality and the time and place of delivery of the commodity named in the contract.

SELLERS 30. A contract calling upon the seller to deliver a security which has been sold within thirty days from the date of sale. See SELLER'S OPTION.

SELLING AGAINST THE BOX. SELLING SHORT against the known ownership of covering shares, in order to provide insurance against large price fluctuations. The practice involves "selling short" (see SHORT SALE) an amount of stock which is no more than the amount actually owned (held LONG in a safe deposit box). Profits made through a rise in price of the stock held long are automatically cancelled because an offsetting number of shares of the same stock have also been sold short, and the same principle applies in a declining market. Moreover, dividends are nullified since payments on the owned stock revert to the lender of the stock borrowed to make the short sale.

Selling against the box is primarily to protect PAPER PROFITS and to postpone the payment of capital gains taxes from one year to another. Whereas such sales could formerly be used against short-term profits for tax purposes, recent legislation has blocked this loophole.

SELLING GROUP. A combination of securities dealers, which operates under the leadership of the SYNDICATE department of an UNDERWRITING firm to participate in the public sale of an issue of securities. See UNDERWRITER.

SELLING OFF. Declining prices. Term may refer to the general market, a group of stocks, or an individual issue. When more shares are offered for sale than there are orders to buy them, prices will decline, and the market is said to be *selling off*.

SELL ON SCALE. A mechanical formula used for AVERAGING sales up in a market which seems too high. An order to sell 1,000 shares on a ¼ point scale up from 47, would involve ten separate sell orders of 100 shares each beginning with 47 and continuing to 49¼. Precedent shows that most stocks and the MARKET AVERAGES will retrace about half the distance between their high-low points and vice-versa; but ultimate success with scale orders leans on the assumption that operators know the approximate values of stocks in which they intend to deal. The fractions or points between sales and the limit to which further offerings should continue are problems for individual decision. The same principle applies to BUY ON SCALE. See SCALE ORDER.

SELL ON THE BID. See ON BID, OR OFFER.

SELL OUT. The sale of enough securities held LONG in an account to satisfy the demands of a MARGIN CALL, or if the owner is unable to pay for securities he has bought. Also, the disposal through sale of all securities held in an individual account.

SELL OUT NOTICE. An urgent notice sent sometimes by a brokerage firm to a client. It represents a final warning that, unless the client deposits enough cash or securities immediately to pay for a previous purchase or maintain adequate MARGIN in the account, the brokerage firm will be obliged to sell enough of his securities to meet the minimum MARGIN REQUIREMENTS.

SELL SHORT. The act of selling that which is not actually in the seller's possession at the time of sale, but which he expects to obtain later. See SHORT SALE.

SENIOR SECURITIES. Bonds and preferred stock which receive prior consideration over the common stock when a corporation fails or is being dissolved.

SENSITIVE MARKET. A market where prices respond quickly and sharply to alternating favorable and unfavorable developments.

SERIAL BONDS. Bonds having the same date of issuance but different maturity dates extending over a series of years, so that the entire debt is not payable at once. A $10 million issue may be redeemable at $1 million annually until the whole issue has been redeemed in ten years.

SESSION. A period of trading activity which coincides with the hours of business on a stock exchange. "The market was strong today in a four million share *session.*"

SETTLEMENT. 1. An arrangement between brokerage houses for the payment or receipt of cash, or securities. It represents the final consummation of a securities transaction and is handled through the STOCK CLEARING CORPORATION.

2. An adjustment made between a client and his broker whereby the former pays the debit balance in his account to the broker or the latter pays the credit balance to his client.

SETTLEMENT DATE. The date on which the final consummation of a securities transaction takes place and payment is made, usually four full business days following the DATE OF TRADE.

SHADE. A small concession; a marking down of prices.

SHAKE OUT. A sudden flurry of selling often accompanied by a LATE TAPE.

SHARE. 1. One of the equal parts into which the capital stock of a corporation is divided. It represents the owner's proportion of interest in the company and is issued to him in the form of a stock certificate. The world's first shares were issued by the Dutch East India Co., a corporation formed in 1602 with a fleet of 64 merchant ships. In order to raise funds to buy ships, docks and warehouses, the company was granted a charter of incorporation (the first limited liability company) that issued registered stock called "actien."

2. In England and Canada, share is generally considered synonymous with the American stock, and the term "stock" denotes Government bonds.

SHARE TURNOVER. Same as VOLUME.

SHIN PLASTERS. Nickname for *fractional currency* issued during the Civil War.

SHOESTRING TRADING. Operating on thin, or barely sufficient, MARGIN. The stock market equivalent of "skating on thin ice."

SHORT ACCOUNT. 1. The total of securities which have been sold short in anticipation of declining prices. See SHORT SALE.

2. An account maintained with a broker to accommodate all transactions made on the SHORT SIDE of the market.

SHORT COVERING. Closing out a "short selling" contract by buying back, or "covering," the same number of shares that was previously sold short. See SHORT SALE.

SHORT INTEREST. The total number of shares which have been "sold short" in anticipation of declining prices and which comprise the SHORT ACCOUNT (1), as of a specific moment of time. Short interest figures have little significance for average investors. Traders, however, are often concerned with the extent of the short interest in a particular stock, or the general market; for, a large short interest would indicate a temporarily oversold condition and might spark a sharp run-up in the price of the stock. Short interest figures have been compiled by the New York Stock Exchange since May 25, 1931. See SHORT SALE.

SHORT LINE. The number of shares "sold short" in an account. The act of selling securities short is sometimes called "putting out a line." See SHORT SALE.

SHORT OF THE MARKET. To maintain a SHORT POSITION in securities in anticipation of lower prices. See SHORT SALE.

SHORT POSITION. The prevailing market position of one who is a BEAR. See SHORT SALE.

SHORT SALE. Any transaction which creates a debt in terms of promised goods: a farmer's contract to deliver unharvested produce, a magazine subscription, or an agreement for future delivery of a new automobile. As applied to securities, the method involves (A) selling something not actually in the seller's possession at the time of sale; (B) borrowing the same number of shares involved to make delivery to the purchaser, in the hope of buying back the stock later for return to the lender at a lower price. The difference between the higher selling price and the lower buying-in, or covering price would represent the short seller's profit in the transaction. However, if the stock that is sold short rises rather than declines, the seller stands to take a loss.

Covering (see SHORT COVERING) purchases are made in exactly the same way as other purchases in the market. Also, the seller may remain short indefinitely, so long as it is possible to borrow stock and the contract's requirements are fulfilled. No interest is charged on a short position. However, it should be pointed out that (A) a premium may be necessary for borrowing the stock; (B) the short seller is liable for any dividends paid during the life of his contract; and (C) if the capitalization (number of shares outstanding) is small, or the stock is closely held, the broker may have difficulty acquiring the amount of stock needed to make delivery. For income tax purposes, the Revenue Code states that a short sale is completed on the date the shares are delivered to close the short sale.

The method of executing a short sale (see ONE-EIGHTH RULE) and the brokerage mechanics involved are always generally identical yet the reasons motivating an original selling order may differ widely. Many transactions constitute a private venture and involve no regular species of securities business. Short sellers of this type are usually broker-members of the Stock Exchange or customers dealing through MEMBER FIRMS, who sell short for a "quick turn" over a period of hours or days, or as a longer term speculation.

Other types of speculative short sales are made rapidly and often (but for relatively small profit) by so-called professionals during the course of their daily business. Considered as contributing to a more orderly and liquid market, they include short sales made by (A) the SPECIALIST who, in his dual capacity of broker and dealer, must maintain a firm and continuous market in one or a limited number of securities; and (B) the in-and-out FLOOR TRADER whose rapid and frequent dealings on the long, or the short side of the market, make for closer, more stable prices.

However, it should be emphasized that not all short selling is speculative. Some short sales represent insurance against large price fluctuations. Others may constitute a temporary condition for facilitating the regular flow of securities owned by the seller and are essentially technical in character. In this connection, the following species of short sale should be distinguished from the more speculative types.

Selling "when issued" stock: Sometimes, when old securities are made exchangeable for new—as the result of a stock split, a stock dividend, or a corporate merger—the new certificates are not immediately available in deliverable form. Without recourse to the short sale, the investor might not be able to liquidate quickly the *when issued* certificates to which he is entitled but has not yet obtained. Although the sale of *when issued* stock is not a short sale in the strictest sense (because it does not require borrowing stock for delivery), it nevertheless involves the sale of property which is not yet actually in the seller's possession and is therefore termed a short sale.

Selling Stock Obtained through "Rights": To protect against the possibility of lower prices (before the new stock made available by "exercising rights" is obtained), individuals sometimes sell short in advance the new stock to which they are entitled. Having sold this stock and borrowed the same amount temporarily for delivery, the seller finally closes the contract by returning to the lender the new stock, when he eventually obtains it from the issuing company.

The above examples differ from other general types of short selling in that no necessity of repurchasing the securities sold short is involved.

Selling Short for "Hedging" Purposes: Used primarily as insurance against large price fluctuations is the short sale for *hedging* purposes, sometimes known as SELLING AGAINST THE BOX. This entails selling short an amount of stock which is no more than the amount actually owned. Because a long and a short position in the same number of shares of the same stock is maintained simultaneously, profits are fictitious. Any profit gained through price appreciation of the securities owned is cancelled automatically by a corresponding loss shown for the same securities which have been sold short, or vice versa. Moreover, dividends have been nullified since payments on the owned stock revert to the lender of the borrowed stock.

Before the early 1930's, when there were no curbs on short selling and the CAPITALIZATION of leading share issues was relatively small, a group of determined BEARS could easily "hammer the market" (drive it lower) by the sheer weight of their persistent selling directed against certain key stocks. But this practice known as "bear raiding" is strictly outlawed today, and the short sale as a bludgeon in the hands of the speculator is entirely a reminiscence. Manipulation in any form is forbidden; in fact, regulations such as the "1/8 Rule" make it impossible with short selling.

Secrecy, the gambler's former ace-in-the-hole, has been trumped by a decree that original selling orders be marked "Long" or "Short," and by regular monthly publication of the outstanding number of shares sold short during the previous four-week period. Higher commission rates, the capital gains tax and tighter margin and loan requirements have further restricted profits for stock market bulls and bears alike. (Excerpted from an article by Peter Wyckoff in *The Analyst's Journal*—May, 1959.)

SHORT SELLER. A stock market pessimist, one who is BEARISH on the trend of securities prices and substantiates his opinion by *selling short*. See SHORT SALE.

SHORT SELLING. The act of *selling short*. See SHORT SALE.

SHORT SIDE. The side of the market favored by pessimists (BEARS) who have backed up their opinion by *selling short*. The opposite of LONG SIDE. See SHORT SALE.

SHORT STOCK. Stock which has been *sold short* and not yet COVERED. See SHORT SALE.

SHORT-TERM. 1. From a tax standpoint, any security held for a period of less than six months and one day is a short-term holding. According to the New York Stock Exchange's periodic *Public Transaction Studies,* about 40% of stock purchases by the general public are closed out within six months.

2. In the parlance of traders in stocks, short-term is one day to approximately two months; intermediate-term means two to six months; LONG-TERM means six months or more.

SHORT-TERM NOTES. Obligations which run from one month to a year.

SICK MARKET. A wobbly tremulous market—one that appears *ill;* generally the effects of previous over-speculation which caused prices to fall sharply. At such a time, with uncertainty and discouragement prevailing, traders in stocks will search anxiously for some news or development that would justify taking a new position in the market.

SIGNATURE GUARANTEED. A practice whereby a brokerage firm or a bank guarantees the signature of the registered owner of a security so that it will represent a GOOD DELIVERY or transfer.

SILENT PARTNER. A person who supplies capital but is not openly declared to be a partner in a business enterprise. Although not active in managing the business, he nevertheless is equally responsible for any debts incurred by the PARTNERSHIP. See ACTIVE PARTNER; GENERAL PARTNER; LIMITED PARTNERSHIP; SPECIAL PARTNER.

SIMPLE INTEREST. Interest computed on the original principal. For example. "A" loans "B" $1,000 for six months at 5%, the *simple* interest amounting to $25. If at the end of that time the interest is not paid, "A" cannot collect additional interest on the $25 for such time thereafter as "B" fails to make the payment. Compound interest, however, would permit the charging of interest on the $25; that is, interest upon interest. See COMPOUND INTEREST; EXACT INTEREST; ORDINARY INTEREST.

SINGLE OPTION. A PUT or CALL as distinguished from a SPREAD or STRADDLE. See OPTION.

SINKING FUND. A fund set aside in the form of cash or securities to retire all or part of a debt (such as bonds or preferred stock) or to replace depreciable assets. Sinking funds are necessary to protect the investor and corporations floating bonds in EXTRACTIVE industries (coal, oil, mining, and lumber). These industries usually make liberal sinking fund provisions in order to retire the entire issue at maturity. The sinking fund makes it certain that as the company's oil or other resource is diminished, its bonded debt will be proportionately decreased.

SIZE OF THE MARKET. The total number of ROUND-LOTS bid for at the highest price showing on the SPECIALIST'S BOOK and the total number being offered for sale simultaneously at the lowest price quoted, as of a given moment of time. Thus, the *size* might be reported back from the trading floor as "5 and 3"; meaning five hundred shares showing at the highest bid price, versus three hundred shares at the lowest offering price.

SKYROCKETING. A precipitous rise in price within a short period of time.

SLAUGHTER. To sell securities indiscriminately at unnecessarily low levels.

SLEEPER. A stock whose price performance in the market has been relatively quiescent but which is, nevertheless, considered attractive for strong potential gains.

SLID OFF. Dropped in price.

SLIPPING. A slight easing of the price. "The market is *slipping*" means it is selling lower.

SLUGGISH. Term referring to a dull, inactive market where the volume of transactions is relatively low. Fewer stocks are traded and prices have difficulty making much progress in either direction.

SLUMP. A sudden drop in security prices or a decline in business activity for a particular industry, or for business in general. It is not as violent as a SMASH and is shorter in duration.

SMALL BUSINESS INVESTMENT COMPANY (SBIC). A form of company, authorized by Congress in 1958, which is licensed and regulated by the Small Business Administration and designed to provide capital to small businesses.

SBIC's may make long-term loans or buy convertible debentures, or stock in small enterprises whose assets do not exceed $5 million, whose NET WORTH does not exceed $2½ million and whose average net income after taxes was less than $250,000 for the two previous years. See CONVERTIBLE BOND; DEBENTURE.

Investors in SBIC's must put up at least $150,000 of their own capital. The SBA lends them an equal amount, up to $400,000 at 5% annual interest. This total (at least $300,000) is the SBIC's initial capital. It can then borrow up to four times this amount, either from the SBA or from banks, to relend to small firms. To encourage private investment in SBIC's, Congress gave them a unique tax advantage: losses on investments in SBIC's are deductible from a taxpayer's ordinary income. Most capital losses cannot be deducted but may be used only to offset capital gains taxes.

Only 49 of the 664 SBIC's operating across the country are publicly owned. Most are called "minimum capital" SBIC's, with only \$300,000 in capital. Eighty-two are wholly or partly owned by commercial banks. The 49 publicly held SBIC's, however, dominate the field. Their total capital of \$301 million is more than half of the \$575 million capital of all SBIC's.

SMASH. A severe decline in the stock market, bordering on panic.

SNOWBALLING. The sequence of transactions which occurs when STOP ORDERS are successively "touched off" and become MARKET ORDERS, during either an advance or decline. For example: the SPECIALIST'S BOOK has orders to sell 1,000 shares at 65 Stop; 500 at 64¾ Stop; 1,200 at 64½ Stop; 300 at 64¼ Stop. When a transaction takes place at 65, the order to sell 1,000 shares Stop at that price automatically becomes a market order.

Bids at 64¾ are then made and the Specialist sells the stock to buyers at that price. But this transaction touches off the next Stop to sell 500 shares at 64¾, etc. In other words, each sale at declining prices has the effect of changing additional Stop Orders into Market Orders. Aware of the possibility that Stop Orders might influence unusually sharp trading swings in either direction, the Floor Governors of the Exchange have the authority to suspend Stop Orders in individual securities whenever they consider such action to be warranted.

SOFT. The tendency of a stock or the general market to seek lower price levels.

SOFT MONEY. 1. Paper bills or notes as distinguished from coins.

2. The money of any nation which fluctuates over an unusually wide range of value in domestic and foreign exchange. If the credit

of the issuing government is good, its money is referred to as strong; if it is poor, its money is said to be weak or soft.

SOFT SPOT. A sudden decline by specific stocks or by a group of stocks, despite firmness, or even strength, in the general market.

SOLD OUT MARKET. A market which appears to be thoroughly liquidated and due to recover, after being subjected to steady and aggressive selling pressure. It is characterized by gradual relief from offerings of stocks for sale.

SOLVENT. A condition existing when corporate assets exceed liabilities, and resources are available to pay all debts as they become due.

SPECIAL BID. A method sometimes used by INSTITUTIONAL INVESTORS for acquiring a large block of stock. The bid is entered on the floor of the Exchange at a given price which must be equal to or above the last transaction, or the current quotation, whichever is higher. The buyer pays a special commission and the seller pays none. The order may be filled during trading hours by MEMBER FIRMS selling stock for their clients to the buyer's broker. See EXCHANGE ACQUISITION.

SPECIAL DIVIDEND. A dividend in cash or stock declared in addition to the regular payment. Virtually the same as EXTRA DIVIDEND.

SPECIALIST. A broker-dealer member of the Stock Exchange who is charged with executing orders entrusted to him by other brokers and with maintaining fair and orderly markets in the stocks he services. Another of his key functions is helping to execute large orders by (A) accepting or providing all or part of the stock for his own account at a price coinciding as closely as possible with the previous market price; (B) locating buyers and sellers for the stock; (C) helping to handle the order on an agency basis for a reasonable time; (D) buying or selling stock for his own account with the approval of the Exchange, in order to fill a large bid or offer outside the regular auction market. See SPECIALIST BLOCK PURCHASE; SPECIALIST BLOCK SALE.

The first specialist was a broker with a broken leg, who did such a huge business dealing in one stock (Western Union) from a designated spot on the trading floor in 1879, that other brokers began also to specialize in individual issues. There are 350 specialists on the New York Stock Exchange today.

SPECIALIST BLOCK PURCHASE. An OFF-THE-BOARD purchase made by a SPECIALIST for his own account. This may take place only when the sale of a large block of stock cannot be made at a reasonable price on the Exchange itself, and if such purchase will assist the specialist in performing his normal duties.

SPECIALIST BLOCK SALE. The sale of a block of stock made outside the exchange, and at a price higher than that prevailing there, for the SPECIALIST's account.

SPECIALIST'S BOOK. A book composed of orders to buy and sell "away from the market." Each stock has a separate book, and there will be as many books in a stock as there are SPECIALISTS in it. The orders are entrusted to the specialist by other brokers who are unable to execute them, because they are limited to a price other than the one prevailing in the market at the time they were entered.

SPECIAL LOAN. A loan involving unusual collateral, such as OVER-THE-COUNTER securities. Loans of this nature generally command a higher rate of interest.

SPECIAL OFFERING. A method of selling a large block of stock which could not otherwise be sold within a reasonable time or without unduly affecting the market price. Special offerings must be approved by the Stock Exchange and must meet with certain rules; such as number of shares involved, total market value, price range, volume of shares traded in the past, and general interest in the stock. If approved by the Exchange, a notice of the offering, stating the commission involved and the gross price, will be printed on the TICKER TAPE. Brokers handling the order receive a special commission, which usually is higher than the commission ordinarily paid. Should the offering be OVERSUBSCRIBED, allotments will be made according to the size of each bid and the size of the block being offered. See EXCHANGE DISTRIBUTION; SECONDARY DISTRIBUTION.

SPECIAL PARTNER. A partner of a brokerage firm whose liability is limited to the amount of his interest in the firm and who is not active in its management. See ACTIVE PARTNER; GENERAL PARTNER; LIMITED PARTNERSHIP; SILENT PARTNER.

SPECIAL SITUATIONS. Securities whose attractiveness depends upon certain features that imply large capital gains, regardless of the general market's action. They should meet four requirements: (1) reflect a specific corporate development; (2) sell at a discount from inherent values; (3) have a readily definable profit potential; (4) be priced at a minimum risk level. According to "How to Profit from Special Situations," by Maurece Schiller (Published by American Research Council, Larchmont, N.Y.) there are ten basic types:

(A) Reorganizations.
(B) Liquidations.
(C) Mergers.
(D) Court orders.
(E) Spin-off of assets.
(F) Government regulations.
(G) Undervalued assets.
(H) Hidden earnings.
(I) Acquisitions.
(J) Management policies.

SPECIALTY STOCK. A stock belonging to no particular industry group which attracts attention by advancing independently of the general market.

SPECIE. Metallic money as opposed to paper currency, checks, and notes. Same as HARD MONEY.

SPECULATE. To invest enthusiastically; to buy, or sell, securities with the intention of making a profit over a relatively short period of time and with little regard for growth possibilities or income producing capacity of the stock concerned. Term is used in contradistinction to GAMBLING; INVESTMENT.

SPECULATION. A calculated risk taken to gain a quick profit; an operation where intelligent foresight is employed for the purpose of deriving a profit from price changes. The greatest losses in the stock market are caused by: ignorance, over-trading, dreams, deceptive appearances, speculation in CATS AND DOGS, misleading opinions, and mechanical speculation. See GAMBLING; INVESTMENT.

SPECULATOR. A person who is willing to risk loss of principal in the hope of acquiring large capital gains. There are four general classes of speculators: FLOOR TRADERS, professional operators (THEY) and others in close touch with the market, persons who deal in SPECIAL SITUATIONS on the basis of inside knowledge, and the public. See GAMBLING; INVESTOR.

SPILLING STOCK. Term meaning to throw stocks on the market for sale; such as when they are disposed of from necessity, i.e., *spilled.*

SPIN OFF. The splitting of a corporation by distributing or apportioning all or part of its assets to another company in exchange for the latter's capital stock, and the immediate distribution of such stock pro rata as a dividend to stockholders of the former company.

SPLIT CLOSE. 1. Term referring to price discrepancies, the range of trading in prices of commodities, at the close of any market session.

2. A variance existing between the closing average price of any one of the three major market indices (Industrials, Rails, and Utilities). A higher closing price for the Industrial and Utility averages, but a lower closing price for the Rail average would indicate a *split close.*

SPLIT COMMISSION. A commission which a broker has divided with his customer or with someone else who procures business for him. Splitting commissions is strictly prohibited under New York Stock Exchange regulations: a REGISTERED REPRESENTATIVE may lose his license for life. However, this should not be confused with the situation in which a member or member organization of the Stock Exchange executes a buy or sell order and "gives-up" another member or member organization. See GIVE-UP ORDER.

SPLIT DOWN. See REVERSE SPLIT.

SPLIT ORDER. An order to buy or sell securities which is split in two or more parts and executed separately at different times.

SPLIT QUOTATION. Dividing a stock's smallest regular fractional quotation in half. Thus 1/8 becomes 1/16, and a stock may be quoted: "3/8 bid, offered at 7/16."

SPLIT STOCK. The new OUTSTANDING shares of a corporation created by a STOCK SPLIT.

SPONSORSHIP. The interest known to stand behind a particular issue of securities, such as that provided naturally by the original UNDERWRITER of the issue.

SPOT. Term used in the commodity markets and meaning immediate delivery for cash, as distinguished from future delivery. See FUTURES.

SPOT NEWS. Sudden news or a development which influences market prices momentarily.

SPREAD. 1. The difference between the BID PRICE and the ASKED (OFFERING) price. When a stock is quoted "50 bid, offered at 52," a two point spread is said to exist.

2. The difference between the price of the same security or commodity in one market and the price in another market.

3. A double STOCK OPTION CONTRACT, consisting of a separate PUT and a separate CALL, whereby the owner has the privilege of "putting" at one price and "calling" at another, the stock named by the contract within a specified period of time. The purchaser of a spread is actually "playing two ends against the middle."

4. A commodity market term, meaning to be *Long* of one contract and *Short* of another contract of the same commodity simultaneously, but in different months. For example, a spread would exist if a long position in July wheat and a short position in December wheat were maintained at the same time. See SHORT SALE.

SPREADING THE RISK. Distributing the risk involved in any securities venture by purchasing several stocks rather than just one. The opposite of "putting all your eggs in one basket," and virtually synonymous with DIVERSIFICATION.

SPURT. A short, sharp advance in price.

SQUEEZE. 1. The culmination of a CORNER in a stock, or commodity.

2. Term referring to a condition which arises when those who have sold stocks short in a rising market are obliged to cover, or

buy back, at a loss to themselves in order to fulfill their short selling contract obligations. See SHORT COVERING; SHORT SALE; TWISTING THE SHORTS.

3. A *money squeeze* is caused by a temporary shortage of loanable funds. Money becomes difficult to borrow and interest rates are high.

STABILIZE. 1. To keep prices from fluctuating or changing radically; one of the principal functions of a stock exchange SPECIALIST, who is obligated to maintain a fair, orderly and stable market in the stocks in which he specializes at all times. In general, unless a specialist is stabilizing the market in well over 80% of his trades, the New York Stock Exchange is not satisfied with his performance.

2. To make firm or stable; such as when a SYNDICATE manager enters supporting orders to buy a certain number of shares of stock at one point, two points, and so on down to five points below the issue price; and also to sell shares of the same stock at one point, two points and so on above the issue price. This would accommodate any investor wishing to buy or sell the security and would stabilize the market in it.

3. A general market term describing a flat condition existing after a period of severe price changes and heavier volume.

STAG. London Stock Exchange term for one who subscribes for shares of a new securities issue with no intention of retaining his allotment, but only of selling immediately at a profit, and especially if it rises to a PREMIUM in its "after offering" market.

STAMPED SECURITY. A security which has been *stamped* to indicate a change, or provision, made since it was originally issued, as a change in interest rate, maturity or CALLABLE date.

STAMPS (TAX). Stamps representing the amount of tax levied by the Federal Government and some states on the issue, sale or transfer of securities. Federal stamps are issued by the Commissioner of Internal Revenue and state stamps by state tax commissions. Certain commercial banks are designated as sales agents for the stamps.

STANDARD & POOR'S CORPORATION. A leading statistical organization which publishes dividend and corporation records and stock and bond reports, and provides other information and services in the field of finance.

The Company's history dates back to 1860 when Henry Varnum Poor published America's first financial reference: *History of Railroads and Canals of the United States,* later retitled *Poor's Manual of Railroads*. The first coverage of industrial stocks was *Poor's Handbook of Investment Securities* in 1890. Standard Statistics (founded 1906) merged with Poor's Publishing Co. to become Standard & Poor's Corp. in 1941. Home Office: 345 Hudson Street, New York, N.Y. See BEST, ALFRED M. & CO. INC.; FITCH INVESTOR'S SERVICE; MOODY'S INVESTOR'S SERVICE.

STANDARD & POOR'S 500-STOCK PRICE INDEX. A well-known gauge of stock market movements, computed by STANDARD & POOR'S CORPORATION and determined by the price action of a carefully selected list of 425 leading industrial issues, 25 railroads and 50 utilities.

It is based on the relationship between the average market prices of these stocks during 1941–1943 (the base period) and the average prices prevailing for the same stocks at any specific moment of time today; such as hourly, or closing, prices. (1) Multiply the current market price of each stock used in the Average by its number of shares OUTSTANDING to get their aggregate value; (2) Divide this aggregate value by the aggregate value of the base period and multiply the result by ten. Whenever a stock used in the Average is split, or a stock dividend is paid, a comparable adjustment is made in the base year price of the stock, so that index readings are consistent at all times. Standard & Poor's 500-Stock Price Index and the industrial, railroad and utility indices are quoted in leading newspapers and financial publications and hourly on the American Stock Exchange STOCK TICKER. They are computed every five-minutes on the Ultronics System (a form of quotation instrument). See DOW-JONES AVERAGES.

STANDARD STOCKS. Stocks of well known corporations. See SEASONED STOCKS.

START-UP COSTS. The costs involved in putting a new plant or production facility into operation for the first time. They result from conditions that are not expected to occur regularly, or in the foreseeable future, and are therefore regarded as NON-RECURRING EXPENSES.

STATED VALUE. The value of a corporation's stock CAPITALIZATION as stated and carried on its books in the event that the stock has no nominal or PAR VALUE.

STATEMENT OF ACCOUNT. See MONTHLY STATEMENT.

STATEMENT OF CONDITION. See BALANCE SHEET.

STATEMENT, THE. Term usually referring to the ANNUAL REPORT of a corporation. See BALANCE SHEET; MONTHLY STATEMENT; PROFIT AND LOSS STATEMENT.

STATISTICAL POSITION. Term referring to certain external forces which influence market movements (labor and material costs, corporate profit margins, dividend payout, taxes, price-earnings ratios). Also called *Fundamental Position.* See TECHNICAL POSITION.

STATISTICIAN. A trained financial analyst whose opinion of the general market and the prevailing, or potential, value of a single stock or group of stocks is based upon his interpretation of certain mathematical data and computations. Also known as a *Fundamentalist.*

STATISTICS. Mathematical data and computations respecting past or future trends of a single stock or the general market.

STEADY. Term indicating that market prices are firm with little tendency to fluctuate much in either direction.

STIFFENED. Firming tendencies in the market with an indication toward slightly higher prices.

STOCK. A certificate of ownership; a contract between the issuing corporation and the owner which gives the latter an interest in the management of the corporation, the right to participate in profits and, if the corporation is dissolved, a claim upon assets remaining after all debts have been paid. According to the New York Stock Exchange: "When you own a share of stock, you own a share of business." See ASSESSABLE STOCK; AUTHORIZED CAPITAL STOCK; BLUE CHIP; BONUS STOCK; BORROWED STOCK; CAPITAL STOCK; CLASSIFIED STOCK; COMMON STOCK; CONVERTIBLE PREFERRED

STOCK; CYCLICAL STOCKS; DEFENSIVE STOCKS; DEFERRED STOCK; EIGHTH STOCKS; FLOATING STOCK; GROWTH STOCK; GUARANTEED STOCK; HIGH GRADE STOCK; HYPOTHECATED STOCK; INACTIVE STOCK; ISSUED CAPITAL STOCK; LISTED SECURITIES; LOANED STOCK; LONG STOCK; MISCELLANEOUS STOCKS; NON-ASSESSABLE STOCK; NON-VOTING STOCK; NO-PAR STOCK; PENNY STOCKS; PIVOTAL STOCK; PREFERRED STOCK; PREMIUM STOCK; PROTECTIVE STOCKS; QUALITY STOCK; QUARTER STOCKS; SECONDARY STOCKS; SHORT STOCK; SPECIALTY STOCK; STANDARD STOCKS; STOPPED STOCK; TEN SHARE UNIT STOCK; TREASURY STOCK; UNISSUED STOCK; UNLISTED SECURITIES; VOTING STOCK; WATERED STOCK.

STOCK AHEAD. Orders to buy or sell which were received by the SPECIALIST and written in his "book" at specific price limits ahead of subsequent orders entered at the same price. *"Nothing done, stock ahead"* means that an order has not been executed because other orders with priority at that price have not yet been filled. See PRECEDENCE OF ORDERS; SPECIALIST'S BOOK.

STOCK BORROWED. Stock which is borrowed by one broker from another to effect delivery (such as when securities have been sold short) and which is subject to prevailing interest rates and premiums. See SHORT SALE.

STOCK CERTIFICATE. An engraved piece of paper representing legal evidence of ownership of a stipulated number of shares of stock in a corporation. See CARE OF SECURITIES; LOST CERTIFICATES.

STOCK CLEARING CORPORATION. A subsidiary of the New York Stock Exchange, which *clears* securities transactions for

MEMBER FIRMS in the same general way as a bank clearing house clears checks for member banks. With the use of a clearing system, it is not necessary to deliver all securities sold to other firms for their customers. Moreover, each firm may settle its payments with other firms with a single check for all transactions instead of issuing thousands of checks to pay for the individual transactions.

The Stock Clearing Corporation also collects and pays security transfer taxes on all cleared securities and serves as receiving agent for transfer taxes on other security transactions in which a tax liability is incurred. In addition, the corporation settles floor commissions between exchange members. A number of members employ other members on the trading floor to help in handling transactions. The corporation has a system by which the payment of such commissions may be made through its facilities. The first successful clearing system was instituted by the Philadelphia Stock Exchange in 1870. The New York Stock Exchange clearing plan was introduced in 1892, but the Stock Clearing Corp. was not established until April 26, 1920.

STOCK DIVIDEND. A dividend payable in shares of stock and generally disbursed in lieu of cash by corporations wishing to conserve capital for expansion or other purposes. A 10% stock declaration means that ten additional shares will be distributed for each 100 shares held.

STOCK EXCHANGE. See AMERICAN STOCK EXCHANGE; NATIONAL STOCK EXCHANGE; NEW YORK STOCK EXCHANGE; REGIONAL EXCHANGE.

STOCKHOLDER. The owner of one or more shares of corporate stock who is entitled to: (A) a proportionate share of the issuing company's undivided assets; (B) dividends when declared by the directors; (C) the right of proportionate voting power, and frequently; (D) the opportunity to subscribe to additional stock before public offerings are made.

STOCKHOLDER LIST. An alphabetical list of a corporation's stockholders showing the name, address and number of shares held by each stockholder entitled to vote in the affairs of the corporation. See HOLDER OF RECORD.

STOCK LOANED. Stock which is loaned by one broker to another, the loanee paying interest according to the prevailing market value of the stock.

STOCK MARKET. See AMERICAN STOCK EXCHANGE; NATIONAL STOCK EXCHANGE; NEW YORK STOCK EXCHANGE; OVER-THE-COUNTER.

STOCK OPTION CONTRACT. A negotiable contract paid for in advance, which gives the purchaser the right to buy (Call) or sell (Put), usually 100 shares of the stock named in the contract at a fixed price during a period running from a minimum of twenty-one days to a year or more. Also known as a "Paper" or "Privilege." See CALL; PUT; STRADDLE.

Options can be used to reduce risks, thus minimizing the dangers of speculation since the risk is limited to the price of the contract. Contract prices are determined by supply and demand and they are subject to negotiation, as is the price of a stock, a house, or used car. Other factors influencing contract prices include the market history, prevailing market price, quality of the stock involved, the duration of the contract, and the demand existing from others for similar Calls or Puts. Generally, the better the quality, the less the percentage cost. The best market for contracts usually exists in medium-to-higher-priced active securities.

STOCK OPTIONS. A method whereby the owners of businesses grant executives and key employees the incentive of partnership interest and the opportunity to share on a capital basis in the increased value of the company as reflected in the price of its common shares.

From the company's viewpoint, stock options provide a vehicle with which to attract, retain and stimulate executive talent and at the same time properly reward competent and promising executives and employees. From the latter's standpoint, stock options represent additional compensation taxed on a capital gains basis, a proprietary interest in the company, and to some extent, a status symbol. Furthermore, unexercised options, in case of death, may be exercised by the beneficiary or estate. The main criticism of stock options is that they hitch the executive's star to the vagaries of the market, and to that extent, tend to divert his attention from his primary responsibility—that of building and fortifying the enterprise itself.

The past fifty years have seen a healthy growth in understanding on the part of the owners of businesses in the advantage of stock ownership by executives who are responsible for profits. This was especially true in the 1930's. Then companies that were in difficulty and required strong management to get them out but couldn't afford the necessary salaries to attract top executives could bring a man in at a modest salary and heavy stock options. A few years ago, the New York Stock Exchange reported that over 40% of the firms listed on the Exchange had stock option plans.

Section 421 of the Internal Revenue Code of 1954 prohibits optionees from taking up their stock in less than two years and requires that they hold it for at least six months before selling. (Excerpted from an article entitled "Stock Options—an Incentive in Reverse," by David L. Jones in the *Financial Analyst's Journal,* November–December 1962.)

STOCK (BOND) POWER. A "detached assignment"; a separate piece of paper, identical in form with that found on the back of a stock certificate, which includes an exact description of the certificate to which it refers. When properly filled out and accompanying the unsigned certificate, the detached assignment has the same power as that printed on the certificate. Sometimes also called an "Assignment in blank."

In mailing an unsigned, uninsured certificate, there is always the possibility that it may be lost or fraudulently used. However, by sending the unsigned certificate in one envelope and the stock power, properly endorsed, in another envelope, the addressee will, upon receipt of the two, be able to transfer the security or use it as collateral. Since neither of the enclosures has value without the other, no real lasting harm would be done if one should be lost or mislaid in transit. The same method may be employed with Bond Powers and REGISTERED BONDS.

STOCK PURCHASE WARRANT. A privilege granted by a corporation which gives the holder the right to purchase a specific number of shares of stock (usually of the same company) at a certain price until a stipulated future date. Warrants may have a market value, particularly a speculative value, based on a possible rise in price of the stock named in the warrant. *Detachable* warrants may be bought and sold in the open market, regardless of the security they are involved with; *non-detachable* warrants, notwithstanding the value of the security to which they are attached, cannot circulate alone in the market and may be traded only as a part of the security they accompany.

Assignment Separate from Certificate.

For Value Received, ...

hereby sell, assign and transfer unto ....

....

....

....(...................) *Shares of the* ....

Capital Stock of the ....

standing in ....*name on the books of said* ....

....*represented by Certificate No* ....*herewith*

and do hereby irrevocably constitute and appoint ....

....*attorney to transfer the said stock on the books of the within named*

....*with full power of substitution in the premises.*

Dated .... SIGN HERE ....

STOCK QUOTATION INSTRUMENT. The original name for stock ticker. See TICKER.

STOCK SPLIT. A division made of the capital stock of a corporation to create more shares, primarily to improve marketability and heighten investor interest. Stock splits generally are on a two-for-one basis (two shares of new stock are made exchangeable for one share of old). A two-for-one split would leave the owner of 100 shares of old stock worth $90 per share, with 200 shares of new stock worth $45 per share. All a split actually does is increase the number of OUTSTANDING shares. See REVERSE SPLIT.

STOP LIMIT ORDER. A form of STOP ORDER which sets a specific limit on the price the seller will accept in the event that the stock named in the order reaches the STOP PRICE. If XYZ is selling at 47 and a trader enters an order to "Sell 100 XYZ at 46 Stop Limit," it means that he will accept no less than $46 per share for his stock. However, since a Stop Order automatically becomes a MARKET ORDER as soon as the stock concerned reaches or sells through the Stop Price, the trader might instruct the broker to "Sell 100 XYZ at 46 Stop, Limit 45½," if he is worried that he might miss the market entirely at 46. The same general principal applies to the buying side. See STOP ORDER.

STOP LOSS ORDER. A standing instruction left with a broker to sell a stipulated number of shares of stock if the price declines to a certain level. When this occurs, the order automatically becomes a MARKET ORDER. Although the broker will try to execute the order at the STOP PRICE, he cannot guaranty to do so. Stop Loss Orders are primarily intended to prevent, or minimize, a loss; but full protection against loss cannot be guaranteed. See STOP LIMIT ORDER; STOP ORDER.

STOP ORDER. An order to buy or sell that automatically becomes a MARKET ORDER as soon as the stock concerned reaches or sells through the price specified in the order.

The device may be used to initiate trades at critical market levels, protect PAPER PROFITS in a topheavy market, or insure against large loss in the event of a decline. For example, if a trader buys 100 shares of stock at 48 and wishes to limit his possible loss to two points, he will enter an order to "Sell 100 shares at 46 Stop." This means that whenever 100 shares of the same stock sell at 46, the Stop will become effective immediately and the broker will try to execute at 46, the STOP PRICE, although it is not guaranteed that he will be able to do so. See STOP LIMIT ORDER.

STOPPED AT. A price for a stock that is sometimes guaranteed to a buyer, or a seller, by the SPECIALIST in it. For example, the following message might be relayed from the trading floor: "On your order to buy 100 XYZ at the market, the stock is quoted '45 to 45⅜.' You are *stopped at* ⅜." See STOPPED STOCK.

STOPPED OUT. Term signifying that a STOP ORDER has been executed at the best price obtainable after a sale of 100 shares or more of the same stock has taken place at or below the STOP PRICE.

STOPPED STOCK. A service performed usually by a SPECIALIST for a COMMISSION HOUSE broker wherein the specialist will try to execute an order at a better price than might otherwise be obtained if the order was executed immediately.

Assume that a broker has 100 shares of stock to sell AT THE MARKET, where the last sale was 25¼. The stock is quoted "25 bid, offered at 25¼." Rather than HIT THE BID at 25, the broker believes he can do better for his client, so he asks the SPECIALIST if he will STOP 100 shares at 25. The Specialist agrees, thereby guaranteeing a minimum price of 25 if the stock sells at that price. On the other hand, if it becomes possible to sell the stock at a higher price, the Stop is automatically cancelled.

STOP PRICE. The price at which a STOP ORDER becomes a MARKET ORDER.

STRADDLE. 1. A double STOCK OPTION CONTRACT with identical STRIKING PRICES, which entitles the holder to deliver (PUT), or demand (CALL), the stock named by the contract on or before a fixed date.

2. A purchase and a sale made simultaneously of the same commodity in two different markets, or the purchase of one commodity made against the sale of another commodity whose price movements are normally geared closely together.

STRADDLE THE MARKET. A situation which exists when a person is SHORT of one or more stocks and LONG of another, or others, simultaneously. It is a form of insurance for protecting one's position when the near-term market trend is uncertain. The long and the short position cancel each other out, since the loss incurred by being long in a declining market is approximately offset by a profit made at the same time by being short. See HEDGING; SELLING AGAINST THE BOX; SHORT SALE.

STRAP. A combination of STOCK OPTION CONTRACTS consisting of two CALLS and one PUT. See STRIP.

STREAKS OF RUST. Colloquialism referring to railroads or railroad securities. The first railroad stock to be traded was Mohawk & Hudson in 1830.

STREET. Term denoting New York's financial district in general and specifically the Wall Street area.

STREET CERTIFICATE. A securities certificate issued in a STREET NAME. See ASSIGNED IN BLANK.

STREET NAME. Title of a recognized brokerage house, such as a MEMBER FIRM of the New York Stock Exchange. Securities bought on MARGIN are carried in a Street Name (the name of the broker) for his customer's account, rather than in the name of the customer himself.

STRIKE FROM THE LIST. Term describing the action taken by a stock exchange in canceling all trading privileges in a security, suspending it from further dealings. See DELIST.

STRIKING PRICE. The price at which a CALL or a PUT OPTION is written. With a Call, it means the fixed price at which a stock named in the contract may be bought; with a Put, it means the fixed price at which a stock named in the contract may be sold.

STRIP. A combination of STOCK OPTION CONTRACTS consisting of two PUTS and one CALL. See STRAP.

STRONG. An advance in price to higher levels. "The market is strong today": In other words, it is selling higher than yesterday.

STRONG HANDS OR WEAK HANDS. Terms referring to a technical condition in the general market. *Strong hands* means that the majority of recent purchases were made by true investors for long-term holding, i.e., the stocks involved are not likely to be offered for sale for six months or more. *Weak hands* means that the securities are loosely held by traders and speculators who will sell at a small profit on any further rally or bail out promptly in the event of a decline. The portfolios of INSTITUTIONAL INVESTORS are said to be held in strong hands, compared with the general public's holdings, which are said to be held in weak hands.

SUBJECT TO CALL. Term referring to a provision in the document under which a corporate bond is issued (INDENTURE), that gives the issuing corporation the right to redeem (call for redemption) in whole or in part, the bond named in the contract at a fixed minimum price, at any date or dates before the issue matures.

SUBJECT TO REDEMPTION. Term designating securities which may be called (redeemed) with prior notice to the holders thereof.

SUBSCRIPTION PRICE. The price at which new or additional securities issued by a corporation are offered for sale.

SUBSCRIPTION WARRANT. A certificate granting stockholders of record the right to subscribe to certain securities at a specific price, within a stipulated time period, or perpetually. See HOLDER OF RECORD.

SUBSIDIARY COMPANY. A company whose operations are managed and controlled by another corporation. Ownership of the majority of capital stock usually establishes the control.

SUBSTITUTION. Withdrawing a security, or securities, originally deposited as collateral against a loan, and substituting another, or others, of equal value.

SUPPLY AREA. The price area indicated on the chart of an individual stock or the general market where previous advances faltered and were turned back. Same as RESISTANCE LEVEL.

SUPPORT LEVEL. Technical market term meaning the price level indicated on the chart of an individual stock or the general market which contained several previous declines and sparked a recovery. The opposite of RESISTANCE LEVEL or SUPPLY AREA.

SUPPLY. To provide (offer) for sale. When stocks are in large supply, offerings are numerous and prices are generally lower.

SUPPLY AND DEMAND. The basic forces which influence changes in stock market and business cycles or day-to-day price fluctuations.

SUPPORT THE MARKET. To enter buying orders at or slightly below prevailing market levels in order to STABILIZE the price and perhaps set the stage for a rally.

SUPPORTING ORDERS. Buying orders entered to support the price of a specific security or the general market, such as by the SPECIALIST in his role as a stabilizer of prices in the stocks in which he specializes or, for example, by the BANKER'S POOL, which tried unsuccessfully to bring order out of panic during the 1929 market break.

SURPLUS. Accumulated (undivided profits) which have been reinvested in a business. See ACCUMULATED SURPLUS; EARNED SURPLUS; NET SURPLUS; OPERATING SURPLUS.

SURPLUS EQUITY. The difference between the market value of securities held in a brokerage account and the amount needed to meet MARGIN REQUIREMENTS.

SUSPEND TRADING. To prohibit securities dealings in a stock for an indefinite period. Sometimes the prohibition is prompted by a sudden influx of buy or sell orders which threatens to stampede prices and upset the orderly flow of the market; as when President Kennedy was assassinated November 22, 1963.

SUSPENSION. The prohibition of a broker's privileges for a stated period. A stock exchange may suspend any broker found guilty of violating its constitution.

SWIMMING MARKET. A strong, confident market where everything is buoyant.

SWINDLERS. Unscrupulous persons dealing in worthless or doubtful securities and distorting the true facts.

SWING. The price movements, up or down, of a certain stock or the general market.

SWITCHING. Selling one security and purchasing another to improve yield, strengthen a portfolio position or enhance the prospects for price appreciation.

SYMBOL. See TICKER SYMBOLS.

SYNDICATE. A group of UNDERWRITERS dealing in securities first hand from the issuing organization.

T

T. The Ticker abbreviation for American Telephone & Telegraph Company.

TAKE A BATH. To go through the "financial wringer"; incur a large loss.

TAKE A FLIER. To plunge recklessly in a stock, hoping to make a large profit, but understanding that a substantial loss is also possible.

TAKE A POSITION. To commit oneself to the Bullish, or Bearish, side of the market by buying stocks in expectation of an advance, or Selling short on the theory they will decline.

TAKE IT. An expression used by brokers on the trading floor of a stock exchange. It indicates willingness to buy a stock that is being offered for sale at the price stated. For example, when a broker with a Market order to buy 100 shares of U.S. Steel approaches the Post where Steel is traded and asks: "How's Steel?" the Specialist, or person making a market in the stock at that time, may reply "8 to ⅛" (meaning 48 bid, offered at 48⅛). Since a market order is involved and the best offering price is 48⅛, the broker says: *"Take (it)* 100 at ⅛," to which the other broker replies, "Sold," thus closing the deal.

TAKE ON A LINE. To acquire a substantial amount of the stock of one or more companies systematically and usually over a period of time, in expectation of higher prices. The opposite of PUT OUT A LINE.

TAKE UP. 1. To pay in full for securities purchased originally on MARGIN.

2. Term used by participating UNDERWRITERS to indicate they will accept certain securities for direct sale.

TANGIBLE ASSETS. Real property; things that have substance —such as buildings, land, machinery, cash, and inventories. See INTANGIBLE ASSETS.

TAPE PRICE. The last sale of a security as printed on the TICKER TAPE.

TAPE READING. Forecasting price movements solely from information conveyed by the TICKER TAPE. The pure tape reader overlooks basic statistics, tips, news and outside advice, and draws his conclusions only by price, volume, time, activity and breadth, as indicated by the tape.

TAX-EXEMPT BOND. An obligation issued by any of various political units of the United States promising to pay back, with interest, money borrowed; such interest is exempt from present federal income taxes. The political units that issue tax-free bonds are: (A) states, territories and possessions of the United States; (B) counties, cities, villages, school and other districts within the several states, territories and possessions; (C) public authorities incorporated under the laws of the United States or under one or more states or territories, or under city or town ordinances.

In addition to being free from federal income taxes, interest on bonds issued by a state or any political subdivisions of the state, generally is free from state income and local taxes if owned by residents of such state.

TAX-FREE BOND. A bond on which the federal income tax (usually up to 2% of the COUPON) is paid at the source by the issuing corporation. Interest on bonds issued by a state or any political subdivision of the state generally is free from state income and local taxes if owned by residents of such state. However, the tremendous increase in income taxes over the past few years has reduced the significance of such a provision, and new issues now seldom impose this share-the-tax obligation on corporate borrowers.

TAX SELLING. Disposing of securities that show a loss in order to reduce or offset the tax liability on CAPITAL GAINS which have been realized. Tax selling is especially heavy during the fourth quarter of the year and frequently has a temporary depressing influence on the market price of certain securities. However, it may be done to realize profits also. This selling is often prevalent in the first part of January because many investors have deferred profit taking until the new year for various tax reasons, or they believe the market is poised for a decline.

TECHNICAL DIVERGENCE. The failure of one MARKET AVERAGE to confirm the prior action of the other. See DOW THEORY.

TECHNICAL MARKET ACTION. The market's overall price performance as it is influenced by so-called technical factors. These include the rise or fall of volume, size of the SHORT INTEREST, ratio of new highs to new lows achieved daily by individual stocks, the ratio of ODD-LOT purchases to sales and other internal conditions—as opposed to psychological factors, or basic statistics and fundamentals which also affect price movements.

TECHNICAL POSITION. Term referring to the prevailing status or position of the market as it is influenced at any given moment by various internal forces called *technical* factors: volume, character of the buying and selling, quality of the leadership, activity in low priced stocks, size of the SHORT INTEREST, relationship between ODD-LOT purchases and sales, ratio of new individual highs achieved daily to new lows, etc. It relates to the balance between supply and demand existing at any given moment and does not include psychological or business and economic factors, which constitute the external forces.

For example, when the ratio of new highs to new lows and the index of daily odd-lot purchases to sales are unfavorable, and when the preponderance of market activity is in low-priced speculative stocks, with the volume of trading diminishing as stocks have difficulty in advancing further on good news, the technical position is said to be poor, or weak. See OVER-BOUGHT; OVER-SOLD; STATISTICAL POSITION; TECHNICAL MARKET ACTION.

TECHNICIAN. A CHARTIST, or an individual whose market forecasts or securities transactions are based mostly upon changes taking place in the TECHNICAL POSITION of various stocks he studies closely and/or the general market.

TENDENCY. The inclination of the market, or an individual stock, to move higher or lower.

TENDER. A formal offer presented for acceptance, as when a company offers to buy a certain amount of its own securities at a stated price within a specified time limit.

TEN SHARE UNIT STOCKS. The common or preferred issues of companies in which the full unit of trading is ten shares. See ODD-LOT; POST 30.

TERTIARY MOVEMENT. One of the classifications of price movements developed by Charles H. Dow (founder of the *Wall Street Journal* and originator of the *Dow Theory*), which includes daily fluctuations caused by trifling developments. Also called *underlying movement*. See DOW THEORY; PRIMARY MOVEMENT; SECONDARY MOVEMENT.

THEY. A vague and shadowy term referring to all those who supposedly have access to advance information. The so-called "powers behind the market." See INSIDERS.

THIN MARGIN. A small and narrow MARGIN which gives the owner only very little protection in the event of a decline in price.

THIN MARKET. A volatile market where BID AND ASKED prices are usually well below or above the price of the last sale.

TICKER. A mechanical device which prints the volume and prices of security transactions within minutes after they have taken place on the trading floor. The ticker, or "Stock Quotation Instrument," was first introduced in 1867 and printed a stock's full name and price in a straight line. Printing the name and price on two lines was started in 1873. Just as the old, glass-domed, 285 character-per-minute stock tickers of 1929 have been outmoded, so the 500 character machines have been made obsolete recently by 900 character machines that eliminate lateness at volumes up to 10 million shares a day. A separate ticker system for bonds was installed on January 2, 1919.

TICKER SYMBOLS. Abbreviations for stocks as they are printed by the stock TICKER. Symbols are intended to speed the dissemination of prices and all stocks traded on the New York Stock Exchange and the American Stock Exchange have them. For example: Polaroid (PRD); Crucible Steel (XA); Firestone Tire & Rubber (FIR); du Pont (DD); New York Central (CN). Each symbol is different and is associated as closely as possible with the security it represents. The fewest possible letters are employed, with a single one for usually active stocks. To avoid confusion in hastily written reports of transactions by brokers on the trading floor and to reduce possible errors caused by "blurring" over the telephone or telegraph, the letters used in symbols are unlike one another in shape.

TICKER TAPE. A narrow band of paper about one-half inch wide on which are printed, within minutes after they occur, the report of transactions that have taken place on the floor of a stock exchange.

TIE-IN SALES. An agreement made by an UNDERWRITER with his customer, whereby the customer will receive a certain number of shares of a new issue at the offering price, if he agrees to buy additional shares at a higher price when the issue becomes publicly traded. These subsequent purchases often push up, or at least help stabilize, the price of the stock. They violate the anti-manipulative provisions of the *Securities Exchange Act* and are looked upon with disfavor by the SECURITIES & EXCHANGE COMMISSION, The NATIONAL ASSOCIATION OF SECURITIES DEALERS and the New York Stock Exchange.

TIGHT MONEY. A condition existing when interest rates are high and credit is stringent. Also called *Dear Money* and the opposite of *Cheap Money,* or EASY MONEY. The availability of credit is controlled, through interest rates by the Federal Reserve Board, which has the delicate task of keeping credit tight to dampen down inflationary pressures but must also guard against making it so tight it throws the economy into a downturn. If the Board supplied banks with funds freely in a period of economic expansion, it obviously would have immediate inflationary effects. The total money supply would climb, thus tending to reduce the buying power of the dollar. Speculation would be encouraged and in some cases ready money would be bidding for goods in short supply, thus pushing prices up.

TIMING. The art of deciding upon the exact moment to buy before an advance gets underway, or to sell before a decline. Timing is perhaps the most difficult of all market factors to achieve correctly. The wrong timing of a purchase or sale is a major factor responsible for loss in the stock market.

TIPS. Supposedly advance (inside) information concerning the price action of a particular stock or a pending development that will yield a profit to the person who acts quickly upon it. The majority of all tips are worthless and should never be followed without thorough investigation.

TIPSTER SHEET. A form of tout sheet (advertisement) of one's ability to furnish "information" on stocks that will produce a harvest of profit for those who follow it. No legitimate broker would do, or is permitted to do, anything of this kind. There is no such thing in the financial world as "a sure thing."

TO COME—TO GO. Term describing the exact number of shares remaining to be bought (to come), or to be sold (to go) from an original order. If 600 shares of a 1,000 share order have been sold, the FLOOR BROKER will report back that there are "400 *to go.*"

TOPHEAVY MARKET. A market which seems too high on the basis of existing FUNDAMENTAL or TECHNICAL conditions and is likely to react (decline).

TOP OUT. The gradual levelling of market prices after a sustained upward movement; the opposite of BOTTOM OUT. It also, refers to a market, or a stock, which appears to have reached a temporary peak and is unlikely to carry much higher immediately.

TOP PRICE. The highest price reached by the general market, a group of stocks, or an individual stock during a particular period of time under discussion.

TOPPY. Refers to a market, or a stock, which appears topheavy; a setback may be expected.

TOUCH OFF THE STOPS. See SNOWBALLING.

TRADER. One who buys and sells securities for his own account, generally on a short-term basis. About 14 to 15% of stock purchases by the public are sold within 30 days, about 25% are sold anywhere from one to six months, and the balance is held for six months or longer. According to the National Security Traders Association, the perfect trader should be "one who is endowed with a rare combination of abilities itemized as mental keenness, perception, courage, knowledge, analytical ability, quick decision, good humor, winning personality, great physical stamina, loyalty, gift of gab and salesmanship . . . efficient, patient, honest and wise."

TRADE DATE. See DATE OF TRADE; SETTLEMENT DATE.

TRADER'S MARKET. A market which fluctuates within a narrow range and has no extended movement either way. Such a market offers numerous advantages for active trading.

TRADING TEMPER. The condition of the public mind in respect to its willingness to be tempted to adopt a certain course in the market.

TRADING UNIT. See UNIT OF TRADING.

TRANSACTION. The purchase and the sale of a security. It makes no difference which is made first. See SHORT SALE. For every seller there is a buyer.

TRANSFER AGENT. An officer or clerk of a corporation; an outside individual, bank, or trust company trusted with keeping the stock certificates, books and stock ledgers of a corporation, with issuing original certificates and, when certificates are presented for transfer, with canceling the old ones and issuing new ones in the name of the transferee. As soon as this is recorded on the company's books—dividends, financial reports, notices of meetings, proxies and other pertinent information will be mailed direct to the owner. The Chase Manhattan Bank's physical plant for stock transfer and related activities requires 1,000 employees (57 percent of them women) in the dozens of controlled steps involved in moving a stock certificate from the former owner to the new owner. The maze of machinery runs from electronic computers to "Rippling Ralph," a sort of automated secretary that can count a stack of 500 fresh certificates in 24 seconds.

TRANSFER AND SHIP. To change the title of ownership appearing on the face of a stock certificate and then to mail to the new owner.

When a stock is sold, the seller delivers the certificate representing the number of shares to his broker, who sends it to the TRANSFER AGENT. The transfer agent cancels the old certificate and issues a new certificate in the name of the buyer. Both certificates are then forwarded to the REGISTRAR of the company concerned, who returns the new certificate to the transfer agent.

The latter sends it to the buyer's broker, who forwards the certificate to the new owner.

TRANSFER TAX. A federal and state tax paid by the seller and levied on the sale, or transfer, of securities from one person to another.

Federal: The tax is imposed at the rate of four cents on each $100 (or major fraction) of the actual value of the stock involved in the sale or transfer. There is a minimum tax of four cents per transaction and a ceiling of eight cents per share on stocks selling for more than $200 a share. For example: The tax is 4 cents if the value of the stock sold or transferred is $150 or below; 8 cents on value from $150.01 to $250; 40 cents on $1,000; $2 on $5,000 and $10 on $25,000.

New York State: One cent per share on stocks selling below $5.00; 2 cents on $5.00 but less than $10 stocks; 3 cents on $10 but less than $20 stocks; 4 cents on $20 or above. On transfers not involving a sale, the rate is 2 cents per share.

On all bonds expect Government, State and municipal bonds, the rate is 5 cents per $100 FACE VALUE. There is also an SEC fee of one cent for each $500 or fraction thereof of the principal amount of money involved in sales on any registered exchange.

TREASURY STOCK. Stock issued by a corporation and later reacquired, usually by purchase. It may be kept in the treasury, or disposed of in any manner deemed suitable by the company. However, it has no voting power and receives no dividends while it is so held.

TREND. Any continuing price movement in a given direction; usually classified according to duration in time, direction, or amplitude. BULL or BEAR, markets are classed as MAJOR TRENDS; the corrective phases of major trends are called INTERMEDIATE TRENDS and day-to-day fluctuations MINOR TRENDS.

A trend is based upon what traders, investors and speculators presume will happen immediately or in the future as a result of current conditions. The market is always trying to discount the future anywhere from six months to a year in advance. See LONG-TERM; NEAR-TERM; SHORT-TERM.

TREND LINE. A line drawn upon a chart that indicates direction in which a particular stock or the general market is trending.

TRIPLE TOP (BOTTOM). The highest point attained by the market, or an individual stock, which virtually duplicates the level reached on two previous occasions. To the market TECHNICIAN, this creates a *triple top* and indicates that a formidable barrier of overhead resistance has formed, which may bring about a change of trend.

TURNED OVER. Disposed of or sold.

TURN IN THE MARKET. A change in the trend of prices.

TURNOVER. Term synonymous with VOLUME, meaning the number of shares traded in an individual stock or the general market during a given period.

TWISTING THE SHORTS. Causing the price of a stock in which there is a large SHORT INTEREST to advance suddenly and sharply, so that those who are short of it may be compelled, or frightened into closing their contracts at a loss. A form of manipulation currently prohibited. See SHORT SALE.

TWO-DOLLAR BROKER. A broker-member of the Stock Exchange who executes orders for other brokers, especially when the market is very active or at the opening when numerous orders have accumulated overnight. The name, *Two-Dollar Broker,* stems from the fact that his fee for these services used to be $2.00 per hundred shares. Today it varies with the price of the stock.

U

U. The TICKER abbreviation for The United Corporation.

UNCOVER THE STOPS. To depress the price of a stock to a level where many STOP ORDERS are known to be entered. Since Stop Orders become MARKET ORDERS whenever 100 shares of the stock concerned sell at the STOP PRICE, this additional selling may further lower the price to the next Stop Orders. See SNOWBALLING. The practice could involve manipulation and is therefore closely supervised. The term is synonymous with GATHER IN THE STOPS.

UNDERLYING MOVEMENT. Same as PRIMARY MOVEMENT. See DOW THEORY.

UNDERTONE. The basic condition of the market—strong or weak.

UNDERWRITE. To act as a middleman and guaranty the sale of a new issue of corporate securities to new investors. See INVESTMENT BANKER; SYNDICATE.

UNDERWRITER. An investment banker. One who *underwrites* or guarantees the sale of an issue of corporate securities. The underwriter either buys the whole issue and sells it to investors through his own organization or forms a SYNDICATE to help dispose of the securities.

UNDIGESTED SECURITIES. Securities issued beyond the capacity of buyers to absorb them, such as those remaining unsold on the books of SYNDICATE members after a public offering has been made. The term was originated by the late J. P. Morgan.

UNEARNED INCOME. Income derived from rent, interest, dividends or other factors not directly associated with personal or corporate effort. It also infers income or advances received for future value or services to be rendered.

UNEVEN LOT. Same as ODD-LOT.

UNISSUED STOCK. The difference between AUTHORIZED STOCK and that which is ISSUED AND OUTSTANDING.

UNIT OF TRADING. The minimum basic quantity established by a stock exchange in which the market in a security may be made. See ODD-LOT; POST 30; ROUND-LOT.

UNLISTED SECURITIES. Securities which are not LISTED on an organized stock exchange, such as those traded OVER-THE-

COUNTER. There are about 25,000 unlisted stocks, but only about 7,000 are traded with any regularity. All stocks traded on the New York Stock Exchange are listed. See LISTING REQUIREMENTS. The Stock Exchange has long advocated elimination of the double standard which differentiates between listed and unlisted stocks in the fields of MARGIN REQUIREMENTS and disclosure rules. Banks are not regulated in making loans on unlisted stocks, while the rule for listed stocks is based on prevailing margin levels. Unlisted companies below a certain size are not required to publish annual reports or earnings statements, or disclose insider information about officer's dealings in the company's stock.

UNLOAD. To dump overboard or sell, usually in large amounts, in anticipation of declining prices.

UNREALIZED PROFITS. PAPER PROFITS which have not yet been made actual.

UNSECURED BOND. A bond which is not backed up by any pledge of assets that the debt will be paid; the debtor merely pledging his credit standing . . . "secured by full faith." Government bonds and most corporate DEBENTURES are in this category.

UPSIDE GAP. A formation appearing on a stock chart caused by the highest price of any market day remaining below the lowest price of the succeeding day with sufficient margin to form an open space or gap.

UP TICK. A transaction made in a security at a price that is higher than the previous price. This is important to a person trying to SELL SHORT because short sales may only be made on an up tick. Also called plus tick. See ONE-EIGHTH RULE; SHORT SALE; ZERO PLUS TICK.

UTILITY. See PUBLIC UTILITY.

V

VALUES OF STOCK. See BOOK VALUE; MARKET VALUE; PAR VALUE.

VARIATIONS IN PRICE. Security price fluctuations created by changing supply and demand factors. On most stocks the minimum allowable price change is ⅛ point, or 12½ cents a share.

VENTURE CAPITAL. Capital which is subject to more than a normal degree of risk, usually associated with a new business or venture. Also called RISK CAPITAL.

VERBAL REPORT. A report from the trading floor, transmitted verbally rather than in writing, that an order to buy or sell a security has been executed. Verbal reports are not as firm or binding as written reports. However, the phrase "Take a *verbal*" means that the order has very probably been executed at the price stated.

VICINITY OF THE EXCHANGE. According to the New York Stock Exchange: "that part of the Borough of Manhattan, City of New York, located South of Fulton Street."

VISITOR'S GALLERY. A balcony overlooking the New York Stock Exchange trading floor where the public is admitted. The Exchange was first opened to public view in 1938, and the first Exhibit Room was opened in 1952. On May 29, 1962, when the market was unusually active, 8,231 visitors were recorded. Visitors are not admitted to the trading floor, except by permission of an officer of the Exchange.

VOLUME. The aggregate number of shares traded during a given period. Volume is always heaviest in a falling market. The first time a day's volume topped one million shares was on December 15, 1886. During the Blizzard of 1888, with only thirty-two brokers on the Exchange, it dipped to 15,800.

The largest share turnover in New York Stock Exchange history was 16,410,030 shares traded October 29, 1929. The all-time low was 31 shares on March 16, 1830 (26 shares of U.S. Bank and 5 shares of Morris Canal & Banking Co. Value: $3,470.25).

VOTING RIGHT. The right of a stockholder to participate in the affairs of his company by voting in the election of directors or in other corporate matters requiring a vote. Common stockholders of record are usually entitled to one vote per share held. Preferred stock generally has no voting power, except when the dividend is in default.

VOTING STOCK. Stock in a corporation the holders of which are entitled to vote for the election of the directors of such corporation.

VOTING TRUST. An agreement whereby the majority of a corporation's voting stock is deposited in the custody of trustees for a fixed period. The *voting trustees* are empowered to vote the stock in accordance with stipulations prescribed by the *voting trust* agreement. The trustees issue certificates to the stockholders (in lieu of their stock), which may be traded or transferred in the same way as stock certificates. They become exchangeable for stock again upon termination of the trust. Voting trusts are usually created in connection with reorganizations; but they may also be necessary in a merger, in raising capital, or in carrying out a judicial decree. See VOTING TRUST CERTIFICATE.

VOTING TRUST CERTIFICATE. A negotiable certificate issued to stockholders by the voting trustees of a corporation as a receipt for stock certificates deposited with them under terms of the VOTING TRUST agreement.

W

WALL STREET. The financial district in New York City, often called The Street. Name derived from the wall, or stockade, that the early settlers built across Manhattan Island near the present site of Wall Street. The stockade was to protect against surprise attack by Indians and to keep cattle from straying.

WANTED FOR CASH. A phrase printed sometimes on the TICKER TAPE, indicating that someone will buy a certain number of shares of the stock designated and pay for it the same day (as contrasted with the normal 4-day delivery period). This may be because a one-day cash transaction is necessary to make good on a SHORT SALE, or a customer has failed to make delivery on a stock, or a broker is obliged to BUY IN to make good on a sale.

WAR BRIDES, OR WAR BABIES. The securities of companies engaged in manufacturing armaments.

WARRANT. A certificate which entitles the holder to buy a specific number of shares of a company's stock at a certain price within a stipulated time limit, or perpetually. Warrants have no direct claim on earnings, no voting rights, and they pay no dividends.

They are highly speculative and usually highly *leveraged.* See LEVERAGE.

WASH SALE. 1. Buy and sell orders instigated within a short period of time by the same person (sometimes by two persons), which have little or no effect on that person's interest in the security or commodity, but are primarily intended to create the impression of activity and strength and induce the public to buy. This is a form of manipulation currently prohibited.

2. Term refers also to a loss on the sale of securities, which is not allowed for tax purposes. This occurs if substantially the same securities (or options to buy them) are obtained within thirty days prior to, or following, such sale by persons who are not dealers in securities, or traders in them.

WATCH MY NUMBER. A request made to a broker by a fellow broker, who has occasion to leave the trading floor. Each Stock Exchange member has a number and when his number is "up," or "flashed," it means his presence is required immediately at the booth his firm maintains on the rim of the trading floor. See ANNUNCIATORS.

WATERED STOCK. Term referring to a now historic method of overstating asset values and thus increasing the apparent value of shares; this was done during the period when market values depended greatly on asset valuation. Term originated from a former practice of drovers feeding cattle large quantities of salt to make them thirsty, and then letting them drink all the water they could hold before they went to market. The heavier and fatter the cattle, the more money they would bring.

WEAK HOLDINGS. Securities held on MARGIN by speculators and traders, who will use any excuse to sell out. See STRONG HANDS or WEAK HANDS.

WEAK MARKET. A market that is trending lower under the weight of aggressive selling pressure.

WENT TO THE WALL. Applies to individuals or corporations which have failed. The liabilities of companies failing crossed $1 billion for the first time in 1959. The principal reason for most failures recently has been increasing competition.

WHEN ISSUED. Term referring to a transaction in a security that has been authorized but not yet actually issued. This occurs sometimes when old securities are made exchangeable for new (as a result of a STOCK SPLIT, a STOCK DIVIDEND, or a corporate merger) and the new certificates are not immediately available in deliverable form. A stock sold "w.i." means it is deliverable when, as and if issued.

WHIPSAWED. Term meaning that a double loss has been incurred: first in buying at the top of a rise, and then in reversing position and SELLING SHORT at the bottom of a decline or vice versa.

WIDE MARKET. A market where BID AND ASKED prices are unusually far apart. The opposite of a CLOSE MARKET. Also, a market where LISTED STOCKS are available to a greater number of investors.

WILDCAT SCHEME. A speculative venture which appears to have little hope of success.

WINDOW DRESSING. A practice whereby certain companies temporarily arrange their affairs, in order to create a more favorable public impression as of the date when the next financial statement is issued. This applies especially to annual statements, either calendar or fiscal year.

WIPED OUT. Term meaning that all available cash and MARGIN are exhausted.

WIRE HOUSE. Usually a large brokerage firm with many branch offices and correspondents linked together by PRIVATE WIRES.

WITH INTEREST. Same as "and interest", or "added interest". See INTEREST.

WITHOUT INTEREST. Term applied to bonds and meaning the same as FLAT. See INTEREST.

WORKING CAPITAL. The excess of CURRENT ASSETS over CURRENT LIABILITIES; the amount required to carry on a business.

WRITE OFF. An accounting procedure which cancels a debt or a claim. When the value of an uncollectible debt is reduced to zero, the entire asset is charged as a loss and removed from further consideration.

X

X. The TICKER abbreviation for United States Steel Corporation.

Y

Y. The TICKER abbreviation for Alleghany Corporation.

YANKEES. London Stock Exchange term for American securities.

YIELD. The ratio of dividends paid on a stock for the past twelve months to its current market price. Yield is obtained by dividing the indicated dividend on a stock by its market price. Thus, a stock paying $2.00 and selling at $40 a share would yield 5%. The yield on a bond is the annual percentage of return it pays in INTEREST.

YIELD TO MATURITY. The YIELD, or return, provided by a bond to its maturity date; determined by a mathematical process, usually requiring the use of a "basis book". For example, a 5 percent bond pays $5.00 a year interest on each $100 PAR VALUE. To figure its current yield, divide $5.00 by $95—the market price of the bond—and you get 5.26%. Assume that the same bond is due to mature in five years. On the maturity date, the issuer is pledged to pay $100 for the bond that can be bought now for $95. In other words, the bond is selling AT A DISCOUNT of 5% below par value. To figure yield to maturity, a simple and approximate method is to divide 5% by the five years to maturity, which equals one percent pro rata yearly. Add that 1% to the 5.26% current yield, and the yield to maturity is roughly 6.26%.

$$\frac{5\%\quad\text{(discount)}}{5\quad\text{(yrs. to maturity)}} = 1\%\text{ pro rata, plus }5.25\%\text{ (current yield)}$$

$= 6.26\%$ (yield to maturity)

Z

Z. The TICKER abbreviation for Woolworth (F. W.) Company.

ZERO PLUS TICK. Term used by ODD-LOT brokers and meaning the sale of a ROUND-LOT which is one of a continuing series of sales made at a price that is higher than the last different price. See UPTICK.